I0605054

PLANNING THE MURDER of ANNE BOLEYN

As always, for

Grayson, Torben,
Adora, and Alice,

who understand unconditional love better than any king

PLANNING THE MURDER of ANNE BOLEYN

CAROLINE ANGUS

First published in Great Britain in 2024 by
PEN AND SWORD HISTORY
An imprint of
Pen & Sword Books Ltd
Yorkshire – Philadelphia

ISBN 978 1 39903 186 8

A CIP catalogue record for this book is available from the British Library.

Typeset in Times New Roman 11/14.5 by
SJmagic DESIGN SERVICES, India.
Printed and bound in the UK by CPI Group (UK) Ltd.

Pen & Sword Books Limited incorporates the imprints of Atlas, Archaeology, Aviation, Discovery, Family History, Fiction, History, Maritime, Military, Military Classics, Politics, Select, Transport, True Crime, Air World, Frontline Publishing, Leo Cooper, Remember When, Seaforth Publishing, The Praetorian Press, Wharncliffe Local History, Wharncliffe Transport, Wharncliffe True Crime and White Owl.

For a complete list of Pen & Sword titles please contact
PEN & SWORD BOOKS LIMITED
George House, Units 12 & 13, Beevor Street, Off Pontefract Road,
Barnsley, South Yorkshire, S71 1HN, England
E-mail: enquiries@pen-and-sword.co.uk
Website: www.pen-and-sword.co.uk

or

PEN AND SWORD BOOKS
1950 Lawrence Rd, Havertown, PA 19083, USA
E-mail: uspen-and-sword@casematepublishers.com
Website: www.penandswordbooks.com

Contents

Author Note

With every new release written about Anne Boleyn, we all wait and hope of seeing newly-found information. If only the papers around her trial were not destroyed. If only Thomas Cranmer had made it known what his reasons were for annulling the marriage of Anne and Henry VIII. If only Thomas Cromwell had not destroyed all his correspondence in 1536. It is no secret that the royal court of London in 1536 would have been a terrifying place. It has been almost five hundred years since Anne Boleyn was beheaded at the behest of her husband, and the tale does not dim in this intense narrative of injustice and unfairness. On the surface, it looks as if we have little to go on when trying to understand what King Henry wanted, and what Anne Boleyn did, did not, could, and could not do in 1536.

What we do still have are the movements of so many others around the royal court in 1536. While the court wished to appear as a serene swan floating on a pond, underneath it was a panic of splashing, kicking and floundering to stay afloat as courtiers jostled for favour, support and survival. Nobody worked at the royal court by accident. Everyone was there because of their connections, be them familial, financial, educational, or commercial. While Anne Boleyn's voice has been lost amongst the gossip of the last six months of her life, the void has been filled with assumptions, errors, and plain disinformation.

What remains abundantly clear is that Anne Boleyn had precious little to do with her own demise. In the cacophony of voices, hers does not rise above the men and women of the court. Her actions, movements, decisions, mistakes, convictions, and desires are not the ones that shaped those months of 1536. While we are unlikely to ever find any insight into the true nature of the human affairs surrounding Henry VIII's decision to kill his wife, we can see how the royal marriage was only one part in a much wider network of situations that caused an unstable king to snap. While Henry VIII was romancing Jane Seymour in full view of Anne Boleyn, meetings, alliances, choices, and religious worries swirled inside and outside the court, far beyond Anne's control. But while we may never gain full insight into the realities of Anne's arrest, trial and execution, we can see how nobody ever believed guilt played a part in the saga.

As an author, my first thanks always go to my children: Grayson, Torben, Adora, and Alice. Every moment of my life is dedicated to my babies, and their understanding of my constant need to write is what makes all these books possible. This is for our new dreams, plans, futures, and hopefully soon, a new heart too.

The trust and support of Sarah-Beth Watkins and Sarah Hodder at Pen & Sword Books cannot be overlooked. Finding someone who supports my ideas, takes the time to painstakingly work through my words and help me create my impression of the 1530s has made this book a far better piece of work thanks to your insight. I am deeply grateful for the support.

The myriad of historians and authors who have supplied me with vital insight and inspiration could go on forever. Thanks to Natalie Grueninger for her respect and attentive understanding of Anne Boleyn; to Owen Emmerson for his passion and enthusiasm for Anne, and taking the time to critique this book; Diarmaid MacCulloch's limitless insight to religious changes under Thomas Cromwell; Sylvia Barbara Soberton for her commitment to the women around Anne Boleyn, and generously dedicating time to reviewing my work; Sandra Vasoli for her meticulous research into Anne Boleyn's letter from the Tower; Elizabeth Norton's research on Jane Seymour, and Melita Thomas' work on Princess Mary.

Another thank you must go to my early readers who donated their time to read my book – Grayson Angus, Amy McElroy, and Sophie Bacchus-Waterman. Time is a precious commodity and you were kind enough to share.

Finally, to all Anne Boleyn lovers (for she has no haters), while myths and misunderstandings continue to persist even after five centuries, there are plenty of us still researching, still advocating, still reading, and still educating on the realities of 1530s England. No matter how we approach the topic, we all strive for the same thing, and thank you for being the audience to this challenging work.

CHAPTER 1

Defying the Heroes of History

While Katharine of Aragon will forever be known as the Spanish queen, by the time she breathed her last, she had lived in England for thirty-five of her fifty years. Henry VIII's queen for almost twenty-seven years, Katharine hoped she had done her best for England, despite the fact England had not done its best for her. King Henry had been openly trying to rid himself of his wife for a decade and had put Anne Boleyn on Katharine's throne in 1533. Queen Katharine's final years were filled with stubborn refusal, hostile defiance and abject cruelty. Katharine had wanted her husband and throne back, her daughter restored and treated as a princess and heir, and the country to turn back to the Catholic faith. She knew this was unlikely to happen, but when cancer took her life at two o'clock on the afternoon of Friday, 7 January 1536,[1] even she could not have seen how her death would inadvertently lead to another queen's murder.

There is no reason to dispute the records that showed Henry and Anne were a happy couple in early 1536. But outside the relationship between the pair, the political storms had continued to loom. Henry's treatment of Katharine put England at odds with Pope Paul, and with Holy Roman Emperor Charles V, who was Katharine's nephew, King of Spain and the most powerful Catholic ruler in Europe. England's continued drift towards the new faith further inflamed grievances, and made France turn their eyes away from England. The Reformation may have opened the doors to give King Henry the power, and the wife, he wanted, but his actions towards the new religious teachings never seemed to have any strength of conviction. England had spent five years dangling on a precipice as the king pushed ahead out of sheer stubbornness against the Catholic Church, and with the Dissolution of the Lesser Monasteries, yet another of Henry's hasty schemes, relations at home and abroad were about to take another turn.

Kimbolton Castle, where Queen Katharine died, was a seventy-mile ride from Greenwich Palace where the court was celebrating Epiphany.

News reached Vicegerent Thomas Cromwell's desk in the night or the following morning; the king's secretary was a notorious workaholic who was always available to receive correspondence. The letter, signed by Edward Chamberlain and Edmund Bedingfield, was short, explaining the queen had passed and they needed the king's wishes to proceed with preparing her noble body for burial.[2] They also mentioned they had no money at Kimbolton to prepare a funeral and sort through the household.[3] Who shared this news with King Henry went unrecorded, though it was likely Cromwell himself. Richard Pollard, William Portman, Thomas Paulet, William Peter, Thomas Lee and Ralph Sadler were dispatched to Kimbolton to see to the household, and Cromwell dictated the plans for Queen Katharine's funeral to his new secretary, Thomas Wriothesley.[4] Cromwell knew as well as anyone that Katharine could not receive the funeral of a queen, addressing Katharine as 'the right excellent and noble Princesse the Lady Catherin, Doughter to the right highe and mighty Prince Ferdinand, late King of Castle, and late Wief to the noble and excellent prince Arthur, Brother to our Soveraign Lorde King Henry the viijth'.[5] But still, Cromwell laid out specific and elaborate plans, ordering that thirty of her staff should receive black fabric for mourning, and that her body was to be encased in lead and taken in procession to St Paul's Cathedral in London. The funeral was set for Tuesday, 25 January, after the hearse had passed through all the towns on the seventy-mile route, where long torches would be held aloft by men as a tribute to their former queen. Noble ladies were to walk in procession close to the queen, with lords surrounding the women and hearse in protection, all bearing torches. Cromwell also instructed that only mutes could lay Katharine's body out, nine men bearing torches were to stand around Katharine's coffin before she began her journey to London while four knights would hold a canopy over her, with barons at their sides. A chief mourner was appointed to ride on horseback ahead of Katharine, the horse draped in black velvet, with another eight mourners at their back.[6] Cromwell prepared liveries for all dukes and duchesses in attendance, ensured the ladies in mourning were provided for, and that everything down to the saddlers and painters that were needed were itemised and payment prepared. But almost immediately King Henry put a stop to Cromwell's plans. Ralph Sadler, working as the messenger between Henry at Greenwich and Cromwell at his Master of the Rolls office in London, was chastised by the king for such elaborate plans.[7] Henry refused to have a hearse carry Katharine to St Paul's as she had wished; the king did not wish to pay for such a funeral and did not believe Katharine deserved a queen's burial. Sadler politely pointed out that Henry's sister, Mary Tudor, had received a queen's funeral in 1533, 'but that was a bad misstep, producing the snarl that [Mary] was a Queen'.[8] Enough was already being spent on Katharine's funeral, Henry commented sourly. Fortunately, Cromwell had given Sadler a gift to present to the king at the meeting, a novelty lock, which at least spared Sadler from getting too much grief when Henry shot down Cromwell's ideas.[9] The Imperial ambassador at court, Eustace Chapuys noted that Cromwell rescheduled the funeral for 1 February in London, to be so magnificent, 'that even those who see it all will hardly believe it', and that the chief mourners would be the highest-ranked women of the realm, and six hundred mourners would be dressed in black.[10] But once again Cromwell's funeral plans were ceased by the king at once. It surely came as no surprise when Sadler relayed this news to the Vicegerent at his Rolls office.

The recorded response of King Henry upon hearing the news of Katharine's death was, 'God be praised that we are free from all suspicion of war!' Henry believed Katharine's death was good for England, that Anglo-French relations could improve, and that the fractious relationship between England and Emperor Charles could instantly be repaired.[11] Henry also wasted no time in ensuring all of Katharine's valuables were returned to him in London. Given that Cromwell dispatched a letter to France on 8 January, the day the news arrived in London, Henry seemingly first thought of how Katharine's death placed him internationally. Cromwell wrote to his nemesis, Bishop Stephen Gardiner, in Paris, telling him the news about Katharine, and that, as French ambassador, Gardiner had to appear more courteous to King Francis.[12] However, a report from Nicholas Sanders, albeit a highly dubious source, recounted that King Henry wept upon hearing the news and when reading Katharine's last letter to him, which spoke of her love and honour. Both responses could be true; though Henry may have cried for himself, and not Katharine.[13] Anne Boleyn made no attempt to hide her pleasure, giving an expensive gift to the messenger who came from Kimbolton, and expressing that she was now the only queen in England.[14] During the period of her marriage, Katharine had been the queen of England, by the laws of God and of England. Anne Boleyn could say the same thing; two women unwittingly pitted against one another by the whims of a king.

On Sunday, 9 January, the infamous scene of Anne brandished all in yellow clothing, revealed to the court their true feelings. With Anne wearing the colour of joy (and not of Spanish mourning, a myth which has endured), and Henry decked out in yellow silk with a white feather in his cap,[15] they enthusiastically presented their two-year-old daughter, Princess Elizabeth, to all at court and danced with Anne's ladies, before Henry spent several days enjoying activities in the tiltyard. Ambassador Chapuys reported that Anne's father, Thomas Boleyn, and her brother, George, were overheard at court rejoicing over Katharine's death and hoping Princess Mary would be the next to go.[16]

Whether the whole court was as happy as the Boleyns is subject to conjecture; no matter how much had occurred in the years since Katharine's official exile in 1531, threats of harm towards Katharine and Princess Mary were made by no one but the 'new' royal couple. Queen Katharine's autopsy had shown she had a black heart, with a black mass attached, which a grief-stricken Ambassador Chapuys thought could be poison.[17] The whispers that Katharine had been killed continued for months in Chapuys' circles, though never amounted to anything more than anti-Boleyn groups despairing over the loss of their Catholic queen. The fact it was Queen Katharine's heart which gave up also served rumours that she died heartbroken, away from her husband, daughter, and throne. Katharine had been almost universally beloved and respected throughout England and Europe, so the suggestion the court rejoiced in her death may have merely been a facade to appease the king. Chapuys wrote to Emperor Charles that several unnamed people felt indignation towards Henry's joy, which is almost certainly true. King Henry had been alone in believing Katharine and their daughter Mary deserved to be downgraded in rank and living, and to be discarded and treated roughly. Even Martin Luther, who devoted his life to disavowing the Catholic faith, did not believe Queen Katharine deserved to be demoted from her status as queen when England took on the new faith.

Vicegerent Cromwell never shared his own feelings about Katharine's death. Despite being the man who legally ended her marriage to Henry, Cromwell never held any hostility towards her, or vice versa. He had sworn several times to protect Katharine and Mary and had petitioned King Henry often for their welfare.[18] At that time, Cromwell had the fate of England in his hands; he had total authority over anything he liked and took full advantage of the fact. But in January 1536, Cromwell had his hands full and busy preparing a new parliamentary session, the first Reformation parliament; he could not afford to be hindered by issues surrounding the royal marriage. The king's monastery dissolutions were about to get underway, and one of Cromwell's friends, Thomas Bedyll, had recently uncovered a manuscript written by King Edgar for the opening of Ramsey Abbey in 969.[19] The papers showed the monks swore allegiance to their king, not a pope, which could be vastly useful in future arguments involving the closure of non-compliant monasteries. Given that Cromwell was against closing all the monasteries, going as far as voicing his personal opinion and invoking the king's wrath,[20] any document that could help in persuading the king to reform monasteries instead was invaluable. But even Cromwell stopped to reflect on the death of the queen. Re-affirming his admiration for Katharine, he went as far as telling Ambassador Chapuys, 'if not for her sex, she could have defied all the heroes of history'.[21] But Cromwell was one of the rare pragmatic men at court and also admitted that he:

> 'Was not ashamed, in talking with one of [Chapuys'] men, to tell [Emperor Charles] he had no reason to profess so great grief for the death of the Queen, which [Cromwell] considered very convenient and advantageous for the preservation of friendship between [Charles and King Henry]; that henceforth we should communicate more freely together, and that nothing remained but to get the Princess to obey the will of the King.'[22]

International diplomacy was a large part of Cromwell's work and woes. No leaders in Europe ever supported King Henry's argument to leave Katharine or formally acknowledged Anne as queen. Katharine's death meant England could reduce some of their embarrassment over the previous three years and move forward. Stephen Gardiner, a Catholic bishop who had desperately preferred Katharine on the throne over Anne, wrote to Cromwell to discuss how relations with France could now be repaired. Gardiner also crucially mentioned that the lords of Germany, who were forming a league overseen by the Duke of Saxony, would be likely to embrace Henry and Anne's marriage and Henry's supremacy over the Church, as 'wherein God hath given sentence for the most part by the death of the Dowager'.[23]

With Cromwell busy with diplomacy, monasteries and parliament, the plans around Katharine's funeral moved out of his hands. The king's Comptroller of the Household, Sir William Paulet, travelled to Kimbolton with Katharine's comptrollers, Chamberlain and Bedingfield, and the king's universally disliked solicitor, Richard Rich, was also in attendance. Rich was unpleasantly tasked with sharing his legal opinion that as a 'sole' woman, Katharine had the right to distribute her valuables as she saw fit, rather than give them to the crown.[24] Unsurprisingly, Katharine had wished to give items to her daughter Mary, and see that her staff were provided for after her death, from her assets of around 5000 marks (around £1.3 million today).

Princess Mary (styled as Lady Mary by her father for being 'illegitimate') was almost forgotten in the whole event. Not residing at Greenwich where the royal family enjoyed the season, Mary was kept three miles away at Eltham Palace and sometimes twenty-six miles north of London at Hunsdon, under the care of Lady Anne Shelton, a sister of Sir Thomas Boleyn and aunt to Anne Boleyn. Lady Shelton was always under strict instructions from her niece to treat Mary without respect, and even use violence if needed.[25] Ambassador Chapuys sometimes received permission to attend Princess Mary and had a servant visit once a week to relay messages and letters, of which sadly few survive. In January 1536, Chapuys asked to go to Mary at once and tell her the news of Queen Katharine's death but was refused. King Henry initially refused to allow Princess Mary to even hear the news and banned any messengers from seeing her. But Chapuys had been sending small gifts and tokens to Lady Shelton, which caused her to allow a messenger in against the king's orders.[26] On Tuesday, 11 January, four days after Katharine's death, Mary heard the news of her mother's passing through Lady Shelton, without anyone to comfort her. Chapuys wrote as soon as permitted to one of the ladies in Mary's household, who gave Mary his letter of consolation. Princess Mary requested that Chapuys ask the king to remove her from her sister, Princess Elizabeth's household and the Boleyn family, and prepared herself for execution for refusing to sign the Oath of Supremacy.[27] Mary also begged Lady Shelton to petition the king to allow Queen Katharine's physician and apothecary to visit Hunsdon, so Mary could hear the full truth of her mother's death. Henry initially refused, saying the only affliction his daughter suffered was worry.[28] To comfort her, Chapuys sent Mary letters written by her cousins, Holy Roman Emperor Charles, and Queen Mary, Governor of the Netherlands, so she might feel as if she had allies and could see she was not forgotten by the world. Chapuys told Emperor Charles:

> '[Mary] shows great sense and incomparable virtue and patience to bear so becomingly the death of such a mother to

> whom she bore as much love as any daughter ever did to her mother, who was her chief refuge in her troubles.'[29]

Both Princess Mary and Ambassador Chapuys feared King Henry would now increase his force on Mary to sign the Acts of Succession and Supremacy, accepting she was illegitimate, her mother was never a queen, and that the Pope was not Head of the Church in England. But Princess Mary was determined to reject these.

While King Henry rejoiced in his first wife's death, waited for rulers and diplomats to bat their eyelashes at him once again and continued his cruel treatment of his daughter, his second wife was not complacent. Anne wrote to Princess Mary, extending a hand of friendship and told Mary that if she obeyed her father, Anne could be her best friend, a second mother, and that Mary could return to court.[30] Naturally, Mary did not take this message well, and Anne ran out of pleasantries. Anne wrote to her aunt, Lady Shelton, and reminded her that Anne alone knew the king's mind and that neither Anne nor Henry cared what road Mary chose to take now. Anne believed she would soon give the king a son and had simply wished to warn Mary that her obstinacy against her father was going to have unfavourable consequences. Anne told her aunt to continue treating Mary without any kindness, a theme Anne had instructed her aunt to follow for the past several years.[31]

If Henry and Anne were still riding high on the death of Queen Katharine, it was not a ride that would last. By the king's command, Katharine's funeral was moved seventeen miles north of Kimbolton to Peterborough Abbey, with minimal respect given. Ambassador Chapuys refused to attend, as it was not a funeral worthy of a queen; Princess Mary was not permitted to attend at all. Vicegerent Cromwell did his best to ensure what was left of his funeral plans went ahead, and even solicitor Richard Rich was sympathetic to Queen Katharine's ladies. The ladies had been gifted items and apparel by Katharine before her death, and Rich considered it dishonourable to take the items from the women who now had little to nothing to their names.[32] The king had no interest in being sympathetic; he thought many of his troubles were over now Katharine was gone, that his daughter Mary would no longer be a beacon of defiance for the Catholics of his country, and that he was no longer a pariah among European leaders. But Henry was also simply a man going through a middle-aged crisis, and spent more time in the tiltyard, indulging in jousting, despite the fact he was no longer fit or healthy enough to participate.

Whispers that Anne was not so cheerful over Queen Katharine's death soon began to swirl. Married to the king for three years, Anne would have expected to be treated as the queen, now the only queen, of England. As long as Katharine lived, Anne had openly criticised her and Princess Mary, but their existence accidentally made Anne safe as Henry's second wife. While England had two queens, King Henry would never dare set Anne aside and look to another woman, even when he entertained mistresses. Katharine was the Catholic queen, Anne the evangelical queen, and if Henry left Anne, he would need to return to Queen Katharine. Henry's stubbornness would never allow that to happen. With Katharine dead, Henry could now leave Anne and marry another; after all, he had Vicegerent Thomas Cromwell, the man who could undo royal marriages. Both national and international gossip mentioned the possibility of Henry annulling his marriage to Anne,[33] though it was wishful thinking as much as anything else.

Messages between the court of Holy Roman Emperor Charles and the French King Francis suggested King Henry could marry a French princess now that Katharine was dead, just assuming Anne would somehow be dismissed.[34] Anne was wise to be wary; she had played a masterstroke in making the leap from mistress to queen but her position had no precedent. The situation in 1536 was as it has always been; when a man marries his mistress, it creates a vacancy. Henry would never admit he was wrong to marry Anne and break with the Catholic Church, even if he did feel that way. But by all accounts, at that time Henry was happy with Anne; his New Year gifts to her in January were exquisite, Anne was three months pregnant, and they hoped for a boy. Outwardly, the couple had everything to look forward to and Katharine's death should not have shaken the relationship.

But there was another side to the issue. Despite being Henry's queen, Anne lacked power and allies at court. She certainly had those who considered her their patron; she had sponsored and assisted many into prime religious positions. Anne was intelligent, pious, and charming. Even those who considered Anne an enemy called her talented and witty. However, the long-running negotiations to find a French husband and alliance for Princess Elizabeth had fallen to dust, causing frustration for Anne. The French still considered Princess Mary the heir over young Elizabeth and the multiple embassies both in London and Paris had come to nothing. It would not have taken Anne long to realise she could be in political trouble.

CHAPTER 2

Power Vacuum

In 1529, when Cardinal Thomas Wolsey toppled from the king's side, charged with praemunire and treason, a power vacuum opened. It was the chance that the Boleyns needed to rise higher at court, but they failed to capitalise on the position. Anne's father, Thomas Boleyn, Earl of Wiltshire and Ormond, became Lord Privy Seal, the fifth highest office in the land, but as Anne's ascent to the throne continued, his position was increasingly sidelined, and he spent more time away from court. Anne's brother, George Boleyn, Lord Rochford, was at court, close to the king on the Privy Council and a gentleman in the privy chamber, but again he failed to gain any significant positions or offices from the crown, other than working as a diplomat in France. It was Lord Rochford's embassies, alongside his highly experienced father, that had failed to win a French alliance and marriage for Princess Elizabeth.[1] Among those more powerful than the Boleyns at court, none were Anne supporters, not even the Duke and Duchess of Norfolk, unrivalled in their position among the nobility and Anne's maternal uncle and aunt. Thomas Howard, 3rd Duke of Norfolk had also become sidelined throughout 1534 and 1535; politically isolated by Vicegerent Cromwell for his Catholic views, Norfolk was more often than not away from court and not welcome to share his opinions with the king.[2]

The similarly powerful Charles Brandon, 1st Duke of Suffolk, had never supported the king's marital or religious changes; nor did Henry and Gertrude Courtenay, the Marquis and Marchioness of Exeter. The equally Catholic Pole and Grey families would never support the changes. Lord Chancellor Thomas Audley was Cromwell's puppet but rarely said a word in favour of anyone, though Audley was a better ally than his predecessor Sir Thomas More, who had burned reformists before being beheaded himself. High-level support for Anne Boleyn, and the Reformation, was severely lacking. Most at the court simply complied with the king's wishes, which was to accept Anne as the current queen and Henry as Head of the Church. Archbishop of

Canterbury, Thomas Cranmer, was possibly the only exception in the Privy Council. Cranmer believed in Anne's right to be queen, as he was the person to rule Queen Katharine's Catholic marriage to Henry invalid, despite not having the authority to undo a papal-approved union.

But it had been Thomas Cromwell who filled the power vacuum created by Cardinal Wolsey, rising from a common lawyer to the MP running parliament, to private councillor to the king, then Privy Councillor, Jewel-Master, Clerk of the Hanaper, Chancellor for the Exchequer, Chief Minister, Master Secretary to the king, and then Vicegerent of the Spirituals as well as most secular matters; the only person in history to hold such a position. Cromwell was the king's prime minister in every respect; he oversaw all changes and legislations and had the final word on what anyone in the whole court wished to do, say, or even put before the king. The largely silent but powerful feud between Anne Boleyn and Thomas Cromwell would soon be in danger of exploding.

A few weeks before Katharine of Aragon's death, a French rumour had swirled that Anne may have committed adultery. Bishop Stephen Gardiner was still acting as an ambassador at the court of King Francis in Paris, banished from King Henry's sight for his low opinion of the royal marriage and supremacy. Gardiner had spent years in Cardinal Wolsey's service, as a canon lawyer and advisor, and at the same time, Thomas Cromwell had worked for Wolsey as a civil lawyer and advisor. By 1536, the men had known each other for over a decade and had never been friends. Despite this, they wrote to each other with fervent regularity, the letters littered with false courtesies and often outright scorn while they worked for their king.[3] The men were poles apart on most subjects, with their opposed religious choices the sore point. Another issue also lingered; when Cardinal Wolsey was forced from power in 1529, Stephen Gardiner, then only an archdeacon, became the king's new Master Secretary, abandoning his old master after a lifetime of being given a fine upbringing, education and position. Most men abandoned Wolsey in 1529, Cromwell being the rare outlier (a position he regularly held, and seemingly enjoyed[4]). Stephen Gardiner was without doubt an intelligent man; King Henry took Gardiner into his service for his wide range of knowledge, experience with French diplomacy, and sterling reputation. Gardiner was a quiet Catholic who did as he was told, wanted to serve his king, and was named Bishop of Winchester in 1531 for his work.[5] Gardiner was the only clergyman who did not have a litany of mistresses hidden away, he was just a man who got on with his work and feathered his nest with financial rewards.

Thomas Cromwell had no such fine reputation when he and Gardiner met; the king had even spoken openly against Cromwell as early as 1527.[6] It was Cromwell's close personal friends who spoke to King Henry on his behalf; men like John Gage, William Fitzwilliam and John Russell (who was famously rescued from an awkward unnamed situation in Rome many years earlier by Cromwell[7]). Cromwell's openly defiant loyalty to Wolsey in the 1529 parliamentary session, witnessed by Henry, changed the king's opinion of the common lawyer. Cromwell was everything Gardiner was not. Uneducated as a child, Cromwell grew up to become a roguish charmer who had travelled extensively, spoke fluent Italian in addition to his French, Latin and Greek, collected books and art, had amassed a huge personal wealth through merchant business and law, and had little interest in adhering to the standards and expectations of the court.

Cromwell lost his wife, Elizabeth, to sweating sickness in 1528 and his daughters in 1529, and with his only son away studying with his cousins, Cromwell had little left to lose when Cardinal Wolsey fell from power just a month after young Anne and baby Grace Cromwell died.[8] King Henry, despite his reservations, became another person beguiled by Cromwell in parliament (Cromwell charmed so many that his detractors were angry at themselves for liking his speeches[9]). After a single closed-door meeting between the king and Cromwell in February 1530, Wolsey was freed of all charges and sent north to York to live quietly.[10] Cromwell worked as an unnamed personal councillor to the king throughout 1530; given no title, he passed through the palaces in private, all while Stephen Gardiner sat as the man closest to the king. But even Cromwell could not help Cardinal Wolsey in November 1530; when Wolsey's 'treasonous' letters to Katharine of Aragon, Pope Clement, and Emperor Charles surfaced, Wolsey died on his way to what would likely have been his execution in London.[11] With Gardiner as Master Secretary managing the king's day-to-day affairs, Cromwell was given free rein in parliament, and he spent the next several years working on the legal documentation to ensure the Catholic Church could not rule over England; laws which would allow a royal annulment without the need for a papal approval.[12] Cromwell worked largely in peace; he was given rooms and free access to the king but no title, for Anne Boleyn never approved of the man, a commoner too lowly for his position.[13] Cromwell had no care for this; he and Thomas Boleyn had worked together on and off for many years and had a good relationship. Cromwell was the lawyer Boleyn called on when he needed personal matters resolved.[14] Cromwell seemingly enjoyed his persona as a mysterious, private man; his only surviving portrait is a planned testament to disguising the character of a person.[15]

But Cromwell and Gardiner had largely always wanted the same thing; to provide their king with the means to divorce Queen Katharine and marry Anne. Gardiner had been discussing the possibility of annulment without papal intervention since 1529 with Thomas Cranmer and Edward Foxe, all men of Cambridge University.[16] At that time, Cromwell had been busy building Christ Church College at Oxford on behalf of Wolsey and then King Henry. Cromwell and Cranmer had been friends for at least six years by October 1532, when the position of Archbishop of Canterbury fell vacant, and Gardiner certainly would have envied such a role, but Cromwell wanted his friend Thomas Cranmer in the position.

At that time, Thomas Cranmer had been in Germany, collecting support and intellectual opinion on whether a king could break with papal authority and remarry. Cranmer and Cromwell had worked as a pair and had been gently drip-feeding reformist opinions and doctrine to the king for several years by 1532. The Boleyn group similarly liked Thomas Cranmer, his evangelical beliefs fitting well with Anne's, and so Cranmer's new title was assured. By this time, Gardiner was still staunchly Catholic and would never waiver, leaving him ill-placed to hold any sway with the king. Thomas Cromwell was all-powerful by 1532; he ran court and parliament, and among other legislation, had created the Submission of the Clergy, making Henry the Head of the Church in England. Lord Chancellor Thomas More had quit in a rage when the king approved Cromwell's submission, leaving Cromwell to do the work of a lord chancellor and most of Secretary Gardiner's work. Cromwell and Cranmer worked together and had Anne installed as a queen in 1533; Cromwell also had Gardiner regularly dispatched to Paris as an ambassador and installed a puppet lord chancellor, another friend, tepid but pliable lawyer, Sir Thomas Audley.

Cromwell and Gardiner remained an odd duo. Cromwell had his nephew, Richard Cromwell (whom he treated like a son), installed in Gardiner's household until 1533, to maintain an outwardly civil relationship.[17] Cromwell took the official title of Master Secretary from Gardiner in April 1534, when the king banished Gardiner from court for refusing to sign the

Act of Supremacy. But still, Cromwell and Gardiner wrote to one another weekly, sometimes even daily, discussing royal affairs. By Christmas 1535, Gardiner had packed up his London office and moved permanently to France. Gardiner left behind his secretary, Thomas Wriothesley, who transferred into Cromwell's royal offices by mutual consent.[18] Gardiner wrote to Wriothesley as often as he wrote to Cromwell, and in December 1535, Gardiner wrote from the French court:

> 'Certain reports [are] being circulated in the Court of the King of France, and certain letters have been discovered, according to which the Queen [Anne Boleyn] was accused of adultery.'[19]

This record comes from Alexander Alesius, a Scottish man faithful to the Reformation, who taught at Cambridge and worked as a spy for Cromwell on regular occasions. Alesius only wrote of the facts decades later, when looking to gain favour with Queen Elizabeth. Alesius had a theory on why Anne Boleyn died, and while his words were written decades after Anne's death, there is no reason he would lie. He was precisely placed in 1536 to hear what was going on, what was said, and who believed whom. Not everything in Alesius' long letter is correct, the unfortunate byproduct of recalling long-gone matters. But other details in his words are taken as fact even today, filling in the many gaps surrounding the events leading to Anne's death.

Rumours at the French court suggesting Anne Boleyn was an adulterer cannot have been that unusual to hear. France was still a Catholic nation, and King Francis had not supported Henry's second marriage or his changes to the Church. For all the letters, embassies, visits and niceties, Henry and Francis never truly struck up a trusting relationship, and Francis thought nothing of Anne. France's months of fruitless marriage and alliance negotiations with England showed the nation's continuous support for Princess Mary as the heir of England.[20] Supporting Mary as England's heir-presumptive meant France could also rally support and treaties from Mary's cousin, Emperor Charles, easing any threats of war. Random gossip that Anne Boleyn was a whore, albeit lies made in mockery, surely could not have shocked Gardiner's ears. The rumours more likely showed France's lack of respect for England than anything more lurid.

Still, armed with this insult from Gardiner against Anne, Thomas Wriothesley went straight to Vicegerent Cromwell with the story. It was an interesting move; had Gardiner wanted Wriothesley to do such a thing? Cromwell's hatred of the French was well-known on both sides of the sea.[21] Further inflaming Cromwell's dislike would do nothing for French relations, relations which Gardiner was stationed in Paris to nurture. At once, Cromwell took this information to King Henry. There had never been any impropriety on Anne's part, and Cromwell, a well-known champion of wronged women and widows, more than likely took this information to Henry to insult the French rather than to slander Anne.[22] It was no secret that Cromwell and Anne hated each other; all of Europe knew the pair did not get along, and King Henry kept the two mainly apart. But Anne was the queen Cromwell had engineered onto the throne because that was Henry's demand. Cromwell had put his personal opinion aside and done his king's bidding and, in turn, worked night and day without rewards or a title. Producing this French letter to the king was likely to upset the tentative situation at court.

King Henry was naturally angry to hear rumours of his wife's adultery but surprisingly did not erupt with rage.[23] The news probably came at the best time for Anne; she was pregnant, Henry was happy, and Katharine was at her end. The odds of Henry fearing some truth to the rumour and retaliating against Anne were minimal to non-existent. Instead, Henry appointed Cromwell and Wriothesley, and:

> 'Certain others, who, as the report says, hated the Queen, because she had sharply rebuked them and threatened to inform the King that under the guise of the Gospel and religion, they were advancing their own interests, that they had put everything up for sale and had received bribes to confer ecclesiastical benefices upon unworthy persons, the enemies of the true doctrine, permitting the godly to be oppressed and deprived of their just rewards. To them [Henry] intrusted the investigation of the whole business.'[24]

It's very possible that Alesius did not know who was asked to investigate these rumours. If Cromwell decided to destroy Anne with this information, he needed to bide his time. Anne was carrying the king's child, and Henry's whimsical nature could swing in any direction from one day to the next. Given that Alesius references the selling of properties relating to the monasteries, it's likely that the monastery project leaders, Lord Chancellor

Thomas Audley and his protégé Richard Rich, the king's solicitor and head of the new Court of Augmentations, also knew of these rumours. But Cromwell was no fool and did not leak the information, and likely kept his closest men with him on this secret: Richard Cromwell, Ralph Sadler, Thomas Wriothesley, Richard Tomyou, Edward Baynton, Thomas Bedyll, and Thomas Avery. These were not important men at court; they were Cromwell's family and friends. Richard and Ralph were practically Cromwell's sons and were well-liked and respected by everyone at court and could pass through anyone's offices. Thomas Wriothesley had quickly become essential to Cromwell, in need of an experienced secretary, as his other secretary, Stephen Vaughan, spent much of his time in Antwerp and Brussels. Thomas Avery worked as Cromwell's purser and all of Cromwell's vast personal funds went through Avery. Richard Tomyou was a long-time servant to Cromwell and spent time in both Katharine of Aragon and Princess Mary's households. Thomas Bedyll was a friend and one of Cromwell's head monastery inspectors close to London and was always available to help his master. Edward Baynton had the plum role of being Anne Boleyn's Vice Chamberlain, and his wife Isabel was one of Anne's ladies, so anyone coming in or out of Anne's rooms could be reported to the Bayntons. If Cromwell needed anything done, it would happen through his quiet intermediaries. The trouble was that the gossip was based on nothing, so there was nothing to investigate. For now.

CHAPTER 3

Pride Before the Fall

King Henry VIII had long been paranoid about illness. The benefit of this was his interest in medicine, founding the Royal College of Physicians in 1518 and eventually the Company of Barber-Surgeons in 1540. He had a wide team of well-known physicians on hand throughout his life, most notably Sir William Butts, Dr Thomas Vicary, Dr John Chambre, Dr George Owen, Dr Thomas Linacre, and Dr John Clement. Between on-hand medical care, a long-term interest in creating treatments, and practising isolation and social distancing,[1] Henry had managed to escape most of the serious illnesses that plagued England. A tall, healthy, strong man, Henry evaded most, if not all childhood illnesses, only suffering smallpox as an adult in 1514, and the occasional bout of malaria in the 1520s. However, his over-confidence would lead him into the path of injury.

In 1526, King Henry measured just over 6 feet tall (183 cm) and weighted a healthy 90 kilograms (200 pounds/15 stone). He was a man who got through a huge amount of meat, pastries and wine in an average day, but was always physically active. But in 1527, Henry suffered two injuries; first, he damaged his ankle playing tennis, and while this healed, he was never able to wear a full shoe again, adopting soft, calf leather slipper-like shoes. This quickly became the fashion at court.[2] Later in the year, while in Canterbury, Dr Vicary treated Henry's 'sore leg',[3] likely an ulcer which had first appeared more than a decade earlier while isolating from illness (the lesion described has caused some to believe the king suffered syphilis, a now well-disproven myth). In 1527, the ulcer healed without too much cause for concern, earning Dr Vicary a tidy pension.

While Henry's physicians did not keep detailed records, Henry seemed to suffer little illness or injury for almost a decade after the incident in Canterbury. But with the death of Katharine of Aragon, a new threat emerged — the mid-life crisis. After the celebration following Katharine's demise, Henry went to the tiltyard to enjoy some jousting practice, an activity he had not partaken in for some time. He was not the active man he once was, and the beginning of a middle-age spread had begun its passage of time. Henry's activities in the tiltyard were not of any consequence and not recorded, until he fell from his horse on Monday, 24 January 1536. With no record of the actual injury, the truth of the accident has been muddied. Records of the king being unconscious for two hours would lead to the suggestion he suffered a massive head injury, which never occurred. There is no proof to support the theory that Henry suffered a head injury that day. Still, a large man wearing 50 kilograms (110 pounds) of armour, thrown from a large horse was a serious accident, particularly if the horse went down with him. The notion that Henry went 'two hours without speaking' came from Pedro Ortiz, Emperor Charles' ambassador in Rome, who heard the news from someone in France, who heard it from someone in London … not an accurate source.[4] Ambassador Chapuys was the man in London who had first-hand knowledge of the actual incident, writing:

> 'The King, being mounted on a great horse to run at the lists, both fell so heavily that everyone thought it a miracle he was not killed, but he sustained no injury. I think he might ask of fortune for what greater misfortune he is reserved.'[5]

Chronicler Charles Wriothesley, who had the benefit of his cousin Thomas working for Vicegerent Cromwell, also reported that the king 'suffered no hurt'.[6] Cromwell himself mentioned that the king was up and working immediately after the accident and had no injury in his regular dispatch to Bishop Gardiner.[7] But it was the ulcers of Henry's earlier days that burst in the accident and proved to be the injury that he couldn't heal without proper medical treatment.

The final week of January 1536 would have been a fraught time after King Henry fell from his horse. While suffering from leg pain, his all-important pride was also damaged. Jousting was not only an athletic activity, but it was also a symbol of manliness, virility, and patriarchy. Henry had stumbled in the pursuit designed to make him look like a man, a king. A strong jouster was a man who could rule, overpower enemies, control women, and be the most masculine of men in an era when image meant everything.[8] How could a man have honour and power if he were too injured to display such alleged male characteristics? Wriothesley's account of the incident only added further embarrassment; Henry was only training, 'running at the ring', where a rider gallops with his lance aimed towards a ring-shaped target as practice.[9] This was no defeat at the hands of a worthy competitor or riding in the pursuit of glory, but a simple mistake during a task Henry would have done hundreds, thousands of times throughout his life. It was witnessed by his friends and servants waiting on their king, not in front of the queen and court there to witness a grand duel. King Henry's delicate feelings meant a great deal to the court; many had lost their heads due to Henry's outbursts, and plenty more would in the future.

The misinformation of January 1536 continued through the horrific final week of the month. Anne Boleyn said her troubles began when she heard the news of the king's accident, presumably soon after the fact, delivered in haste by the Duke of Norfolk.[10] When Anne's miscarriage began is unclear; she could have been unwell even before Henry fell from his horse. Ambassador Chapuys wrote to Emperor Charles on Saturday, 29 January that Anne:

> 'Cried and lamented herself on the occasion, fearing lest she herself might be brought to the same end as (Katharine). And this very morning, someone coming from the lady [Gertrude Courtney] mentioned in my letter of the 21st of November ultimo, and also from her husband, [Henry Courtenay, Marquis of Exeter] has stated that both had heard from the lips of one of the principal courtiers that this King had said to one of them in great secrecy, and as if in confession, that he had been seduced and forced into this second marriage by means of sortileges and charms, and that, owing to that, he held it as null. God had well shown his displeasure at it by denying him male children. He, therefore, considered that he could take a third wife, which he said he wished much to do'.[11]

For King Henry to have said such a cruel thing about Anne could only have come after the miscarriage of their longed-for son. The couple had been nothing but content until this point, no matter the rumours and disparagement from Anne's enemies. Chapuys' use of the word 'sortileges' has given rise to later accusations of witchcraft, pure disinformation against

Anne.[12] Sortileges could mean magic, divination, sorcery, secrets, simple beguilement, 'feminine wiles', or simply a man in love with a woman. At no time was the theory of witchcraft ever mentioned and does not deserve any further mention in legitimate discussion. But for Henry's words to have been overheard, then spread to Gertrude Courtenay, and then to Ambassador Chapuys would have taken time, at the very least a full day, to say nothing of the opportunity for the tale to become twisted with each retelling.

It was not until Thursday, 10 February that Chapuys wrote to say Anne Boleyn had suffered the loss of a son, around three and a half months into her pregnancy.[13] Where he got this highly detailed information goes unrecorded. Given the medical knowledge of the time, only Anne could have known how far along her pregnancy had progressed, rather than any 'evidence' she produced. As for determining the sex, it only might have been possible to tell. The baby being male plays well into the narrative that this was the turning point of Anne's demise but cannot have a basis in fact. Nothing else suggests Anne lost a son, not even her own words, which go unacknowledged in paperwork. The exact date of Anne's miscarriage cannot be determined, but Chapuys recorded it as Saturday, 29 January, the day of Queen Katharine's funeral.[14] It made for a good story: the 'true queen' was laid to rest and the 'concubine' suffered the loss of a son. But judging by his own words on 29 January, Chapuys has made up the date to suit the narrative. Charles Wriothesley recorded Anne's sad loss and wrote down Sunday, 30 January for her miscarriage, and this might have been the date the information spread publicly. Wriothesley believed Anne to be fifteen weeks pregnant at the time of her miscarriage, by her judgement, but Wriothesley did not mention gender.[15] The other source of information is Nicholas Sander and his imagined tales decades later, suggesting a deformed child, but his writing is so full of slander and disinformation that it is not worth adding at this stage of the tale.

Anne's pain cannot be overlooked; a pain only utterly understood by those fated to suffer such a profound loss. Coupled with the magnificent stress of needing to provide England with a male heir, and the international furore caused by their marriage in the first place, it is little wonder Anne was distressed. King Henry was undoubtedly also devastated to lose a desperately wanted child, but he acted out in typical fashion, anger. With little to say to his beloved wife, Henry told Anne that, 'he saw clearly that God did not wish to give him male children',[16] and left her at Greenwich, and would only speak to her after she recovered. Ambassador Chapuys' little spies heard all and reported back that Anne did her best to put the loss aside and:

> 'Consoled her maids who wept, telling them it was for the best because she would be the sooner with child again, and that the son she bore would not be doubtful like this one, which had been conceived during the life of the Queen.'[17]

The comment does sound like the Anne known during her life at court; the one to hold herself together and maintain her dignity most of the time. Chapuys believed that Anne had mentioned that a child conceived after Katharine of Aragon's death would be preferable, which showed that Anne herself doubted whether Princess Elizabeth was legitimate. This sounds like Chapuys' imaginings more than anything. Chapuys likewise heard that Anne blamed two things for her pregnancy loss: the fall King Henry took in the tiltyard causing great shock (which Chapuys said was a lie, as Norfolk told his niece gently and without panic[18]), and that Henry now 'loved others'. Chapuys wrote on 10 February that courtiers believed Anne feared she could not have male children and that:

> 'The King would treat [Anne] like the late Queen, especially considering the treatment shown to a lady of the Court, named Mistress Semel, to whom, as many say, he has lately made great presents.'[19]

This was the first mention of Jane Seymour. Who shared this information, who believed it, and how long the attention had been on Jane is conveniently omitted from Chapuys' letters. But it was entirely probable that Henry had picked up a mistress, even just in the interest of courtly love rather than physical, while Anne was pregnant. But Anne, having married the king for love, never politely overlooked her husband's behaviour with mistresses. Queen Katharine understood the reality of being married to a king, but Anne did not have Katharine's practical or political experience. The rules of royal marriage did not apply to Henry and Anne; they were a love match. Anne had no support outside Henry's love; she brought no alliances to the table, no internationally powerful relatives, and sadly no son in her womb.

Tales told fifty and one hundred years later speak of Anne ripping a locket from Jane Seymour's neck or witnessing Jane upon Henry's knee (which was injured from his fall at the time), but there is no contemporary evidence to back up any of these claims. Any hint of Anne retaliating against Jane Seymour would have been fodder for every gossip in Europe. Anne had similarly not condemned Mary Shelton and an unknown earlier mistress (possibly Margaret Lee), and there was no reason to believe Anne was foolish now.

But who was Lady Jane Seymour? Born and raised on the approximately 1200 acres of Wulfhall, close to Savernake Forest in Wiltshire, the royal court visiting the Seymour family home in 1535 likely did not benefit Jane Seymour. The Seymour children were already at court; Jane and her younger sister Elizabeth had served multiple queens by 1536. The golden child of the surviving six Seymour children, Sir Edward Seymour had been at court for over twenty years, first serving Henry VIII's sister, Mary, when she became Queen of France for several months in 1514.[20] As a quiet but loyal man, Edward was a good example for his sister Jane, who, at the age of 19, joined Queen Katharine around 1527, when introduced either by her brother, or by their cousin, courtier Sir Francis Bryan.[21] A woman could have no finer role model than Queen Katharine, and Jane had not had much of an education beyond being a gentlewoman. But Jane could read and write and likely knew a little French, but was best known for her exquisite needlework, pieces of which (like Anne's) stayed in the royal collection more than one hundred years after her death. While Jane would have been taught to be obedient and amiable, as men wanted in a silent, fertile wife, she was also an excellent horsewoman, able to join in hunting rides after learning the skill from her father at Wulfhall.[22] In 1527, there would have been little worry about whispers that the king wanted a new wife, and a position in Queen Katharine's household would have felt like a glittering future for a young woman like Jane. It would have also been a suitable time to move from home; Wulfhall had suffered scandal, with Edward Seymour humiliated after his wife Catherine bore two sons who seemingly were not her husband's.[23] Later, unprovable rumours suggested Sir John Seymour fathered the boys with his daughter-in-law.

The turbulent years of Henry and Katharine's royal divorce would have affected Jane Seymour and the other ladies in the queen's household, especially once Katharine was exiled from court in July 1531, and sent to The More in Hertfordshire. While Jane's name does not appear in the papers of the period (sadly lacking throughout 1531 for most people at court), there is all likelihood that Jane followed her mistress into exile, who continued to dine as a queen with thirty maids at her side.[24] But Queen Katharine's household continued to shrink as Henry ordered his wife to move around royal manors, and in February 1533, word came that King Henry had secretly married pregnant Anne Boleyn. Katharine was living at Ampthill in Bedfordshire at the time, and Jane could have been one of the maids at her mistress' side when the news arrived. By August 1533, Katharine's household was broken up and moved again, and Jane's name was not among the ten women moved with their mistress.

By 1533, Jane Seymour was 25 and unmarried. Returning to her family's estate could not have been a promising thought. However, with Anne Boleyn now on the throne, there was space at court again, and Jane and her younger sister Elizabeth were able to serve in Anne's rooms. The drama of Edward Seymour's marriage had died down, and a new wife from a comparative family was later found to create the next generation of legitimate Seymour heirs.

Jane Seymour had many siblings to call upon, though the eldest Seymour child, John, had died as a teenager, and an infant bearing the same name died soon after. Young siblings Anthony and Margery Seymour had both died from the sweating sickness outbreak of 1528, leaving Jane with older brothers Edward, Henry and Thomas, and younger sisters Elizabeth and Dorothy.[25] Henry Seymour had left Wulfhall in 1528 to work in minor noble positions away from court; Thomas Seymour held similar middling positions. Elizabeth Seymour had been given away in marriage at age 12 in 1530,[26] something Jane had escaped, and Dorothy Seymour married and had a child in 1533, aged just 13.[27] The Seymour girls were handed to men at a tender age, yet Jane, almost double her sisters' ages, remained unmarried.

Had the scandal of Edward Seymour's children at Wulfhall affected Lady Jane's marriage chances when she was of an age to find a match? The family had seemingly put all their efforts into finding Edward Seymour a good replacement bride, his adulterous first wife sent to a nunnery where she soon died.[28] Henry and Thomas Seymour remained unmarried until the late 1540s, while the younger surviving Seymour girls were offloaded to the first men who wanted a child bride. Portraits of Jane and Elizabeth Seymour both survive, though they were not known to be as beautiful as their mother Lady Margery (née Wentworth), whose beauty inspired poets.[29]

A surviving remembrance written by Thomas Cromwell in 1532 mentions the possibility of a marriage between Sir Ralph Elderton and 'Lady Seymour', which could have only been Jane, though no other hints about her marriage options survive.[30] Lady Jane Dormer mentioned in her autobiography that her father, William Dormer, once a servant in Thomas Cromwell's household, was mooted as a possible husband for Jane by a mutual acquaintance, Sir Francis Bryan. But the Dormers, a wealthy and well-connected family, wanted better for their only son and sought Cromwell's help in marrying William to Lady Mary Sidney soon after the 1534 Seymour proposal.[31] However, this possible Seymour-Dormer marriage is not mentioned anywhere else and cannot be verified. Jane Seymour was lucky to have the support of her distant cousin Sir Francis Bryan, who was beloved by the king, as one of his most trusted attendants and friends.[32] But the window for marriage was slipping away from Jane, while her teenage sisters were bearing children as fast as their husbands could plant them. Perhaps Jane knew that serving Anne Boleyn was as good as life would get for her, and free of men's attentions, she could have lived a comfortable and quiet life on the peripherals of court, just as her wealthy father had done. In New Year 1534, a 'Lady Seymour'[33] received a gift at court; this was likely Jane, as her 15-year-old sister Elizabeth had just given birth to a son, Henry Ughtred, at Gorey Castle at Mont Orgueil, Jersey.[34]

Fiction has made much of the royal court visiting Wulfhall in September 1535, the Seymour home.[35] Sir John Seymour had served loyally under Henry VII and was knighted at the Battle of Blackheath in 1497. He served in multiple roles as a warden and sheriff in the Wiltshire area for decades and joined Henry VIII in battle in Tournai and Thérouanne in 1513. Seymour became a knight banneret before spending his days in Wiltshire as a commissioner and justice of the peace, and rarely visited court. The royal progress through Wulfhall itself was largely uneventful, as the royal court stopped at many homes, and courtiers near bankrupted themselves to entertain their king. Whether Jane Seymour was travelling with the court and serving Anne Boleyn or had been staying at home at Wulfhall during the visit, she is unlikely to have had any contact with King Henry. She simply was not important enough. If Henry was introduced to any of the Seymour women, it would have been Lady Anne (née Stanhope), who married Sir Edward Seymour on 9 March 1535.[36]

It was only in early 1536 that Ambassador Chapuys heard of Jane Seymour, who had aroused the king's attention likely in December 1535.

Jane, so pale she was considered a little sick-looking,[37] with blue eyes and blonde hair (considered then the most beautiful complexion), was a world away from her mistress Anne Boleyn, in looks and temperament. Judging by Henry's many wives and mistresses, he was a man who liked blondes, and the quiet and obedient daughter of Wulfhall must have caught his eye at court quite by chance. The king had managed to finally get his wife pregnant while on progress and was suddenly in need of a mistress. Had Jane been recommended for the role? For Jane, aged 27, she probably wondered what her quiet life of serving and standing aside would become. The letters Henry once sent to Anne Boleyn were suddenly going to Jane Seymour.

In February 1536, with the king paying favour to Sir John's eldest daughter, it would be expected there would be rewards for the Seymour household, but there were none. While records show Sir John Seymour died on 21 December 1536, it is more likely he died in December 1535, just after the royal progress to his home, as he is unmentioned in records again. It would have come as a shock to the Seymour family, all built around their patriarch. He was a man of 60, but his most recent son, born to a mistress, was only 6 years old. A plaque on Sir John's tombstone recalls the many later accomplishments of his children, which may account for the misdating of his death when placed decades after his death.[38] The news of Sir John Seymour's death at court would spread, where Edward and Jane Seymour were based (there is no proof Henry or Thomas Seymour were at court during this time, and Elizabeth Seymour had just given birth to a daughter at Hexby in Yorkshire[39]). Sadly, the New Year gift list for 1536 does not survive, as Jane's gift may have given some assurance to the start of the king's affection towards her. Ambassador Chapuys noted that 'Mistress Semel' was firmly in the king's affections by late January 1536. If the king showed affection to a lady at court, her father would surely benefit, but Sir John is not mentioned at any stage, rather Sir Edward Seymour was the recipient of the king's favour.[40] This suggests Sir John was already dead when the accidental power struggle between Anne Boleyn and Jane Seymour began. All the powerful Catholic families at court would have been quite happy for a family like the Seymours, quiet, loyal, and without court quarrels or alliances, to catch the king's eye. Lady Jane Seymour was simply an object of courtly love, a game for the king while his wife was pregnant. But with Anne suffering a miscarriage, which came just eighteen months after her tragic stillbirth, the game of courtly love was to become a battleground.

CHAPTER 4

The Empire Strikes Back

Princess Mary had been at Eltham Place when she heard of her mother's passing, and that she had been denied permission to attend Katharine's funeral. By early February 1536, Mary was moved to Hunsdon, where Lady Anne Shelton and the household looked to shield Mary from the news of Anne Boleyn's miscarriage, and subsequent marital troubles. Lady Shelton was saddened by her niece's miscarriage, as were her courtier daughters, along with Anne Boleyn's other maternal aunt, Lady Alice Clere, who also worked in the combined Princess Elizabeth and Mary household. Princess Mary's movements on the day of her mother's funeral are unknown.

It was Katharine and Henry's nieces who were listed to attend as chief mourners, Eleanor Clifford (née Brandon), Countess of Cumberland and Frances Grey (née Brandon), Marchioness of Dorset. Both women were newly married and beginning their annual pregnancies, though Lady Eleanor is noted as chief mourner over her eldest sister.[1] Their stepmother, teenager Catherine Brandon (née Willoughby), Duchess of Suffolk, goddaughter of Queen Katharine, also attended in Princess Mary's place, alongside Katharine's thirteen ladies led by Lady Grace Bedingfield, and fifty servants who accompanied the black velvet-covered coffin, all carrying torches.[2] Queen Katharine lay beneath one thousand candles and was received at Peterborough by four bishops and six abbots.

Bishop John Hilsey gave a sermon about how the Pope was no longer Head of the Church and that Katharine's marriage as a queen was not lawful, grossly inappropriate for the event. Ambassador Chapuys reported that Mary had spent most of January alone in her chambers, and it was probably better she did not hear the details of the funeral. Princess Mary did speak with her mother's physician and apothecary and felt somewhat relieved to hear the details of her mother's passing.[3]

Ambassador Chapuys wrote regularly of Mary's reduced state since she entered Princess Elizabeth's household in late 1533. Chapuys spoke of Mary as if she were almost a prisoner, a servant in Princess Elizabeth's household, which was more dramatic than the truth. Princess Mary certainly lived in a state she did not expect as the daughter of a king, but it was never as bad as Chapuys opined to his master. Though not officially allowed to be called a princess, as Lady Mary she received regular letters, had servants to attend her, medical staff to manage her ongoing stomach problems, and was able to eat in private, something reserved for only high-ranking household members.[4]

Even with the Sheltons looking to shield Mary from the news of Anne's miscarriage and Henry's subsequent outbursts of grief, it was not long before the news filtered through. By 10 February, Chapuys was ensuring his servant, who delivered letters and items to Mary weekly, was interrogating Mary's staff for information, about what Mary knew of the royal marriage, and how the information was handled. Whether Princess Mary knew of Chapuys' ongoing fear that Queen Katharine had been poisoned is unclear or whether she knew Chapuys was considering having her smuggled out of England and safe abroad with Emperor Charles.[5] Princess Mary was staying at Hunsdon, but in the first week of February, Henry changed his mind and moved Mary and her small household forty miles away to Gravesend.[6] A perfect location for Mary to be evacuated out of the country and her father's reach, almost too good to be true. Vicegerent Cromwell and Ambassador Chapuys had been in near constant contact over Mary, with Cromwell more intent than ever to create an alliance with the Emperor and ensure Princess Mary's safety, even offering Katharine's physician a royal position in thanks for his work.[7] Katharine's confessor, Thomas Abel, was in the Tower for refusing the supremacy, and soon, so was Mary's beloved former tutor, Richard Fetherstone. Mary had suddenly become a major player in court negotiations after several years of being largely ignored. Holy Roman Emperor Charles was in mourning in Naples for his aunt Queen Katharine, and expected the same of his wife Isabella, who ruled Spain in his place.[8] The Catholic supporters of England suddenly saw an opportunity for change after Anne's miscarriage, a chance to pounce on power while Henry and Anne grieved for their lost son.

As the power dynamic in England shifted, Europe was also in a state of flux. Emperor Charles and King Francis in France were looking to make alliances but were also prepared to go to war over Milan.[9] Princess Mary and Ambassador Chapuys surely knew that following through with a plan to get Mary to sea and into Flanders would cause a massive uproar, possibly war. Emperor Charles may have listened to Chapuys' potential plans for Mary, but in reality, the Emperor had never once stepped in to help Katharine or Mary as King Henry exiled them and broke the Catholic faith in England. If anything, King Henry had moved Mary to Gravesend as a test to see if she would run. If Chapuys and Emperor Charles were discussing the notion of liberating Mary from England, Vicegerent Cromwell surely knew about it too. Mary was already at risk of the death penalty for not signing the Act of Supremacy and renouncing the Pope and Catholicism. Vicegerent Cromwell had been ordered to move Mary and give her a bigger household more befitting of a princess, including people who served her and her mother during more auspicious years.[10] Cromwell sent Mary 40*l* (almost £17,000 today) from the king, to give to the poor.[11] Fleeing now would be a devastatingly bad decision, especially with so many other plans coming into play.

With Anne Boleyn's miscarriage, everyone's focus had changed. Anne was still recovering at Greenwich, missing the usual Candlemas celebrations at court, and already people were pondering the succession, the same succession they had sworn and signed to uphold on Princess Elizabeth's behalf a year earlier. Sadness over Queen Katharine's death brought Princess Mary into the public consciousness again, and Henry Fitzroy, the king's Catholic illegitimate son, was well-liked and at court regularly with his father.[12] The likely rumours of the king engaging in courtly love with Jane Seymour must have raised spirits in a way conservatives had not felt in years.

But every possible plan or scheme, imagined or prepared, for or against Anne Boleyn, had to go through Thomas Cromwell. Cromwell was a man of contradictions; he was quiet at court, but furious in parliament. He was the man to undo Katharine and Henry's marriage in favour of Anne Boleyn, yet he had been supporting Katharine and Mary in the aftermath of his accomplishment. Cromwell lost faith in the Catholic Church in 1518 on a trip to Rome,[13] and then devoted six years of his life to Cardinal Wolsey. Cromwell was perceived as a dour, limping, black-clad man skulking around the court, but his private life was extravagant; he entertained with lavish parties, restored manors fit for a king, and gave out cash and gifts as if it was his last day on Earth. Cromwell would happily dispatch anyone the king asked him to punish, but would also feed 200 homeless people twice daily from his kitchens at Austin Friars.[14] Both Bishop John Fisher and Sir Thomas More were condemned by parliament and the king; Cromwell saw out the execution orders but was also the man who personally begged both men to repent and gave them multiple chances to save themselves.[15] Cromwell had a vast network of friends and family but was hated at court. So, when it came to destroying the very queen Cromwell placed beside Henry, no one could predict which way he would lean. Plus, no one would be able to enact any sort of plan without Cromwell hearing about it; Cromwellian friends were listening in every language all over England and Europe.

Vicegerent Thomas Cromwell and Ambassador Eustace Chapuys had met many times over the previous six years of Chapuys' time in England, either at court for formal meetings, or when Chapuys turned up at Cromwell's various homes to discuss countless matters.[16] On Tuesday, 22 February 1536, Cromwell sent his nephew, Richard, to see Chapuys at his home; Chapuys' lodgings and Cromwell's Austin Friars home in the 'foreigners' part of the city were only separated by the Austin Friars church and its grounds. Cromwell wanted to meet outside the church to discuss a matter, and a plan formed as Ralph Sadler played messenger between the men. Cromwell would stand outside Austin Friars and Chapuys would just happen to walk by on his way to Katharine's funeral mass on Wednesday, 23 February.[17] Cromwell was not living at Austin Friars at the time due to construction work, but rather living out of his offices designed for the Master of the Rolls, a magnificent manor on Chancery Lane, which he adored and could often disappear into without anyone being able to access him.[18] Chapuys knew things were serious; Cromwell publicly walked alone 'half a league' from Chancery Lane to Austin Friars, and the pair took mass for Katharine's soul before discussing business on the street.

Vicegerent Cromwell had made no secret of his desire to secure a peaceful alliance between King Henry and Emperor Charles. He had told Chapuys so for years; Cromwell made his loyalty and commitment plain, to create an English and Imperial alliance, and Chapuys made this information available across Europe.[19] Cromwell had enacted the Act of Supremacy, ensuring everyone in England had to sign the oath that Henry was the Head of the Church over the Pope, but had worked to ensure 'foreigners,' Spaniards especially, were excluded and did not have to defy the Pope, the Emperor, and God.[20] So far, Katharine and Mary had been able to defy the orders to sign away their consciences, but with Katharine gone, Princess Mary was under increasing pressure, and Mary believed she would die to save her conscience and faith.[21]

Vicegerent Cromwell stood in the cold with Ambassador Chapuys on a Wednesday afternoon and told him they could create an alliance between their nations. Cromwell appealed to Chapuys that he had never entreated with the French and that Bishop Gardiner with King Francis would never say or do anything against Emperor Charles and proved so with letters sent by Gardiner from Paris.[22] Cromwell made a plea that now Queen Katharine was dead, that England and the Holy Roman Empire could be allies, even with Anne Boleyn as queen, and begged Chapuys to tell the Emperor that at last, meaningful peace in Europe could be achieved. Cromwell had been the man to break the Catholic Church in England and usher in the Reformation, but he also wanted lasting safety and support from the Emperor who had the power to hold all of Europe to account in the defence of Catholicism if he wished.[23]

Ambassador Chapuys told Cromwell there were four conditions if England wanted a deal with Emperor Charles: that King Henry would need to return to the Catholic faith; that Princess Mary be ruled legitimate and reinstated as heir; that King Henry would have to help the Emperor fight the Turks; and that England had to side with the Emperor against the French over a war in Milan.[24] In return, Charles would acknowledge Anne as England's queen. These were near-impossible tasks for Cromwell to negotiate, but he was so desirable for an alliance he would not rule out making such a deal. Cromwell was even prepared to ensure that Spaniards and other foreigners would be safe from any further Reformation changes. But as Chapuys wrote to the Emperor the next day:

> 'Cromwell's answer was that I might be sure there was no feint, mystery, or dissimulation whatever in what he had just told me. It would have been foolish on his part to hold such language should it bring neither advantage to his master, nor honour to himself. He would not, for anything in this world, be held as a liar or dissembler. But as what he had just said proceeded entirely from himself, without any mandate from his master, I could easily believe that he had no power to make overtures.'[25]

This was the sticking point, and would have unintended consequences for Anne Boleyn, not that either she or Cromwell would have seen it at the time. Vicegerent Cromwell, for all his powers, could not make entreaties as an ambassador. Terms were settled by kings and only their appointed ambassadors. By creating an alliance, Cromwell was overreaching his powers, something he never did; he would normally have the king personally sign off every list of tasks that needed to be actioned. This decision left Cromwell exposed for the first time in his political career, and Anne Boleyn would soon enough suffer for his miscalculation.

Chapuys finished his tale to the Emperor, reporting that Queen Katharine had left a gold cross necklace to Mary, a valueless piece of consolation. The king had forced Cromwell to take the necklace back from Mary. Chapuys signed off his letter mentioning this action, 'by which act, Your Majesty may well calculate what faith and reliance can be placed in these people's words.'[26]

Princess Mary was a realistic alternative as a conduit to power after her father. Anne Boleyn's halo was slipping, and while it is easy to assume Jane Seymour became King Henry's latest object of affection, ejecting Anne from favour, it was not so simple. Princess Mary was freshly 20 years old, the daughter of a dead queen who martyred herself at the altar of Catholic England. Mary had been living as a forgotten child for three years and now the royal relationship, and who was in it, depended on how Henry treated his daughter. Anne Boleyn had always been suspicious of Mary, and now, those fears started to come to fruition.

CHAPTER 5

Cold Shoulders of the Great Families of England

A letter written in late January 1539, concerning the trial of Sir Nicholas Carew, shows how early in 1536 Princess Mary was seriously considered a replacement as the female power holder at court. As always, it was Vicegerent Cromwell in charge of Carew's 1539 case, so the surviving statements and depositions are thorough, and the handwriting is easy to identify among Cromwell's secretaries. Sir Nicholas Carew was investigated in 1539 for his Catholic and White Rose connections; Cromwell ensured the interrogations were vague, on the king's orders. Among those interviewed was an old servant of Queen Katharine, who wrote of his connection with Princess Mary.[1] Anthony Roke was a long-time servant of Queen Katharine, who found work with Thomas Wriothesley, Cromwell's secretary, in 1536. A deposition written about Carew, which has long since been water damaged, and with no signature attached, bears handwriting just like Roke's, who wrote regularly to his master Wriothesley from his posting at Titchfield manor.[2] But the identity of the writer cannot be conclusively identified, as Roke wrote in secretary script, similar to the handwriting of countless other servants. While the handwriting is listed today as 'likely Anthony Roke',[3] the same volumes have ten years' worth of misidentifying Stephen Vaughan's secretary script as Thomas Wriothesley's hand. These errors remain uncorrected to this day. But Anthony Roke was the ideal man to shed light on the conspiracy against Anne Boleyn.

Anthony Roke was a servant of Queen Katharine until her death and was a free agent when the late queen's household was disbanded by the king. Roke returned to London in search of work, where he was summoned to court by Sir Nicholas Carew.[4] Roke was treated with kindness and confidence by Carew, who showed Roke a letter written in Carew's hand, written to Princess Mary. The letter suggested Mary submit to the king's will, by acknowledging Henry's role as Head of the Church and admitting her parents' relationship was never valid. If Mary did so, then Carew and his unnamed 'friends' felt sure King Henry would welcome Mary back to court as the heir-apparent of England. Roke would be the one to deliver this letter and put the offer to Mary. Roke wrote that he replied:

> 'At which time I made answer, "I durst not, until I did know my Lord's [Cromwell's] pleasure", then being Secretary, who [Carew] bade me not fear, for he would show [Cromwell] his-self, saying that he was sure Master Secretary would give a hundred pounds that [Mary] would consent.'[5]

Roke reported that, on hearing of Cromwell's approval of the plan, he agreed to take Carew's letter to Princess Mary, who was at Hunsdon, twenty-six miles outside London. When Roke arrived at Hunsdon, also present was Richard Tomyou, one of Cromwell's private servants. Tomyou was close to Cromwell, trusted to run Cromwell's private home at Austin Friars alongside Cromwell's brother-in-law, John Williamson. Tomyou had once worked in Queen Katharine's household, just as Roke had, and the men were equally surprised to see each other before Princess Mary.[6] Sir Nicholas Carew had trusted Roke to be his messenger to Mary, and Sir Nicholas' wife, Lady Elizabeth Carew had sent a letter with Tomyou, who was undoubtedly selected by Cromwell as messenger to the princess.

Roke's deposition gave the impression that he had previously delivered letters to the princess from her mother, which had been forbidden by the king. Tomyou had been Queen Katharine's Clerk Controller (and Cromwell's spy) until 1533 and then spent two years with Mary before returning home to Cromwell.[7] Princess Mary would have known, through men like Roke and Tomyou, that she could trust the letters she received. Mary stayed at Hunsdon for only a few weeks in early 1536, so the letters must have been delivered in the first two weeks of February. The fact that Carew, his wife, and Cromwell were all simultaneously contacting Mary was no accident but showed a collaboration of unlikely allies.

Sir Nicholas Carew was one of King Henry's oldest friends. Five years younger than Henry, Carew moved into the then-Prince Henry's household at court at age 6 in 1502 and quickly became a companion and jousting friend to the future king.[8] Carew's jousting feats were almost unmatched, so much so that King Henry gave Carew his own tiltyard at Greenwich. Carew was knighted in 1517 and by 1522, took over as Henry's Master of the Horse, one of the closest positions beside the king, and sat on the Privy Council.[9] Carew was an admitted rake, one of several Cardinal Wolsey sought to separate from the king. After several years of working as a diplomat in the 1520s, with King Francis and Emperor Charles,[10] Carew returned to Henry's privy chamber in 1528 and settled down to become a more astute gentleman.

Why 1528? Cardinal Wolsey was still in power at the time, but Carew had an unlikely connection; he shared a great-grandfather with Anne Boleyn, and that may have prompted Anne to consider Carew an ally. Overruling Wolsey, King Henry welcomed his childhood friend back to the privy chamber. But Carew soon became wary of Anne and her influence at court. Carew had a privileged position; there was little he could do to upset the king, given their close relationship. Given Anne Boleyn's strong relationship with France, she likely wished to keep Carew onside, as he continued to travel to Europe to see King Francis and Emperor Charles on diplomatic missions.[11] Yet, Carew did not want Anne on the throne, and openly stated his allegiance to Queen Katharine and Princess Mary on numerous occasions, his words spreading as far as Ambassador Chapuys' ears. Another childhood friend of the king, Charles Brandon, Duke of Suffolk, was equally disgusted by the royal divorce, and both men had discussed their distaste with Sir Henry Guildford.[12] Despite his continued disrespect for Anne, Carew always held on to his position at court.

Carew was one of the men who prepared the landmark meeting between King Henry and King Francis in France in 1532, but told Ambassador Chapuys before he left for Paris, 'that far from executing his commission with fidelity, Carew will do any and everything in his power to have it put off'.[13] Even so, Carew did his duty to the king, and the trip went ahead (albeit without the longed-for success). King Francis asked King Henry to admit Carew to the Noble Order of the Garter, though all twenty-four spaces were already taken. Only in 1536 was a space available for allocation as George Nevill, 5th Baron Bergavenny, had died in June 1535, one month after the annual Garter meeting.[14] Carew, like all of the noble and ancient families of court, had sat with his mouth closed, only gossiping about his distaste for Anne Boleyn in private for years. Only now, as Anne suffered her miscarriage, did Carew feel safe enough to act on his previous whispers and take action in Princess Mary's name.

At first glance, it might look odd that Carew and his wife both wrote to Mary in February 1536, but with parliament opening, Carew had travelled to London, even if simply to show his face. Carew had never been reliable in attending parliament, and with the previous seven parliaments all loaded with issues surrounding the royal divorce and changes to religion, it is little wonder a staunch Catholic did not wish to attend. Lady Elizabeth Carew was technically one of Anne Boleyn's ladies, but lived at the luxurious Carew Manor, eleven miles south of London in Beddington.

Nicholas Carew may have felt safe enough to write such dangerous letters to Princess Mary, and Lady Elizabeth was equally protected. It was not simply being the wife of Nicholas Carew that protected Lady Elizabeth; her history at court and her family connections meant King Henry would never do her harm. Elizabeth's mother was Lady Margaret Bryan, the royal governess, who had raised Princess Mary, Henry Fitzroy, and now ran baby Princess Elizabeth's nursery.[15] Lady Margaret Bryan (née Bourchier) had been one of Queen Katharine's most favoured ladies-in-waiting, so her daughter Elizabeth grew up around the court with her mother, and her father, Sir Thomas Bryan, worked as Queen Katharine's vice-chamberlain back in the glory days of the 1510s.[16] All three of the Bryan children were regular attendees at court; Lady Elizabeth herself became a lady-in-waiting to Queen Katharine at just 14, becoming good friends with her contemporary Bessie Blount. While Bessie's relationship with Henry became infamous, Elizabeth's alleged affair with the king in their youth is far murkier. It seemed that Elizabeth Bryan and Bessie Blount had been indulging in games of courtly love with King Henry and Charles Brandon in 1514, and so Elizabeth was soon married off to their friend, Sir Nicholas Carew. The Carews became something of a power couple at court, hosting the king and queen on multiple occasions at their home, and no matter the dramas and intrigues at court, nothing ever caused the Carew couple any trouble. Lady Elizabeth's brother, Sir Francis Bryan, was good friends with Nicholas Carew, and was another rake at court that Wolsey had tried to ban.[17] Francis Bryan, famous for his eye-patch after a jousting accident, would soon be needed in his sister and brother-in-law's plans to see Mary reinstated as England's heir. The fact Lady Elizabeth Carew and her brother, Sir Francis Bryan, were cousins to Jane Seymour also helped the situation.

Despite being ardent Katharine and Mary supporters and staunch Catholics, Nicholas and Elizabeth Carew had not come to any harm or even under pressure over King Henry's desire for a new marriage and religion. They were also under no pressure to send their young daughters to court. King Henry had always been generous to Nicholas Carew but also was unusually generous to Elizabeth Carew throughout her life. She would have been one of the few women who could openly petition the king if needed. Likewise, Elizabeth Carew had a good relationship with Thomas Cromwell (as most women did).[18] A supportive letter from Lady Elizabeth Carew, who believed in Princess Mary, would have been a tonic for the young woman.

The Carew letters likely reached Princess Mary before the parliamentary opening on Friday 4 February, just as many in London were busy. By Thursday, 10 February, Mary was already staying at Gravesend. For these letters to have arrived so early in February, Cromwell and Carew must have been conspiring even before Anne Boleyn suffered her miscarriage. It could have been Henry's fall from his horse that spurred thoughts of morality and succession. Princess Mary was now 20 and the perfect option as a royal heir; Henry Fitzroy was almost 17, always near his father at court, and likewise a Catholic option for those still refusing the Reformation.

The group that formed around Princess Mary and away from Anne Boleyn was fraught with contradictions. Thomas Cromwell was undisputedly the ringmaster of everything; he was the one who had ushered in the Church of England and played queenmaker by vanquishing Katharine and putting Anne beside Henry on the throne. There was no question that Cromwell wanted the Reformation to go ahead; he had been reading evangelical works since 1518 and all the heavyweights of all factions of the new religion knew Cromwell personally. Martin Luther wrote to Cromwell praising his, 'goodwill in the cause of Christ'.[19] At the same time, Erasmus wrote to Cromwell as he was, 'a man of dignity and authority'.[20] Miles Coverdale considered Cromwell his humanist patron,[21] and Philip Melanchthon had corresponded with Cromwell for years.[22] William Tyndale, only months from martyrdom, considered a letter from Cromwell the only thing that could spare his life[23] (unfortunately the letter did not arrive in Brussels in time). Yet Catholic Queen Katharine, who wrote to him as, 'my especial amigo',[24] always had Cromwell's support as she lived out her banishment. Princess Mary and those of her small household also wrote to Cromwell on casual and friendly terms.[25] Everything hinged on Cromwell, and when Queen Katharine passed away, the world could start anew. Cromwell still desperately wanted his Imperial alliance; despite the fact it was an alliance that put England onside with the very power fighting to destroy the Reformation.

Thomas Cromwell was a strong reformist and Nicholas Carew was a strong Catholic. The men rarely spent any time together; one a man running the court and parliament, the other a diplomat with a lot of time to spare. While both men were well-known in the court, they had only worked together on one issue. Both men were commissioners for the *Act of Commission for Sewers*, under the Statute of Sewers bill, which passed parliament in 1531. A dedimus potestatem writ went out, appointing Cromwell and Carew the power to handle the aggressive and often difficult matters for managing England's waterways (the term sewers meant all waterways, weirs, damns, and irrigation for livestock and crops[26]). The decision for these two to work together for the king likely surprised them both, but Cromwell was not put off by work that would anger landowners and their water access, and Carew was a man the king could delegate to and feel unconcerned about his management. Whether Carew took his sewer post seriously or not is a matter for discussion; Cromwell spent time out in the field, personally inspecting waterways, rivers, swamps, and marshes, even personally inspecting water access in Calais to ensure clean drinking water, drainage and wastewater was being fairly handled and utilised. Carew eventually disappeared from the project and Cromwell and the king went on to plan an entire new harbour at Dover, so the role cannot have been as boring as the subject may suggest.

By February 1536, all in parliament wished they could discuss issues as simple as sewers. Years of difficulty with Henry and Anne's royal marriage had dominated legislation, and despite heavy workloads each year, 1536 had many issues to work through. With Cromwell's Valor Ecclesiasticus, a wholesale valuation of every religious house and its lands and possessions completed by February 1536, the bill for the Dissolution of the Lesser Monasteries went through parliament, which again put Cromwell and Carew on opposite sides of religious debate. Yet their disdain for Anne Boleyn seemingly eclipsed even their sharp religious divide. Or did it? Was it about Anne Boleyn at all, or simply about protecting Princess Mary? One could argue the situations intertwined.

While Cromwell's motives were not always so clear, Carew's at least were not so complicated. Most families in noble circles had connections and shared relations to some degree. Nicholas Carew and Anne Boleyn's great-grandmothers were sisters. While some kept connections like this as a reason to ally, this was not the case for everyone. Carew had never shown any interest in supporting Anne. The Carew family had fewer noble connections at court than most; they had always been on the fringes of court. Carew's father, Sir Richard Carew, had been the Captain of Calais and had been able to get his son placed in the household of Prince Henry by a stroke of luck.[27] Despite Carew's dislike of Anne, and his strong Catholic faith, Henry had not ejected Carew from court, a sign of their genuine lifelong friendship. This, in turn, made Carew's close noble Catholic friends, like the Exeter and Pole families, happy to see him still in favour, as they had less access to the king due to their support for Princess Mary. Carew was well-placed to hear rumours of King Henry having a mistress, or at least paying attention to a new woman at court. Men like Nicholas Carew who perhaps thought it appropriate to promote Jane Seymour, had little desire to do much more than upset the royal marriage. Did the king find he was suddenly interested in Jane Seymour, or had her cousins Nicholas Carew and Francis Bryan put her name forward to the king as a suitable mistress?

Again, it is Alexander Alesius' words that can only fill the gaps. Henry and Anne would have been hurting through February 1536 with the loss of their child. Coupled with that, Henry's fall likely angered the ulcers on his legs, showing Henry, whose masculinity was almost as important to him as his crown, that he was no longer the young, healthy, strong king he had been not so long ago.[28] Having a flirtation with Jane Seymour may have alleviated that pain somewhat.

At the same time, Henry's grief and anger over Anne's miscarriage may have been enough fuel for Vicegerent Cromwell to enlist others to continue their gossip about Anne's adultery, which had so far not led to any conclusions. Alesius asserted that the interrogation of Anne's ladies was undertaken throughout the month of February, but Alesius conveniently omitted the purpose of the interrogations, or who was involved. Due to the later destruction of everything relating to Anne in 1536, even knowing which ladies were serving at court at that time is hard to determine. But the questioning likely had a point from Cromwell's end; he could stir up serious trouble, and the Carews were happy to help.

The notion that Thomas Cromwell spent time interrogating the ladies around Anne Boleyn has become engrained, but no such proof exists. Not at any stage did Cromwell or any of his men interrogate any ladies at court. It could be that quiet conversations of rumoured adultery or related impropriety could be seen as an interrogation of the queen's court, though no formal interviews took place. What Cromwell could do was plant disinformation. Again, it is Alexander Alesius who told Queen Elizabeth in later years that Anne Boleyn's ladies were interrogated, but he never alluded to when it first began, who was giving or receiving information, or whether anything of substance was ever shared. Alesius wrote of Cromwell's men:

> 'These spies, (because they greatly feared the Queen) watch her private apartments night and day. They tempt her porter and serving man with bribes; there is nothing which they do not promise the ladies of her bedchamber. They affirm also that the King hates the Queen because she has not presented him with an heir to the realm, nor was there any prospect of her so doing.'[29]

There can be no doubt the relationship between Henry and Anne was strained in February, with the king at Whitehall as parliament sat at Westminster, while Anne recovered at Greenwich. The usual Shrovetide celebrations did not take place that year, even though Henry usually took any opportunity to celebrate. Chapuys wrote that:

> 'The general opinion is that the concubine's miscarriage was entirely owing to defective constitution, and her utter inability to bear male children; whilst others imagine that the fear of the King treating her as he treated his late Queen.'[30]

But who were the ladies apparently sharing this gossip? The women around Anne were a large group of noble women, each with familial connections that saw them appointed to wait on the queen in her chambers. The group around Anne had been in place since her coronation in 1533, and some even earlier. There is nothing to suggest any women were planted in Anne's chambers to undermine her. But it was their allegiances and opinions that could have been exploited if Anne were to be put down from her great height beside Henry.

Like all queens, Anne's ladies were in a hierarchy. The highest-ranked women were the Great Ladies of the Household. These women did not serve day-to-day; they had their households and families to care for, and usually not at the royal court. This was a position more of formality. Among these were women mostly connected to the Howard family, Anne's maternal relatives. It is easy to become confused with the prolific Howard family, as Thomas Howard, 2nd Duke of Norfolk, had seventeen children with two women, cousins Elizabeth and Agnes Tilney, over a staggering forty-five-year period. What's more, the first generation of children and the second generation often also shared first names as well as surnames. The duke's eldest son, Thomas Howard, 3rd Duke of Norfolk was beloved by King Henry, and canny in ensuring his family was placed at court. But he was not loved by his niece Anne Boleyn.

Anne Boleyn's mother was one of the Great Ladies of the Household. Elizabeth Boleyn (née Howard), Countess of Wiltshire and Ormond, lived primarily at Hever Castle. Elizabeth Boleyn's brother was the 3rd Duke of Norfolk, and his wife, Elizabeth Howard (née Stafford, daughter of the Duke of Buckingham), was another of the Great Ladies, as was Norfolk's stepmother Agnes Howard (née Tilney), who was also baby Princess Elizabeth's godmother. While the Norfolk couple were oddly not supportive of Anne, none of the Howard family would plot against her. (The Duchess of Norfolk was close friends with Thomas Cromwell, but although she would repeatedly tell him about all she knew, they were not foolish enough to discuss their mutual dislike for Anne.) Having the support of women like the Duchess of Norfolk was important, as it showed legitimacy and strength, and sadly Anne never received this support from her aunt.

Most of the Great Ladies were much older than Anne Boleyn, with one exception; her maternal aunt Anne De Vere (née Howard), who had the misfortune to be married off John de Vere, 14th Earl of Oxford. The earl died in his mid-twenties in 1526, when his wife Anne was only in her mid-teens. But Anne De Vere also had a remarkably strong friendship with Thomas Cromwell, staying at his private home and landing a prime space at Anne Boleyn's side during the 1533 coronation. Sadly, the young Anne de Vere did not live at court, instead busy fighting off her dead husband's relatives from her land and possessions and trying to avoid being poisoned.[31]

Another of the Great Ladies was Margaret Grey (née Wootton), Dowager Marchioness of Dorset. Lady Margaret was also close with Cromwell, treating him as one of the family whilst he worked for Margaret's husband, Sir Thomas Grey, and his mother Cecily Grey. As a result, Cromwell also had strong relationships with many in the huge Grey family. Lady Margaret sent her son, the reckless Henry Grey, the 3rd Marquis of Dorset to court in 1534 to marry Lady Frances Brandon (daughter of the Duke of Suffolk and Princess Mary Tudor) to live under Cromwell's eye. Cromwell also ran Ireland through Lord Leonard Grey, Lady Margaret's brother-in-law. While the Grey family were staunch Catholics, they would still always support Cromwell over Anne Boleyn, no matter what, as religion did not harm their friendships. Lady Elizabeth Fitzgerald (née Grey), the Irish Countess of Kildare, was one of the initial high-ranking nobles gossiping about Anne's potential downfall since December 1535.[32]

Another high-ranking lady who did not support Anne was Gertrude Courtenay (née Blount), Marchioness of Exeter. A Catholic, Gertrude was selected alongside Agnes Howard to be a godmother to Princess Elizabeth, to show unity across the widening religious divide in England, a role Lady Gertrude did not relish.[33] A lady with the highest of pedigrees, Lady Gertrude's highly intelligent father William Blount, Baron Mountjoy served Queen Katharine, and among Lady Gertrude's many stepmothers was Inés de Venegas, one of Katharine's Spanish ladies, and Dorothy Grey, sister-in-law of Cromwell's favourite, Lady Margaret Grey. The notion of Lady Gertrude Courtenay ever serving Anne Boleyn is difficult to imagine; she spent her time mostly away from court, fortuitous since she regularly gossiped about both Henry and Anne's downfalls throughout their marriage.[34] Unfortunately, Lady Gertrude did not share in Vicegerent Cromwell's support and safety, as history would later show. Fortunately, her husband, Henry Courtenay, Marquis of Exeter, was King Henry's cousin, and the two Henrys were raised together with their close friend Sir Nicholas Carew.[35] This meant that, like Carew, Henry Courtenay was largely untouchable and beloved by the king. Lady Gertrude exploited this position several times, courting treason by meeting with prophesiers like Elizabeth Barton to hear predictions about King Henry's death.[36] Lady Gertrude's sister, Lady Mary Blount, married Henry Bourchier, Earl of Essex in 1536, and while she never moved in Anne's circles, this meant another strong noble Catholic figure at court was no supporter either.

Anne Stanley (née Hastings), Dowager Countess of Derby was a rare non-Howard Great Lady of Anne's court. Daughter of the loyal Edward Hastings, 2nd Baron Hastings (taking his title as a teen when King Richard III famously beheaded his father) and granddaughter of the Duke of Northumberland.[37] Anne married Thomas Stanley, 2nd Earl of Derby. (His father was stepbrother to Henry VII and through his lineage, Stanley was related to the illustrious Woodville, Neville, Montagu, Beaufort, and Tudor families.) Anne Stanley lost her husband in 1521, but both she and her husband had been so close and trusted by King Henry VIII that she remained quietly in favour and successfully married her children into the families at court and got her daughter Margaret a place close to Anne Boleyn.[38]

The extended Howard family were high in esteem with the king alongside the Courtenays, the Greys and the Stanleys, and yet Anne could not rely on any of them outside of her mother. All the other Great Ladies and their husbands knew Sir Nicholas Carew and his wife Lady Elizabeth, who were now actively working for Princess Mary's restoration. Even familial bonds could not help the coming tide of anti-Boleyn backlash.

CHAPTER 6

Factions in a Queen's Household

The second tier of ladies at the royal court of a queen were the Gentlewomen of the Privy Chamber. These women, while not permanent companions, would spend time with Anne at court when not with their children and estates. Perhaps the best known of these women is Jane Boleyn (née Parker), Viscountess Rochford, wife of George Boleyn. Jane Boleyn has been much maligned as a spiteful wife and sister-in-law, despite no record of such behaviour. George Boleyn married Jane Parker in approximately 1524,[1] around the same time the king granted Boleyn lands in his own right. Lady Jane's parents, Henry Parker, 10th Baron Morley, and Alice Parker (née St John, whose grandfather was Margaret Beaufort's brother) both came from the prestigious Lovel, Beauchamp and de la Pole families. Henry Parker's uncle had married the daughter of Elizabeth Plantagenet, sister to King Edward IV and King Richard III.[2] The Parker family had strong blood ties to the Yorkist White Roses and their Catholic beliefs, just like the Exeters and Greys. Thomas Boleyn and Henry Parker had been friends for years when they saw George and Jane marry, and the men shared a common mutual friend and lawyer, Thomas Cromwell. Again, strong religious alliances did not appear to harm these relationships, and the marriage to Lady Jane Parker was a huge coup for George Boleyn.

By 1536, Jane Boleyn, known as Lady Rochford, had been nothing but a quiet, loyal, and respectful woman and wife. She and Lord Rochford had no (at least surviving) children, which must have been a blow to them and their families. Where Anne Boleyn went, her brother went too, and naturally, Lady Rochford was usually at court serving her sister-in-law and likely lived with her before her rise in power as well. Lady Rochford was the quietest of women, never causing trouble for anyone or being associated with scandals. She was never suspected of having a bad marriage, but in 1534 she was banished (or self-exiled) from court when King Henry was angered by Lady Rochford's attempts to have Henry's latest mistress (an anonymous woman named the Imperial lady, possibly Margaret Lee[3]) removed from court.[4] Lady Rochford goes unmentioned in Henry and Anne's great royal progress of 1535 but was seemingly back at court by the time Anne lost her child in January 1536. The animosity between Anne Boleyn and Thomas Cromwell did not extend to other family members; Lady Rochford had no problem communicating with Cromwell when she needed him, and as a faithful friend to her father, Lady Rochford would have been well aware of the security of her position under Cromwell.

Alice Parker, as Baroness Morley, was eligible to serve a queen at court even without her daughter Jane marrying a Boleyn. Lady Morley did not attend Queen Katharine or Anne but did visit the court on occasion. The Parkers were a couple in their mid-to-late fifties by 1536 and had three children working around the royal court; Lady Rochford's brother, Henry Parker, was a politician, author, and book lover like his father (who shared Machiavelli books with Thomas Cromwell[5]), though Henry's wife Grace Parker (née Newport) usually stayed away from court. Lady Rochford's sister, Margaret Parker, had married Sir John Shelton and the couple worked overseeing Princess Mary's life/confinement in Princess Elizabeth's household.[6] Baroness Morley likely had enough going on with her children's lives that she did not wish to serve at court too. But had Lady Morley seen or heard anything suspicious about Anne Boleyn, she certainly would have reported it to Thomas Cromwell.

Another gentlewoman who would have had information to share was Isabel Baynton (née Leigh), who married Anne Boleyn's vice-chamberlain, Sir Edward Baynton. Baynton was another long-time friend of Thomas Cromwell and had the distinction of also being friends with Queen Katharine.[7] Baynton was a career courtier and moved into Anne's household in 1533, where his wife Isabel soon followed. The Bayntons hosted Henry and Anne during the 1535 royal progress just like the Seymours and were well connected at court.[8] Lady Isabel Baynton was the eldest daughter of Joyce Culpepper, who had five children with Ralph Leigh before marrying Lord Edmund Howard (another of Anne Boleyn's maternal uncles) and had another six children (one being Katheryn Howard, who would one day be queen and be served by her sister Isabel). Edward and Isabel Baynton had a unique position of serving all six of Henry's queens and caring for Princesses Mary and Elizabeth. The couple had struggled during their first five years of marriage, but by 1536, Lady Isabel was about to give birth to a healthy son, the first of three children whose godparents were Thomas Cromwell and

Princess Mary.[9] Edward and Isabel Baynton shared Anne Boleyn's desire for religious reform but served the crown above all. If Cromwell needed information from Anne's chambers, Isabel and her husband could surely provide it. Another lady likely to feel comfortable sharing or receiving gossip would have been Elizabeth Somerset (née Browne), Countess of Worcester.[10] Lady Worcester was the daughter of the devoted Yorkist, Lady Lucy Neville (whose uncle was Richard Neville 'the kingmaker'[11]). Lucy Neville married Sir Thomas Fitzwilliam and had eight children, before surprisingly remarrying to Tudor supporter Sir Anthony Browne (related to the FitzAlan, Arundel, and Despenser families), by which she had five more children, among them her daughter Elizabeth, and a son, Anthony. The pair, along with one of their half-siblings, Sir William Fitzwilliam, were high-ranking members of the royal court by the mid-1520s (though the family can easily be confusing, as Lucy Neville had two daughters named Elizabeth, two sons named Anthony, and two sons named William).

Elizabeth Somerset, Lady Worcester came from a family of strong women; King Henry VII had feared her mother, Lady Neville, would seize Calais and hold it in her cousin's name; her cousin being Edmund de la Pole, 3rd Duke of Suffolk, the last man to challenge Henry VII for the throne.[12] Lady Neville was wisely quiet during Henry VIII's reign, and her daughter Elizabeth married Henry Somerset, 2nd Earl of Worcester (a line of the Beaufort family), a quiet and loyal man, who had once been married to Margaret Courtenay, sister to Henry Courtenay, Marquis of Exeter. Despite being part of these deeply powerful, conservative, Catholic families, Lady Worcester became close friends with Anne Boleyn, with Anne giving her cash and gifts on occasion. The women were seemingly close friends and allies, and Anne particularly worried for Lady Worcester's health during her pregnancy.

There were certainly other gentlewomen of the privy chamber who would not have been open to gossip about their queen. Anne's cousin Mary Fitzroy (née Howard, daughter of the Duke of Norfolk) was married to Henry Fitzroy, Duke of Richmond and Somerset, and the king's illegitimate son.[13] Both were fervently Catholic and had little to do with one another and equally little to do with Anne Boleyn. While rarely at court, Lady Mary Fitzroy was close with Lady Margaret Douglas, the king's niece, and Mary Shelton, Anne Boleyn's cousin, as the pair shared an interest in multiple artistic pursuits, and both later became published writers.[14]

Margaret Douglas, for all her rebellious behaviour over the years, equally could not be approached about Anne Boleyn. Daughter of Dowager Queen Margaret Tudor of Scotland, Lady Douglas was in her uncle King Henry's care and treated like a princess, given private rooms at Hampton Court Palace just as Anne received, alongside Cromwell and Henry Fitzroy. Equally unlikely to openly gossip about Anne Boleyn was Eleanor Manners (née Paston), Countess of Rutland, who was on her tenth pregnancy in 1536.[15] Lady Rutland and her husband Henry Manners, Earl of Rutland, were career courtiers who had been at court with Anne since at least 1532. Lady Rutland was the granddaughter of Anne Heydon, sister of William Boleyn, making her a cousin to Anne Boleyn. Lady Rutland later remained a confidante of King Henry's following four queens, so she must have been a discreet lady of the court.

There were more Howard women at court as well; Katharine Daubeney (née Howard), the Countess of Bridgewater until her famously unusual divorce in 1536, which came with her maternal niece Anne Boleyn's assistance and blessing. Lady Katherine Howard (née Broughton), was the wife of Anne's uncle, William Howard, and attended Anne's chamber, but when Katharine died in 1535, she was almost instantly replaced as a wife with another of Anne's ladies, Margaret Gamage, a maternal cousin of Jane Boleyn, Lady Rochford.[16] Mistress Gamage continued to serve as a new Lady Howard, while yet another Howard sister, Elizabeth Radcliffe, Baroness Fitzwalter also attended her Boleyn niece.[17] Of course, all these women could only be as loyal as their Howard alliances allowed. With her uncle the Duke of Norfolk increasingly sidelined in 1536, and increasingly angered by his reformist niece on the throne, whether Anne felt safe around these women cannot be known. Were these women allies of Anne like her mother, Elizabeth Boleyn, or against Anne, like the Duke of Norfolk? One can only hope these women were free to make their own decisions.

One exception to the Howard tangle of siblings was Dorothy Stanley, Countess of Derby. Lady Derby married Edward Stanley, 3rd Earl of Derby, the widower of her niece, Katherine Howard, but spent little to no time at court serving her niece Anne, as she was plagued with constant pregnancies.[18] The Derby couple and their ensuing children were more moderate in their religious beliefs, and fiercely loyal to King Henry and all his children who reigned thereafter. Lady Derby could have been a highly ranked and supportive aunt at court for Anne, had her husband ever given her a break from childbearing.

The third tier of women around Anne Boleyn were her Gentlewomen Attendants, a mixture of married and unmarried women (the Maids of Honour) who would spend the most time around Anne, completing any tasks she needed doing, being companions, and ladies that Anne would consider her day-to-day friends. The women would sometimes return home and so worked almost in a series of shifts spanning months at a time, either to Anne's needs, their needs, or of course, the semi-permanent state of pregnancy the married women had to endure. Many of the women around Anne had plenty in common with her and with each other.

Up until 1536, the inclusion of Jane and Elizabeth Seymour at Anne's court went by without mention. Jane Seymour had barely received a mention until the king, for reasons unknown, took a liking to her in December 1535. Elizabeth Seymour had a hard early life. The eighth of the ten Seymour children, Elizabeth was married at just 12 years of age to Sir Anthony Ughtred, then aged 52, and was widowed by 1536, with two young children sent away to her late husband's estates.[19] Jane and Elizabeth Seymour both remained at court while King Henry pursued the eldest Seymour sister. It was not long before Elizabeth Seymour put quill to parchment and requested land and a new husband from Thomas Cromwell (who came through for her, setting her up with his teenage son, Gregory[20]). While it is common knowledge that court life would have been exceptionally awkward for Anne Boleyn and Jane Seymour in 1536, poor Elizabeth Seymour was similarly caught in the crossfire before she was transferred to her sister's new court. Elizabeth probably would have said anything Cromwell needed to hear about Anne Boleyn to alleviate her position.

Anne Boleyn had many cousins, two of whom spent time at her court, Mary and Margaret Shelton being the best known. While it is commonly assumed that Margaret Shelton was King Henry's mistress in 1535, it now appears unclear. Margaret Shelton, daughter of John and Anne (née Boleyn) Shelton, lived at court with her cousin and was briefly, and informally, engaged to Henry Norris of the king's privy chamber. Mary Shelton was different to her quiet sister, with a love for poetry, she was popular and beautiful.[21] By 1536, she was contributing to the Devonshire Manuscript, a collection of poetry composed by many courtiers of the period, as was her dear friend Mary Fitzroy, Duchess of Richmond. Mary Shelton had caught the eye of poets Sir Thomas Wyatt, Henry Howard (the married son of the Duke of Norfolk), and her cousin, Thomas Clere. Margaret Shelton, meanwhile, was politely flirting in the queen's rooms with Henry Norris and Francis Weston in 1536, leading a life that would have been forgotten in the annuls of history had their mother not begun to interfere with their lives at court and inflame gossip.

One more reliable lady that Anne could trust was Mary Zouche, daughter of John, 8th Baron Zouche of Harringworth, and Dorothy Capell. Lady Zouche got a job at court through her maternal cousin, Sir John Arundell, and two of her paternal aunts, Katharine Carew and Jane Hungerford, had both served Queen Katharine. Lady Zouche wished to follow in their footsteps. A rarity at court, Lady Zouche never married, though her brother John Lord Zouche did, to one of the ladies his sister worked alongside in Anne Boleyn's household, Catherine St Leger. In 1533, Catherine St Leger was in negotiations to marry Richard Cromwell, Thomas Cromwell's nephew. The Boleyn and St Leger families were intertwined; Margaret Butler had married William Boleyn, while her sister Anne Butler had married James St Leger. But the St Leger family were close friends with Thomas Cromwell, and his father Walter before him.[22] Catherine's uncle, Anthony St Leger, had been friends with Thomas Cromwell since his childhood, and Cromwell ran Ireland through intermediaries like St Leger. Anne Boleyn intervened with Mistress St Leger's marriage plans, not wanting her lady to 'marry low' to a Cromwell and arranged for her to marry John Lord Zouche instead.[23] Whether the new Lady Catherine Zouche maintained her allegiance to her St Leger family or followed the pro-Anne Boleyn alliance with her new sister-in-law, Lady Mary Zouche, is a matter of conjecture.

Familial ties continued to get even tighter in Anne's household. Lord Zouche's nephew, George Zouche, looked for a wife in Anne's household as well, marrying Anne Gainsford, one of Anne's most trusted friends and ladies.[24] These families were all intertwined; Anne Gainsford shared a grandmother with Catherine St Leger even before they married the Zouche uncle/nephew duo. Catherine St Leger had been married before she became a Zouche, and her first husband, George Courtenay, was the stepson of Anne Gainsford's sister Mary Kingston (and to top it off, in 1536, Lady Kingston was married to the son of the man about to arrest Anne Boleyn[25]).

Given the interconnectedness of all the women in Anne's daily household, she probably felt quite secure with the people around her, with the exception of the Seymour sisters. Another of Anne's ladies was Elizabeth 'Bess' Holland, who had been in a relationship with Anne's uncle, the Duke of Norfolk, for around ten years and was in her mid-twenties in 1536. Despite being a mistress, she was also the daughter of Norfolk's long-time treasurer and steward, John Holland, and niece of John Hussey, 1st Baron Hussey of Sleaford, and Mistress Holland lived as a lady in the queen's household. Bess Holland has been slandered by history as a laundress, when it should be more relevant that she physically assaulted Norfolk's wife, Elizabeth Howard, Duchess of Norfolk, in her own home on multiple occasions.[26] Bess Holland could be Norfolk's eyes and ears when he was not at court, and it is hard to tell who she supported, as she would turn even on the Duke of Norfolk a decade later. But Anne Boleyn's surviving Book of Hours has Bess Holland's married name, Elizabeth Reppes, inscribed, so perhaps the pair had been close in the lead up to Anne's final days.[27]

Most of these women could be relied upon for their discretion. There could be no benefit to them in telling secrets or slandering Anne Boleyn, not even the Seymour sisters in February 1536. But three other ladies at Anne's court are not as convincing. One was Jane Astley (often spelled Ashley, a common mix-up plaguing the whole Astley family), whose relationship with Anne was more obscure than others. Anne Boleyn's paternal uncle, Sir James Boleyn, married Elizabeth Wood,[28] whose maternal cousins were Jane Astley and her brother, London merchant turned royal court attendant, John Ashley. In addition to Jane Astley working in Anne Boleyn's household, her brother John worked in Princess Elizabeth's household (and later went on to marry Princess Elizabeth's infamous tutor/companion Katherine Champernowne, known to history as Kat Ashley[29]). While it initially looks as if there would be no benefit to a low-level courtier like Jane Astley betraying her mistress and a very fortunate position at court, Anne Boleyn's death would later see Jane Astley rewarded with an elevated and wealthy marriage and position alongside one of the king's privy chamber men and one of Thomas Cromwell's most trusted diplomats, Peter Mewtas.[30] That alone makes Jane Astley's situation suspicious, despite being Anne Boleyn's second cousin.

Another woman known to betray Anne Boleyn was Nan Cobham. Nan was a nickname for Anne, and while usually only used by people close to one another, given the sheer volume of ladies named Anne at court, Nan may have been used in a wider circle simply for ease. While her identity has never been officially confirmed, Nan was almost certainly Anne Brooke (née Braye), Baroness Cobham. She had been married to George Brooke, 9th Baron Cobham for almost twenty years and had her thirteenth of at least fifteen children in 1536, despite being the same age as Anne Boleyn. Lady

Cobham had been with Anne Boleyn since the coronation in 1533, the same year she gave birth twice, the first time in January and again by the year's end.[31] The daughter of Edmund Baron Braye and his wife Jane Halliwell, Anne Braye married into the Brooke family in Kent, who lived near the Boleyn and Wyatt families.[32] Her husband, George Brooke, Lord Cobham was the eldest grandson of Anne Heydon, sister of William Boleyn, making him one of Anne's cousins, while his father, Thomas Brooke, was from the noble Neville and Beaufort families. A loyal courtier, Lord Cobham had been to France multiple times to represent England, including with Princess Mary Tudor when she married King Louis in 1514. Meanwhile, Lord Cobham's sister, Elizabeth Brooke, had married neighbour Sir Thomas Wyatt (who was in love with fellow neighbour, Anne Boleyn). Elizabeth Brooke became famous for the adultery scandal that saw her separated from Wyatt,[33] which fortunately brought little shame personally to her family (though their Wyatt family loyalties would later bring much trouble). A fervent supporter of the Reformation, Lord Cobham was well-liked and respected by Thomas Cromwell, the pair being close for the majority of the 1530s and Cromwell was godfather to the Cobhams' youngest children. But Nan Cobham's close friendship with Anne Boleyn was very well known, and for her to turn from her queen to her husband's supporters would have come as a cruel surprise.

Another lady close to Anne Boleyn was Margery Horsman, possibly the only lady at Anne's court without a familial tie. Mistress Horsman's family are harder to trace and the Horsman name is not associated with any of the large Boleyn and Howard families. Margery and her brother, Thomas Horsman, were niece and nephew (their father possibly named John) of Roger Horsman, Abbot of Coverham and Vicar of Sedburgh,[34] and Leonard Horsman, Fellow of Christ's College in Cambridge.[35] The family, through Leonard Horsman's career at Cambridge and with Cardinal Wolsey, were well connected to Thomas Cromwell and his close ally, Rowland Lee, Bishop of Lichfield and Coventry.[36] Margery Horsman's brother, Thomas, married Elizabeth Hussey, daughter of Sir Robert Hussey and Anne Say, a fervently Catholic family (not to be confused with Hussey's other daughter also named Elizabeth, who was born to his second wife Jane and became the infamous puritan 'Mistress Crane'). The Horsmans were a religious family from deep in the Catholic north, but readily complied with the religious changes of Cromwell and Bishop Lee in return for favours. With Margery Horsman's family being well-known to Cromwell and Lee, and through her sister-in-law Lady Elizabeth Hussey, Mistress Horsman likely used these connections to gain a place at court. Her sister-in-law would provide great connections; Lady Hussey's cousin was Sir Philip Calthorpe, Anne Boleyn's uncle, and Lady Hussey's great-aunt, Anne Wentworth, was Jane Seymour's grandmother.

Margery Horsman came to be one of Anne Boleyn's closest ladies at court and was still single in 1536. Given her marriage to a Catholic, Michael Lyster, in January 1537, her close relationship with Jane Seymour,[37] and her connections to the Hussey family, we can assume Mistress Horsman was also Catholic. (Also, Michael Lyster's father was a Chief Justice of the King's Bench during Anne Boleyn's trial.[38]) As Lady Margery Lyster, she saw her children (born after Anne Boleyn's death) married into the Catholic Wriothesley family and were later in favour of Queen Mary I.[9] At the same time, Lady Lyster's nephew, Thomas Horsman, lived with reformist, William Cecil, Lord Burghley (Queen Elizabeth's right-hand man, and a former Seymour supporter) making Mistress Horsman one of the most unusual choices as a lady in Anne's court. But in 1536, Margery Horsman was the ear of Anne Boleyn, and probably one of the first to hear of rumours about her queen at court. She was probably the best woman to pay favour to if a courtier wished for an alliance to remove Anne as queen. Mistress Horsman also often worked as an intermediary between Catholic Lord and Lady Lisle and Anne Boleyn.[40]

Lady Lisle was desperate to get her daughters in the queen's court, in fact any queen's court. It is unlikely Margery Horsman had much of a personal relationship with Lady Lisle (though Margery probably knew Lady Lisle's agent, John Lord Husee, quite well), but it shows another Catholic connection to Margery, despite being able to call on the favours of Thomas Cromwell through her uncles. But most ladies likely had to put their own religious beliefs aside to wait on Anne Boleyn, the same way many men had to do the same to serve Thomas Cromwell. Perhaps Margery Horsman believed she could only rely on herself.

The channels of potential gossip and slander in February 1536 cannot be traced. Why any woman at court would risk their position to harm a queen is a question that cannot be answered. None of the ladies at court would gain much advantage from seeing Anne destroyed beyond being spotted as potential wives for noblemen. The servants, attendants and gentlemen ushers whispering in hallways cannot be identified, though the leaders of Anne's household were all well-known men. Thomas Cromwell was

Anne's High Steward and oversaw her household from a distance, so the household was run by her Lord Chamberlain, a violent misogynist named Thomas Baron Burgh, a cousin of Nan Cobham's husband[41] (and briefly the father-in-law of Catherine Parr). Burgh was a hateful man, but passionate about the new religion and his passion for that may have hidden his violent rage against his own family from Anne Boleyn's sight.[42] It would have been unlikely that Burgh would want a reformist queen supplanted for a Catholic queen in 1536, and given his propensity to be hated by those around him, he would not have been privy to the gossip they shared outside his office. The equally reformist, but far calmer and gentlemanly Edward Baynton, acted as Anne's Vice Chamberlain and with his wife Isabel in Anne's chamber, this could have been a prime way for gossip to leak. John Uvedale acted as Anne's secretary, while her uncle James Boleyn was her chancellor. William Coffin was Anne's Master of the Horse, a man who took his role overseeing household staff very seriously,[43] while lawyer George Taylor was appointed Anne's Receiver General, and John Smith as her surveyor. It would have also been these men or their trivial attendants around the court who whispered rumours or accepted little bribes in return for gossip about Anne in February 1536. A mixture of confusion and stereotypes have also always assumed it was Anne's ladies who turned against her, when it easily could have been gossiping men on the edges of the royal rooms who passed around lurid details about a queen stationed far above them.

Any man who worked in the king's chamber would know that Henry now favoured Jane Seymour — knights such as Nicholas Carew, Francis Bryan, Edward Seymour, Thomas Heneage, Henry Norris, and Richard Page — and they could all simply spread a rumour to any of their attendants, which would soon spread like wildfire about the court. Cromwell had an army of attendants who could plant information. Anyone who had grieved Queen Katharine's loss, and that was the majority at court, and those who pitied Princess Mary could take up tales of King Henry and Jane Seymour. Throughout time, whispers have always acted the same way; they start as one story and quickly change, with any number of real or imagined extravagant details added as news passed from one person to another. Sadly, for Anne, the rumours of Henry's fondness for Jane Seymour were real in February and March 1536 and combined with the loss of her son, perhaps Anne Boleyn, like Margery Horsman, thought she too could only trust and rely upon herself.

CHAPTER 7

Dissolution of True Reform

In 1536, the royal court was not completely dedicated to the gossip or even mention of Anne Boleyn. While Anne was away at Greenwich recovering from her loss, the rest of the court were busy with their jobs. Thomas Cromwell opened parliament on 4 February 1536 for a two-month session, which had a heavy workload.[1] With thirty-five private acts and eighteen public acts, it would have come as a relief to Cromwell to finally get non-royal marriage laws passed, after he had worked himself almost to death the year before, catching malaria while trying to manage the government. Each bill could need up to one hundred pages of work, and 1536 would be the second most productive parliament in England's history.[2] Everyone could finally move on from whom the king had married, and who would be his heir, at least for now. But how the new legislation would eventually pass in parliament would inadvertently cause the final fracture between Anne Boleyn and Thomas Cromwell.

The initial thirty-five private acts going through parliament were in the usual simple tone; all were acts concerning the sale or surrender of lands to another party or the crown, or widows or heirs receiving their inheritance. Several acts concerning Church lands were also settled (with two whose acts are still in force today), and the king also had Cromwell put through several private acts on his behalf, bestowing lands as gifts. King Henry assured Baynard's Castle in London to his son, Henry Fitzroy, as he was almost 17 and finally permitted to set up his own house outside of court.[3] Anne Boleyn also received a generous assurance of Collyweston Manor in the north, which had once been Margaret Beaufort's favourite home and had been in Henry Fitzroy's possession for ten years.[4] The dissolution of the monasteries had begun and Thomas Boleyn, Earl of Wiltshire received the Bishopric of Norwich, an enormous amount of lands and buildings, earning 3000*l* a year just in rent (£1.2 million today, not a bad side hustle[5]). Boleyn was also extended a lease on land in Essex, and George Boleyn, Lord Rochford bought in with his father.[6] Rochford was also high in the king's favour at the time; when Thomas West, 9th Baron De La Warr fell ill and was unable to appear in the House of Lords at short notice, the king asked Cromwell to put Rochford in the House of Lords to vote on De La Warr's behalf. From the outside, everything was again fine with the Boleyns. Anyone outside the immediate circle of rumours would have had no idea that anything had been wrong within the royal marriage.

But England, Wales and Ireland were all about to go through a dramatic upheaval thanks to the work Cromwell had spent years drafting in his offices. This was Cromwell's theatre, and he knew how to play an audience. He accepted the simple position offered of Gatekeeper of Westminster Abbey (he was already the Steward), and since parliament was in session, Cromwell was the man who could now control who was in the Commons or the Abbey area, and more importantly, who could be kicked out when it suited him. Parliament had simple things to work through for the benefit of England; they debated new laws around fabric imports, rope and metalwork standards, perjury rules, making sure apprentices did not have to pay to gain their positions, theft punishments, anti-piracy measures, wine prices, clergy benefices, and public disturbance and anti-violence measures.[7] The Treason Act of 1534 was updated; it became treason to 'marry or become engaged to the King's children, sisters, paternal aunts, or his nieces or nephews without the King's written permission, or to deflower any of them being unmarried'.[8] This was particularly relevant to the king's niece, Margaret Douglas, who was discovered having an affair with one of the Howard brothers. But Cromwell also had half a dozen more serious laws to enact, all of which would have repercussions, and would raise the ire of Anne Boleyn.

While Thomas Cromwell had set up the Church of England in 1532 and 1533 through various laws, many of the steps forward needed by reformists had not yet happened. Power had been transferred to the crown instead of the Church, but only in a limited fashion, enough to make sure King Henry could marry Anne Boleyn. Now, the parliament of 1536 would take a step further, consolidating the power of the Church into the hands of the king, and making changes to who could work for the Church, how they became qualified, and how they conducted their offices. The See of Rome Act 1536, or *An Act extinguishing the authority of the bishop of Rome*, was a direct attack on those who still believed in the authority of the Pope in England. Cromwell's preamble opened with:

> 'if any person or persons ... shall, by writing, ciphering, printing, preaching or teaching, deed or act, obstinately or maliciously hold or stand with to extol, set forth, maintain or defend the authority, jurisdiction or power of the bishop of Rome or his see, heretofore used, claimed or usurped within this realm … for every such default and offence shall incur and run into the dangers, penalties, pains and forfeitures ordained and provided by the statute of provision and praemunire.'[9]

It was high treason to preach or even believe in the Catholic teachings of the Church and was punishable by death. Everyone in England, whether they held a religious or secular office, or anyone beginning a college degree had to take an oath renouncing the jurisdiction of Rome and swear the Oath of Royal Supremacy. From now on, the reformist teachings could better infiltrate churches and those beginning their time in the Church would learn that England's king was the Head of the Church, not the Pope.

The *Ecclesiastical Licences Act* also sought to tidy up religious legislation passed in 1532 and 1533. Cromwell had cut off Queen Katharine's right to appeal her marriage in 1533 by the *Act of Restraint of Appeals* and cut off tithes sent to Rome through the 1532 *Act of Restraint of Annates*.[10] Combined with Cromwell's *Submission of the Clergy* and the *Royal Supremacy Act*, King Henry now had full power over England, and the 1536 bill went further in solidifying these laws, ensuring doctrine could be changed in England, and cancelled all bulls, briefs, faculties and dispensations which had been granted by papal authority. All paperwork could be renewed under the new laws, swapped out under the Archbishop of Canterbury's authority rather than the Pope's, and changed at the Court of Chancery. Given that Vicegerent Cromwell ran the Chancery and Thomas Cranmer was the Archbishop of Canterbury, the two men could control all religious men and women, their roles, offices, benefices and powers. The *Tithe Act 1536* was also passed, ensuring the First Fruits payments went to the king instead of Rome, and controlled the speed and manner of payments that went to the crown, rather than lingering in Church coffers.[11] The Church had total power in England until 1532, controlling the land they used or rented out, and dispensing justice and creating laws, but by 1536 they had been whittled down to almost no power at all, thanks to Thomas Cromwell. Meanwhile, a new law called the *Statute of Uses*, a tax simplification bill Cromwell created to streamline tax payable on land and inheritance, removed much of the old feudal system rules and made new guidelines on the way land was given through wills.[12] The bill passed with little argument in parliament, but would explode in anger with the public months after parliament was closed, resulting in the Pilgrimage of Grace.

Anyone in England who believed in the Reformation, from a layman through to Anne Boleyn herself, could not have many issues with these changes. The changes were not an attack on religion itself, but an attack on organised religion and the Church's power, and how they routinely abused said power. It was a chance for England to overcome so much of the corruption within the Church; to reform not only its behaviour, but also its teachings, and how justice was administered throughout the country. The problem was that King Henry, a man not prone to making sound decisions or having any courage of conviction, would be the Supreme Head of the Church and its management, which meant these changes could not be carried out in the rational, equal, or methodical way Cromwell and his men planned.

From the opening of parliament, the issue of the jurisdiction of bishops needed to be debated. Bishops' rights to dispense justice needed to be completely moved to legal officials, which Cromwell and parliament had been working towards for several years. Bishops and archbishops had always been appointed by the Pope until 1533 when Cromwell moved power to King Henry, and while post-1533 appointed bishops knew how to tow the royal line, those sworn in before 1533 were not so pliable. But completing the act to oversee the justification of bishops was so overwhelming that completing the changes to canon law (religious law and justice) into civil law would not be completed for another 400 years.

The Valor Ecclesiasticus, the Church Valuation, a census counting all religious men and women in England, their monasteries, churches, abbeys, friaries and convents, as well as all their possessions and enormous land estates, had laid bare the serious issues in religious houses all over England. Many were not fit to be delivering even a Sunday sermon, let alone justice or the saving of souls. Greed was out of control, many religious houses were filled with mistresses and illegitimate children, and drunken, disorderly behaviour, bribery, and many other issues were discovered upon inspection.[13] The Valor Ecclesiasticus had been largely complete since September 1535, and King Henry and Cromwell had begun work on reforming religious houses, though the pair had wildly different views on the subject. Cromwell had sent out letters to all houses a month earlier, calling out their behaviour as untrustworthy and negligent.[14] King Henry sent out letters calling for all preaching licences to be replaced under the new Church of England, and Cromwell added a note to these letters, reminding the clergy of his power, saying, 'I write frankly, compelled and enforced, both in respect of my private duty and for my discharge … whose office is an eye to the prince'.[15] It was clear it was Cromwell who would be making the decisions, not the king. Cromwell wrote to the bishops to:

> 'put you in remembrance of his highness' travails and your duty to change orders to be taken for preaching, to the intent the people may be taught the truth … preaching in England, breed(s) contention, division, and contrariety in opinion in the unlearned multitude, rather than edify or remove from them, and out of their hearts, such abuses as the corrupt and unsavoury teachings of the bishop of Rome and his disciples.'[16]

Those keen to advance the Reformation were ready to purge the Catholic teachings, idolatry, corruption and greed from monastic houses. Those loyal to the Catholic faith were considerably more dubious about any plans to change religious establishments. But to stand up in parliament for the Catholic faith now meant to stand up against King Henry, which was treason punishable by death. Only the Reformation could win. Months of scepticism and misinformation from both sides of the argument littered the air, so when it became time to vote on the *Act of the Dissolution of the Lesser Monasteries*, what was eventually created bore no resemblance to Cromwell's early drafts. Regardless of the amount of power held by King Henry or by Cromwell, England was not a dictatorship; all laws had to pass their readings in the House of Commons and House of Lords. What became the Dissolution of the Lesser Monasteries has been forever laid at Cromwell's feet, when his original ideas were entirely different. These changes in parliament are what eventually caused Vicegerent Cromwell and Anne Boleyn to come to (verbal) blows.

The original documents for the dissolution legislation are written in secretary Robert Warmington's hand (as Cromwell did not have the time to personally write most of his work) but mirrored Cromwell's legislations, which tended to ramble on, including every idea and detail as it came to mind.[17] Most of Cromwell's senior monastery inspectors were routinely away from London, though Robert Warmington was the one able to sit in Cromwell's offices and discuss the incredible data collected by inspectors. Cromwell's Valor Ecclesiasticus data showed that not every religious house was corrupt and that not all religious men and women were guilty of crimes. The information gathered gave an incredible amount of insight, catalogued to show where problems popped up, why they were happening, and what caused so many issues.[18] As a result, Cromwell's initial draft showed how several issues were causing greed and deception; through the use of false relics, pilgrimages, and so-called miracle images, houses siphoned money from the faithful into the Church through deception. Cromwell was adamant those guilty of such crimes needed to be removed, as did the relics and idolatry, as the valuation showed the reality; that religious relics were simply lies and tricks created to extort money from visitors.[19] What Cromwell was initially writing for parliament was the *Suppression of Religious Houses Act*, to close houses of ill-repute and remove clergymen and women who were at fault, and reorganise their religious houses so they could flourish as reformist churches and colleges, rather than simply closing down the monasteries and abbeys (all convents were exempt from closure on Cromwell's orders).

Cardinal Thomas Wolsey had dedicated much time in the 1520s to closing monastic houses which were underperforming for a range of reasons. Thomas Cromwell had been the man to reform or close these houses.[20] Once in power himself, Cromwell had quietly closed some 150 monasteries between 1532 and 1534 when their leases came up for renewal, and their land and buildings were given to the king's accounts rather than back to the Church.[21] In just three months in 1532, Cromwell made 12,000*l* (£5.3 million today) from closing houses and leasing out the land on behalf of the king, enough to pay for a quarter of Anne Boleyn's extravagant coronation bill.[22] No one argued with Cromwell's quiet and methodical closures. They went largely unnoticed and were managed in a relatively simplistic way; when it became time for a monastery and its lands to change hands, usually when its abbot passed away, the lands and income simply reverted to the crown.[23] Those living in the house would move to another monastery, and the royal coffers benefitted when the land was leased out to those looking to purchase a quiet little earner. Cromwell's system of closing monasteries was very similar to Wolsey's system; Cromwell's plan simply had more time to see out much of Wolsey's vision.

From the outset in 1536, Vicegerent Cromwell looked set to continue his selective closure or reformation of religious houses, albeit without the cloak of invisibility he had enjoyed in his first five years at court. Cromwell, as Vicar-general of the Monasteries, had absolute power to do as he pleased, but now the public eye was on his plans, and King Henry had his eyes on potential plunder. Cromwell had been attempting reform in many monasteries; one of the prime examples was his desire to save and reform the London Charterhouse of Carthusian monks.[24] Cromwell wished to close the monastery as it was known and reopen it as a flourishing school of the new religion, with the monks re-educated and reformed, living in the ways of the new doctrine, and teaching and preaching as evangelicals instead of Catholics. But the Charterhouse monks, like so many in other houses, did not like any of Cromwell's new ideas, and despite routinely harsher measures, nothing was working. Cromwell had grand plans for many religious houses, particularly for turning the large abbeys into colleges, places to educate adults and children, heal the sick and help the poor, all of which were recorded by George Wyatt decades later.[25]

A letter written by William Popley recorded Cromwell's mood over the monasteries in February 1536. Cromwell and Popley had been friends since Cromwell acted as Popley's lawyer in early February 1522, and the pair became friends while Popley worked for Lord Lisle in Calais. By 1536, Popley was working as one of Cromwell's private attendants, dealing with Cromwell's personal finances and administration from Cromwell's office at The Rolls. Popley had remained on friendly terms with Lord Lisle, who wrote to his old agent, trying to sniff out details on potential abbeys being leased or sold[26] (and included grovelling letters to be given directly to Cromwell, and a small bribe for Popley). In early 1536, Lisle wanted to purchase Beaulieu Abbey and its 3,441 hectares in Hampshire. Beaulieu Abbey was the jewel in the Cistercian crown, and had it been available, many highly ranked nobles would have fought for its valuable lands and buildings. But William Popley knew what was happening with Cromwell's attempts to reform monasteries, as one of his most trusted men, and sales or endowments were not Cromwell's primary objective. The dissolutions had not officially begun, but noblemen were already looking to scavenge lands in a deal Cromwell had not even set up in parliament. Some small religious houses were already being privately closed, such as on the Duke of Norfolk and Duke of Suffolk's lands, the men ejecting monks from their homes and enjoying their wealth themselves. Popley wrote back to Lord Lisle on Tuesday, 22 February:

> 'I see no likelihood that the abbey of Bewley [Beaulieu] will be suppressed, or any other of like lands, forasmuch as at the session of this Parliament they ordain statutes and provisions for the maintenance and good order of the clergy, both religious and secular; but if I see a chance for your commodity, I will be vigilant.'[27]

What Vicegerent Cromwell wanted for the monasteries, and what the *Act for the Dissolution of the Lesser Monasteries* became were two different animals. It was no secret Cromwell wanted to crush the Catholic hold over religion in England, and how much he thought the Pope's influence needed to be removed. His ally, Archbishop Thomas Cranmer, had been appointing new bishops, but those already in power had been unwilling to listen to the archbishop, leaving him politically and theologically isolated.[28] The Reformation had begun solely to aid Henry and Anne's marriage and had stagnated as parliament needed to constantly deal with the fallout of the marriage, changes to the Church, and the need for Princess Elizabeth to be seen as the legitimate heir of England. If Cromwell's control increased over monasteries and their religious lives and teachings, then the Catholic faith would finally be under threat. Many knew this, the same people who were voting over whether the Vicegerent, a commoner among noblemen, should have that much power over religion. A great many men in power still had not converted to the new religion, even if they had given lip service to King Henry and accepted the Royal Supremacy Act. Voting through Cromwell's moralising legislation about reforming monasteries would mean giving the commoner even more power. Cromwell's power was quickly diluted, and the vultures began to circle monastic houses. Had Cromwell's original plans gone ahead, he and Anne Boleyn, while enemies, would not have needed to clash over the monasteries in early 1536.

Things were moving swiftly to prevent Cromwell's plans for reform. By 3 March, plans had changed; legislation stated that all abbeys and priories that earned less than 300 marks a year (200*l*) and had fewer than twelve men living there would be closed without possibility of reform.[29] This was similar to the plan Vicegerent Cromwell had been enacting in private for King Henry, and similar to the plan Cardinal Wolsey also envisaged for monastic reform, but smaller houses had been amalgamating, not simply closing down until now. Parliament had spoken, and Cromwell was forced to concede and be pragmatic about monastery closures; not the only time his grand plans would be thwarted by the members of the 1536 parliament. By 9 March, William Popley was writing again, updating his former employer of the changes, but it seemed nothing had been signed in parliament.[30] But Lord Lisle instantly snapped into action, wanting the Benedictine Glastonbury Abbey in Somerset, a holy site for almost 1000 years at that stage, home to the legend of King Arthur. Popley immediately poured cold water on Lisle's dreams, saying Cromwell had:

> 'No intention to put down the monastery of Glastonbury or any worshipful house, but it is thought all houses under 300 marks shall be suppressed, for the maintenance of certain notable persons of learning and good qualities about his Highness.'[31]

Popley mentioned rumours that some monasteries had suddenly surrendered themselves and he was correct; both Bilsington Priory in Kent and Tilty Abbey in Essex,[32] being worth less than 200*l* and less than twelve men living there, gave up voluntarily and had their items given to the king, the men able to gain a pension. Cromwell was not going to get this chance to reform the monasteries, so he opted to ensure Wolsey's minimum of twelve monks, an ode to the twelve apostles, were required to keep a house open.

Again, the Valor Ecclesiasticus came in helpful, as the data collected could help salvage some of Cromwell's plans. The information showed the vast majority of poor behaviour going on behind closed walls happened at the smaller monastic houses. The larger the abbey or monastery, the harder it was to hide your mistresses, children, and stolen cash.[33] Both the Commons and Lords were satisfied with these conclusions, and agreed to only close the small houses, while saving the larger ones so Cromwell could continue his dream of reformation. It was the best deal Cromwell could negotiate in the face of both houses of government. The MPs and Lords involved could also exempt any house they felt deserved special treatment, sweetening the deal to make them close only small houses. The Gilbertine order of canons and nuns living together, the only monastic order of English origin, was spared, even though they were not above the debauchery of other orders. All friaries were exempt, not even mentioned in the legislation, despite those houses struggling financially at the time, and all convents remained untouched. While there would be changes to many rules surrounding nuns, the convents were safe (until 1538 when King Henry decided to make all nuns homeless on a whim[34]). Of the 814 monastic houses in England, 1536 would see the closures of 201, all of which would then belong to the crown. Cromwell had once promised to make Henry the richest man in England,[35] and he seemed to have found a way to achieve this much faster than planned.

By the end of March 1536, Cromwell had no choice but to accept the large-scale closure and changes to his monastery programme. Such a revolutionary project needed serious administrative oversight, one even Vicegerent Cromwell could not undertake alone. It was likely around late February or early March when the new monastery oversight project began to take shape, instigated by Lord Chancellor Thomas Audley and the king's solicitor-general Richard Rich. Audley had been the puppet Lord Chancellor for three years, had done little with his office, but had annoyed Cromwell on many occasions. The Vicegerent was not afraid to give the Lord Chancellor a written dressing down, which always received a grovelling apology from Audley.[36] Richard Rich was no such pushover, but nor was he so important that his opinion had ever previously mattered. It was no secret King Henry wanted to remove the power of the Church, and the financial rewards of monastery closure were at the forefront of his mind. It was Audley who was prepared to stoke the king's desire for money and power, and Rich was the lawyer happy to oversee such changes.[37] While Cromwell and Audley remained friendly during their terms in office, Rich did not ever have Cromwell's friendship; a rare occurrence, considering Cromwell gave most people multiple chances to be his friend or at least a respected colleague.

The Court of Augmentations, created to oversee the financial gains of the dissolutions was soon created and pushed through parliament, a government department modelled on the Duchy of Lancaster, which brought money into the king's accounts. George Wyatt later wrote that the Court of Augmentations only had friends and servants working there, so no one could apply for a position, and it was Richard Rich's friends and servants initially placed there, not Cromwell's.[38] Richard Rich had been under the patronage of Chancellor Audley for several years, and the paperwork and legislation for the office did not come from Cromwell, but from Audley.[39] By Tuesday, 28 March, news was spreading that it was Richard Rich who needed to be petitioned if men wanted to receive land from the king, not Cromwell (not that this fact stopped the endless letters instead going to Cromwell's offices). Richard Rich, given a knighthood for his new role in 1536, was known as, 'always reputed light of his tongue, a great dicer and gamester, and not of any commendable fame',[40] and was the man to give false testimony against Sir Thomas More in 1535.[41] Rich's lasting legacy was a 'reputation for immorality, financial dishonesty, double-dealing, perjury and treachery rarely matched in English history… a man of whom nobody has ever spoken a good word'. It would not be long before Rich was busy being insolent to Vicegerent Cromwell and his monastery inspectors, and generally got underfoot with his dubious attitude.[42] Cromwell could have easily destroyed Rich at his leisure, but instead seemingly let Rich run his little administrative fiefdom to keep him out of the way and planted Cromwellian servants and receivers in the offices to keep eyes on the project.[43]

By the end of the parliament session in early April, Ambassador Chapuys wrote to Emperor Charles about the changes in religion, saying:

> 'I am told, besides, that although Cromwell was at one time the adviser and promoter of the demolition of the English convents and monasteries, yet perceiving the great inconveniences likely to arise from that measure, he has since made attempts to thwart it, but that the King had resolutely declined to make any modification of it whatsoever, and has even been rather indignant against his Secretary for proposing such a thing.'[44]

It was not a good time to get on Vicegerent Cromwell's bad side. The monasteries were not the only loss for him in the parliamentary session after the collapse of his *Act for Punishment of Sturdy Vagabonds and Beggars*.[45] This would do no good for Anne Boleyn either. Cromwell had undertaken to completely overhaul the way the poor were managed and aided in England, an entire revolution of care that would essentially give birth to the welfare system. The bill was several years of solid planning, and all that remains of Cromwell's plans are sixty-six pages, double-sided, written in pencil in a non-secretary script.[46]

Before 1536, the Poor Law in England stated there were whipping punishments for beggars.[47] Cromwell presented an ambitious plan to the House of Commons, and asked King Henry to attend the session in February 1536, a sign of Cromwell's power and support for his law, which would tackle poverty right at the root. (There have been suggestions Anne Boleyn also asked Henry to listen to Cromwell's law; a fact that is without evidence but is entirely probable.) The Poor Law bill went into fine detail — those who could, had to report for work starting at Easter 1537, through to Michaelmas 1540, a time of experimentation of the new law. Jobs would be created, such as making roads, digging waterways, repairing ports, jobs whose results would benefit the population. The workers would be paid a fair wage, along with meat and drink, and a clothing allowance.[48] Salaries were already set out for those overseeing the projects. How to afford this new welfare state was set out as well: six forms of tax would cover the costs; ecclesiastical dignitaries would be taxed; and the temporal lords and laymen would be taxed on different rates depending on their land values and movables.[49] Doctors would be arranged for the sick and injured who could not work; medicine, beds, food, and warm fires would be provided for those who needed them. Children between 5 and 14 could be apprenticed into jobs, but only those over 12 would be whipped for failure to work.[50] All people had the chance to reform, with a three-strike system in place for those who failed to live up to expectations. But the punishment for failure to work was to burn the ball of a man's right hand in public. Other punishments included jail time for those unable to provide a good reason for not working.

Cromwell's Poor Law broke down the costs involved, the men needed, the dates, the figures, the projects, and everything for such an enormous plan. It was needed; with the monasteries being dissolved, more people were about to become homeless and jobless. Cromwell had unique access to all the minute details held in his Poor Law draft and personal knowledge of the realities of being poor. After Cromwell had the Valor Ecclesiasticus completed in 1535, he knew exactly the state of England's people, who often found shelter in monasteries. Cromwell had already been planning what might be done about England's poor for a year before the Valor Ecclesiasticus papers were finished by his inspectors.

The surviving draft of the Poor Law was likely written by William Marshall, one of Cromwell's agents. Marshall was an extreme reformist with an interest in the regulation of the monasteries and a translator with a licence to print in London. In April 1534, Marshall sent Cromwell books on destroying Rome's authority, and begged for money, as he often had none to live on or to print his books. Cromwell must have paid him, for Marshall printed three books in 1534.[51] In 1535, Marshall printed a book entitled *The Forme and maner of subuention of helpyng of pore people, deuysed and practyced in the cytie of Hypres in Flaunders, whiche forme is autorised by the Emperorur, and approued by the facultie of diuinite in Paris*. The book is a translation of work in Ypres, of the systems planned and being implemented to help the poor in the Low Countries during the late 1520s. Many of the initial ideas which appear in Cromwell's draft also appear in this translation. Cromwell must have been fond of Marshall's work, as he then paid 34*l* (£15,000 today), the highest fee ever for printing at the time, for Marshall to translate and print *The Defense of Peace*, and Bishop John Fisher himself read a copy over several days before burning it prior to his execution.[52] Marshall also printed several translations of Erasmus, Joye, and Luther, and a book on idolatry and destroying relics, a book which caused much alarm in 1535. *The Images of a verye Chrysten bysshop, and a counterfayte bysshop* shocked many, including Lord Chancellor Thomas Audley.[53] Cromwell had allowed the book to be published in London and did not seek to have Marshall punished for it, despite the book's extreme Lutheran views, but had to send Marshall to live in Calais with Lord Lisle in 1537, for his safety.[54]

The House of Commons was not interested in taxes and organisations that required the wealthy to start helping the poor. The legislation that eventually passed was a skeleton of what Cromwell had prepared. This was not the compromise Cromwell accepted with the monasteries, this was an all-out failure. *The Act for Punishment of Sturdy Vagabonds and Beggars* which passed stated that 'sturdy vagabonds' had to be put to work. The constables, mayors, JPs, sheriffs, and anyone in control of a district/parish had to look after their own poor. The poor were not simply punished for being poor, and the men in power would be punished if they did not aid beggars.[55] Taxes were not levied to cover these costs, but collections were organised through a common box, to pay for people to be put to work, for the sick to be helped so they could recover and find work, and those who could not work were not left to beg. The poor were to stay within their parish, and in return, they could receive help. There were still harsh punishments in place for those who refused to abide by these rules, but this was the birth of aid for the poor. But it was not enough, and it was not what Cromwell wanted. The men in parliament were the same landowners who needed to help the poor, who had to pay the taxes that would go to the poor, and so they did almost nothing and continued to have the opportunity to push tenants and peasants around at their leisure.[56]

Marshall's translation of Poor Laws which Cromwell had been using to help his initial plan was dedicated to Anne Boleyn. It was common to dedicate a book to the monarchs reigning at the date of printing. Had Anne talked with Marshall about his translations? Possibly. Had Anne read Marshall's published works on Poor Laws or idolatry? Given Marshall's mention of Anne specifically, it suggests the pair either met or traded letters. Anne had access to anything she wanted, and with several dozen of Marshall's books in existence in London, maybe she discussed these issues. While translating this new Poor Law work to go with Cromwell's plans and costings, Marshall wrote a note to Anne, in the hope she would help him gain the support Marshall needed from the king:

> 'My very mind, intent and meaning is (by putting of this honourable and charitable provision in mind) to occasion your grace (which at all time is ready to further all goodness) to be a mediatrix and mean unto our most dread sovereign lord… for the establishing and practicing of the same (if it shall seem so worthy) or of some other, as good or better, such as by his majesty or his most honourable council shall be devised.'[57]

Thomas Cromwell and Anne Boleyn seemed to fundamentally agree on what was best for monasteries, and what was best for the poor and sick of England. Yet parliament managed to undo all the good intentions and looked set to accidentally pit these two passionate reformers once again against each other.

CHAPTER 8

Rise of the Seymours

The enormous changes going through parliament in February and March 1536 did not stop plans and schemes elsewhere for Henry, Anne, or Cromwell. The king was primarily distracted by two things in March: making money in parliament, and Jane Seymour. As early as Monday, 6 March, Spain's envoy in Rome, Dr Pedro Ortiz, wrote to the Holy Roman Empress Isabella with worries about Princess Mary and remarked on gossip he likely received from Ambassador Chapuys in London. Ortiz seemed well informed, telling Empress Isabella:

> 'Anne Bolans is now in fear of the King deserting her one of these days, to marry another lady… it must be owned that though the King himself was not converted like St. Paul after his fall [who fell from his horse in Damascus and heard the word of God], at least his adulterous wife has miscarried of a son'.[1]

To be casually making comments about Anne's misfortune suggests the rumour had taken root abroad, at least among Anne's detractors. Ortiz wrote to the Empress again on 25 March, reiterating that:

> 'Of Anne, the news is that she begins to fear that the King may desert her one of these days, and that to prevent that she feigns to be [carrying] a son, lest the King, perceiving that [if] she is only capable of conceiving daughters, should entirely repudiate her'.[2]

It was not as if European rulers had nothing else to do; talks of war, alliances and visits with various kings and queens, and the Empress' nephew had recently died, causing tremendous grief for the family. But letters between the Emperor, Empress and their many ambassadors still took the time to wish for the downfall of England's royal marriage. The Catholics were scared;

they also discussed 'heretical' book-spreading in England, how monks in England refusing the Royal Supremacy Act would be martyred, and how England was spreading lies in Germany through Bishop Edward Foxe.[3]

But it was not all talk about religion and international alliances, as the Emperor and Empress liked to hear gossip and lies about Anne Boleyn as much as, if not more than, any commoner. Chapuys had been listening to rumours in the final days of March 1536 with George Elyot, a cloth merchant who had been friends with Cromwell since they met in Middleburg in 1512.[4] On Saturday, 1 April, Chapuys received a letter from the Marchioness of Dorset, but he did not specify who he was referring to — the king's niece Frances Grey (née Brandon), Marchioness of Dorset, or more likely, Margaret Grey (née Wootton), the Dowager Marchioness of Dorset, who was friendly with Chapuys. The latter was still very much involved in court gossip, was Princess Elizabeth's godmother, and had been close with Cromwell for around fifteen years. Lady Frances Grey had married Lady Margaret's son Sir Henry Grey and having lost two babies in just three years of marriage by 1536, was largely absent from court, and not prone to gossip at that time. But Lady Grey was close to her cousin, Princess Mary, and had adored her aunt, Queen Katharine, so either woman could have easily written to Chapuys. Both George Elyot and the Marchioness of Dorset told Chapuys the same tale of Jane Seymour.

On the weekend of 1 and 2 April 1536, the court was at Greenwich, while Chapuys remained at home in London. This letter likely flew quickly five miles upstream to London, reporting on the new love match of King Henry and Lady Jane Seymour. It was the day of the infamous purse full of sovereigns, along with a summons to become the king's mistress.[5] Nothing had seemingly occurred between Henry and Jane other than glances, comments, and perhaps the odd letter until that point. But after four months, Henry made his feelings plain. Unfortunately, the identity of the messenger who delivered the purse from Henry's rooms to Jane goes unrecorded, and the list of possible gentlemen of the privy chamber carrying out the task is a long one. But Chapuys' rumours told how Lady Jane did not open her letter from the king, a wise choice indeed if it asked Jane to visit the royal bed. Reading the summons would have made it much harder to refuse. Jane kissed the letter and gave it, and the purse, back to the messenger, and:

> 'Then falling on her knees, begged the royal messenger to entreat the King in her name to consider that she was a well-

> born damsel, the daughter of good and honourable parents without blame or reproach of any kind; there was no treasure in this world that she valued as much as her honour, and on no account would she lose it, even if she were to die a thousand deaths. That if the King wished to make her a present of money, she requested him to reserve it for such a time as God would be pleased to send her some advantageous marriage.'[6]

The messenger could have been Sir Richard Page. Page had been working in King Henry's privy chamber for twenty years, often worked as vice-chamberlain for the king's son Henry Fitzroy and had been chamberlain for Cardinal Wolsey in the 1520s.[7] Page was also a lawyer, held high legal posts in several counties, and was personal friends with Thomas Cromwell, as they had been colleagues in many pursuits. Crucially, Richard Page's stepdaughter was Lady Anne Seymour (née Stanhope), the new wife of Edward Seymour. Page's wife, Lady Elizabeth (née Bourchier) had connections of her own; she was a cousin of Baroness Margaret Bryan, the governess who raised the king's children. Lady Bryan's son, Sir Francis Bryan, was in the privy chamber with Sir Richard Page, as was her son-in-law, Sir Nicholas Carew, the man who had been wooing Princess Mary for favour for months. A Seymour beside the king would be good for everyone in the Page-Bryan-Carew-Bourchier families. Plus, given how Page's year would soon play out, it is likely he was personally deep in the plot to install Jane Seymour. But Page had been a supporter of Anne Boleyn for some time, albeit from afar. Page spoke in favour of Anne as far back as 1527 when he still worked for Wolsey. He was regularly a letter courier between Anne and Cromwell, who famously saw one another very little. Everyone's motives were still murky.

Jane Seymour's gesture of returning Henry's gift had only happened within a few days of Chapuys' letter on 1 April, but it had turned the world on its head. It would be unusual for a lady to refuse the king's orders, or for her friends to encourage such behaviour. But Chapuys reported that Jane had:

> 'Been well tutored and warned by those among this King's courtiers who hate the concubine, telling her not in any ways to give in to the King's fancy unless he makes her his Queen, upon which the damsel is quite resolved.'[8]

But it may have been Jane's decision as much as anyone's to refuse the king's advances. Much has been made of Jane Seymour's decision to refuse the king. After all, the king had overthrown a queen to marry a mistress in the past. Lady Jane Seymour was around 28 in 1536 and was no stranger to court. Jane had a ringside seat to the royal divorce, the making of Anne Boleyn, and the destruction of royal and religious life as everyone knew it. Jane had quietly served Anne Boleyn since 1533 and would have been wise enough to make her own decisions around the king's overtures. The Seymour family were of a respectable, noble lineage, but were quiet on the fringes of the royal court. Jane was one of a long line of Seymours, a family that stretched back to the conquest of 1066, and hundreds of years further back as the St Maur family of France.[9] Through their mother, Margery, the Seymour children could trace their ancestors back seven generations to King Edward III through his son, Lionel of Antwerp, and thus back through all the kings of England.[10] King Henry could make the same connection; he was related to Edward III though Lionel's brother John of Gaunt.[11] This made King Henry and Jane Seymour fifth cousins, not enough to cause any problems, but enough that the king still ensured there were no issues of consanguinity between him and his new love interest.

Ambassador Chapuys noted on 1 April that Jane was 'well tutored' on how to act around the king, probably by her brother Edward and their privy chamber allies. But Jane had to juggle a king who liked the thrill of the chase but was less interested in making a relationship work. Through the gossiping letter from the Marchioness of Dorset, Chapuys spoke of how the king loved Jane's 'innocent' rebuff of his advances; it played into Henry's game of chasing a maiden, and Chapuys mentioned:

> 'In consequence of this refusal, the King's love for the said damsel had marvellously increased, and that he had said to her that not only did he praise and commend her virtuous behaviour on the occasion, but that in order to prove the sincerity of his love, and the honesty of his views towards her, he had resolved not to converse with her in future, except in the presence of one of her relatives, and that for this reason, the King had taken away from Master Cromwell's apartments in the palace a room, to which he can, when he likes, have access through certain galleries without being seen, of which room the young

> lady's elder brother and his wife have already taken possession for the express purpose of her repairing thither'.[12]

It is important to note that Chapuys received this information as gossip and had no proof any of this was true. How did the Marchioness of Dorset get such detailed information? Both marchionesses could have been at court. Lady Margaret was one of the most noble women in England; her daughter-in-law was the king's niece, so both had free access to attend court and visit the queen if they desired. They of course both knew Sir Nicholas Carew and Thomas Cromwell very well. Sir Henry Grey, Marquis of Dorset spent much time at court, though was not in the king's inner circle, but was guarded by Cromwell, to protect him from his own stupidity. It is unlikely any of the interactions between Jane and Henry, or Jane and her co-conspirators happened in front of these guests. Edward Seymour and his wife Anne now had rooms close to the king, so they likely heard and saw everything, and that information likely went straight to Thomas Cromwell. Lady Francis Grey had her cousin Lady Margaret Douglas at court in 1536, which could be another source of information which spilled out of Anne Boleyn's rooms.

The information from the Marchioness of Dorset to Ambassador Chapuys went even further. Chapuys told Emperor Charles that Jane, 'had been advised to tell the king, frankly, how much the people of England hated Anne Boleyn and their illegitimate marriage, and that if Jane were to say such things in front of high-ranking men of the court, they would back her up in this opinion, and swear on their fealty that they, "abominate the marriage"'.[13] For Jane, a quiet woman who had never spent time with a suitor, who had never had a say in politics or religion in England, to openly say such critical things to the king, or worse, in front of an audience with the king, is an idea of total fantasy. Jane Seymour was known to speak her mind to her husband, post marriage, but at this early stage of their relationship, the notion that she could slander Anne Boleyn without consequence in such a way is fanciful. No one would be safe if they spoke ill of Anne in front of Henry unless they were certain he had turned against her. In early April 1536, not a single person had that sense of safety. All the court had were rumours, fast getting out of control, that the king wanted a new mistress. Missing from Chapuys' letter is who told Jane to speak so freely, but was likely again Carew, Page, Bryan, and her brother Edward. None of the women of Anne's chamber would have said something so openly critical; there was no benefit for them.

Now Sir Edward Seymour and his wife Lady Anne were suddenly living right beside King Henry, presumably so Jane could stop by any time for supervised visits. The inner rooms of the royal palaces were very particular in their allotments: the king and queen had their separate rooms; Lady Margaret Douglas as the king's niece had rooms; and Thomas Cromwell had his so that he could be available for Henry at all times and move around the court without encountering others if wished. Everyone else at court had to use the outer rooms assigned to them. Even with Edward Seymour working for Henry in the privy chamber, being assigned personal rooms, especially rooms at Greenwich so close to the king that Cromwell occupied them, was no small gesture. Hoisting a banner emblazoned 'Queen Jane' would have been more subtle.

Naturally, if the king asked Cromwell to make space for the Seymours, he would have without any hesitation, despite how much work it would be to move his behemoth of attendants. But was it King Henry's idea to move Edward Seymour close to the royal bedroom, or was it Cromwell's idea? The Vicegerent cannot have gone far; he needed space to be at court on the first weekend of April, so the Seymour couple likely received little more than a parlour and perhaps a bedroom of their own, with Cromwell's household adjusted into the rest of his quarters. All Seymour needed was the private hallway through to the privy chamber, and Cromwell still needed that access as well. This move of Edward and Anne Seymour, and the handy visiting place this gave Jane, showed the monumental shift in Henry's behaviour through 1536, and Anne needed to make a shift of her own.

CHAPTER 9

Two Sides of the Same Reformed Coin

On Monday, 13 March 1536, Thomas Cromwell sent his son Gregory away from London. Gregory had been regularly away from home for his education since 1528, usually with his cousins Christopher and William Wellyfed, and Nicholas Sadler.[1] But this plan had stalled over the last few years, with Gregory instead spending summers with his father's friends. In 1534, Gregory spent the summer hunting in the West Midlands with Rowland Lee, Bishop of Lichfield and Coventry. In 1535, he spent the summer with his relative John Williams in Rycote, Oxfordshire, making friends, helping said friends woo girls, and hunting rather than studying. In 1536, Cromwell decided to send Gregory away again, to Sir Richard Southwell in Woodrising, Norfolk, with Henry Duwes, Gregory's weary tutor who used to teach Princess Mary, who was to educate the boy.[2] It was much earlier in the year than usual to send Gregory away. Cromwell treated his rather middling teenage son as a precious jewel and was angling at getting Gregory a summer in the Duke of Norfolk's home, an attempt to foster a relationship.[3] But Cromwell liked to keep his son close as much as possible, so sending Gregory away early suggests Cromwell wanted his son far from London. It may also suggest that Cromwell was starting to feel nervous about his position beside the king. It was entirely possible; Anne Boleyn had never relented and accepted Cromwell's place at court. Despite working more than anyone for the king, Cromwell received no rewards other than the roles he worked in, and was not even a knight. All his landholdings were those he purchased or leased, all paid for; including land transactions approved by the king, as none were gifted. Cromwell had worked his way into being the king's Master Secretary and Vicegerent of the Spirituals, and happily took on small administration roles at court to help boost his power and salary, but without a title, a knighthood, or any outward sign of favour from the king it meant he was still just a commoner. Anne Boleyn had been born in wealth and favour, and her influential education in France was skilfully negotiated by her well-connected father. Her mother was born into one of the most powerful noble houses in England. King Henry (and to some extent, his father) was unlike other monarchs before or after his reign; he elevated commoners for their work, not for their family ties and ranks. That continued to irritate those who believed their birthright was to rule. Anne Boleyn thought similarly about Cromwell; the commoner who once worked for Thomas Wolsey would never be enough in her eyes.[4] Cromwell had always been indirectly against Anne's elevation under Wolsey's reign, and despite being the man who eventually put Anne into power, Cromwell would simply never be enough for her. He would always be too lowly. But even Anne did not have the royal favour to displace Cromwell.

Anne had not been discreet in her hatred for Cromwell. Ambassador Chapuys noted multiple times how Anne had mentioned she wanted rid of the Vicegerent.[5] An incident often attributed to 1536, when Anne and Cromwell argued and Anne said, 'she would like to see [Cromwell's] head cut off', actually occurred in early June 1535.[6] Cromwell had done his best to avoid Anne, and probably vice versa, but the pair getting into public slanging matches over the course of her reign probably came as no surprise. The 1535 argument was not the first time Anne told Cromwell she wanted to see the back of him, and it was not to be the last.

How Anne felt about Cromwell was not unusual; he was someone people either loved or hated and seemed to have no issue with that persona. Cromwell was not a man many people knew well, but those who did know him, usually those he knew away from the royal court, loved and trusted him. In times of joy or crisis, Cromwell tended to turn to his own people, his personal friends and family. He had left England as a teen in search of adventure, fought alongside the French in Italy, before becoming educated in merchant business, banking, and law in Florence as part of the Frescobaldi family.[7] After a stint as a self-employed merchant in the Low Countries, he returned home to his family and worked as a lawyer. Cromwell did not seem particularly interested in court life or those who were not self-made; he lived in the Italian quarter of London and created a massive personal wealth through working for a living. A working trip to Rome in 1518 made Cromwell question the Catholic faith, which he admitted to never supporting anyway, and took on the new religion at home.[8] After doing work with his brother-in-law for Thomas Grey, 2nd Marquis of Dorset, he was spotted by Cardinal Wolsey while petitioning for the Greys in parliament.[9] A legal career and personal friendship with the cardinal dominated Cromwell's late-1520s, until Cromwell lost his wife and two daughters to illness. While the wide Cromwellian extended family supported him, Cromwell also lost Wolsey to the king's whims, and had only reached out to King Henry in desperation for his friend.[10] A royal life had come to Cromwell more by accident than design, and while Cromwell had a wide circle of friends and colleagues, aside from Ambassador Chapuys, Cromwell spent almost no time with noblemen at court, aside from the friends he had made in his younger, less royal, years. Cromwell, crucially and strategically, never remarried, despite enquiries and letters about doing so, thus never gaining support from any well-placed family around the court. Cromwell specifically kept himself as a common outsider with a thriving life outside the court.

Thomas Cromwell and Anne Boleyn could have been friends, almost should have, given their similar outlooks. They collected the same books, wrote to the same people, and believed in the same changes to the Church. Anne whispered in one of Henry's ears, while Cromwell whispered in the other. But neither of them ever got over their time with Cardinal Wolsey. It is little wonder Anne felt aggrieved by Wolsey's treatment of her, telling her she was too socially inferior to marry the future Earl of Northumberland when she had the chance.[11] While it may have been technically true in 1523, the Percys of Northumberland were crucial to the security of the north, and hearing your possible marriage was denied due to your social position cannot have been easy to stomach. The match between Anne Boleyn and Henry Percy was seemingly a love match planned between them, which only hurt the pair more. All Anne could do was slink back onto the sidelines of the court working as a lady to Queen Katharine. Anne's sister was known to be the king's mistress at the time, which likely did not help Anne's desire to be seen as 'worthy' of a position or respect at court. Henry Percy was married off to Lady Mary Talbot, who hated the plan as much as Percy, and by 1536, the pair had been unhappily married and living apart for well over a decade (with Mary unable to secure an annulment while living with her father, the Earl of Shrewsbury[12]). The Talbot family were staunch Catholics, as were the Percys, and had Anne married and become the Countess of Northumberland, she may have never been able to enjoy her reformist ambitions. Perhaps in hindsight, Anne got at least a little lucky, but when her time came beside the king, it was again Cardinal Wolsey unable, and unwilling, to ensure Anne's second chance at marriage. While Wolsey's civil lawyer, Thomas Cromwell, did not care whether the king was married to Katharine or Anne, he did care that Wolsey was made the scapegoat of the royal annulment affair and told the king so in parliament.[13] It is no surprise that Anne might have harboured disdain for Wolsey and Cromwell over the entire debacle. She was never destined to be a quiet wife tucked away on an estate, but the opinions of men had seriously hampered Anne's life in England.

Anne Boleyn's religious beliefs were perhaps the largest part of her personality. She may have been beautiful, witty, talkative, and unpredictable, but it was her education that set her apart from others.[14] Her mind captured Henry's attention as much as her outward appearance. Only in 1536 could she feel like a legitimate queen with the loss of Katharine, and yet Anne had already been through hell in the first few months of the year. A decade after the king first fell in love with her, Anne's crown was slipping away, her husband was looking to another, and the Reformation was proceeding without her input. She could not stop Henry from looking at Jane Seymour, but maybe she could save the souls of England by 'righting' the course of the Reformation.

Anne certainly knew how to discuss religion at a legislative level. Few English women could boast such an illustrious education. In 1513 she was sent with messenger Claude Bouton, Seigneur de Courbaron, to Margaret of Austria; because of the confusion over Anne's year of birth she could have been as young as 6 or as old as 12. Margaret was the Governor of the Habsburg Netherlands, her royal household an unrivalled finishing school in Burgundy for children being educated and raised alongside the next generation of Habsburg children. Charles of Burgundy was also being raised by his aunt Margaret, and Anne Boleyn met the Burgundian court staying at Mechelen in Brabant (in what is now Belgium[15]). Charles would one day be Holy Roman Emperor Charles V, ruling the Roman Empire, Spain, Austria, Italy, the Low Countries and the Americas invaded by Spain, and the household was one of the finest in Europe. In 1513, young Charles was also betrothed to Princess Mary Tudor, sister to King Henry VIII. Anne Boleyn was the youngest daughter of King Henry's ambassador to the Netherlands and France, and her mother was one of Queen Katharine's ladies, so she was a perfect addition to diplomacy between the countries.

Anne arrived to be a maid to Duchess Margaret, who ruled the Low Countries on behalf of her father Emperor Maximilian. Margaret was charged with holding a kingdom and maintaining peace with the border with France, as well as raising the next Holy Roman Emperor. Anne was at Margaret's side, placed there to learn French, the language of the nobility of Europe, and continental manners and behaviour. Duchess Margaret was also sister-in-law to Queen Katharine back in England, having been briefly married to Katharine's brother Juan, Prince of Asturias, and Anne was in a prime position to learn how a woman could rule. Anne quickly delighted Margaret and wrote home to her father about how well she was getting on with his plan to see her elevated in social graces and education.[16] Anne could not have asked for better; Margaret ran a strict but generous court. There was no gossip or ill-behaviour, everyone was to be educated in all religious and humanist subjects, and the arts, dances, pageantry, customs, music, and maintaining a good reputation. No harm could come to Anne under Margaret, but her father was forced to recall Anne in August 1514, as she was needed as an English and French-speaking attendant to the new queen of France, Princess Mary Tudor. Not only had King Henry of England betrayed his arrangement with Duchess Margaret to marry his sister to her nephew Charles, but now Princess Mary had married Margaret's enemy, the French King Louis. Mary Boleyn travelled to France to witness the French wedding, and Anne joined the court soon after. But by January 1515, the French king was dead, and Mary Tudor went home to England married to Charles Brandon, the same man Anne Boleyn had seen flirting with Duchess Margaret in an awkward meeting a year earlier.[17] Somehow, Anne managed to stay behind in the French court, a lady to the new queen, Claude, while everyone else in Mary Tudor's court went back to England. Queen Claude and Anne Boleyn had both been ladies in Mary Tudor's household and were likely friends.[18] It would be a post that Anne maintained for seven years as she watched her friend Claude suffer annual pregnancies and endless betrayals by her husband King Francis.

Among the ladies of the French court was King Francis' sister, Marguerite d'Angoulême. While nothing points to their friendship at the time, it was later, when Anne married King Henry, that shows Anne and Marguerite's close friendship. One letter from Anne to Marguerite showed that Anne's, 'greatest wish, next to having a son, is to see [Marguerite] again'.[19] While Anne was in France with Claude and Marguerite, the Reformation was still in its infancy. But Marguerite had already gained an excellent education and was interested in humanism, reading, and studying the likes of Jacques Lefèvre d'Étaples, Erasmus, and Guillaume Briçonnet. This is likely where Anne picked up her humanist leanings and the belief that the Catholic Church needed to be reformed for the benefit of the people. There were plenty of books on humanism in France; Martin Luther's fight against indulgences began in 1517, and Erasmus' updated second edition of the New Testament Bible was released in 1519. Marguerite was an early adopter of many of these beliefs, dedicating the rest of her life to protecting those advancing the French Reformation.[20]

Thomas Boleyn rushed Anne home in around late 1521 when Anglo-French relations soured, and Anne would never see her grand French life again. But the fire lit in Anne would never be extinguished. Change was happening in Europe and combined with the education, customs, pageantry, and glory Anne had witnessed, a mundane English life would simply not suit. She burst onto the court scene in London in April 1522, dancing alongside her sister Mary and future sister-in-law Jane Parker.[21] Anne was destined for an Irish marriage to help quell cousins infighting, including Anne's father, as the Butler family scrambled for the claim to the earldom of Ormond. Anne's uncle, Thomas Howard, Duke of Norfolk, was the first to suggest sending Anne to marry one of her Irish cousins to solve multiple issues in the region.[22] Anne came home from France under the pretext that she would be exiled to a very Catholic life in Ireland. Given that relations between England, France, and the Holy Roman Empire (now ruled by Charles, once Anne's contemporary in the Netherlands) were suffering, going home was not such a bad move, but it would have been a tough pill to swallow for educated Anne. Fortunately, the Irish marriage idea eventually fell through, around the same time as Anne's love for Henry Percy was in full swing, and before Henry VIII appeared in Anne's romantic life. But her faith, her belief in the new religion, the creation of English religious texts, and a reformation of the Church sat quietly in her mind.

There are various reports of Anne owning reformist books, such as William Tyndale's *Obedience of a Christian Man.* Published in October 1528, it is unknown when or how Anne first purchased the book, but a colourful tale comes from John Louth, an evangelical archdeacon who was only a young child when Anne was in King Henry's life. Louth was educated at Oxford but was steered to the new religion by the works of the early reformist, later martyr, John Frith.[23] Louth believed around early 1529, Anne Boleyn acquired her copy of William Tyndale's *Obedience of a Christan Man.* The book was a guide to God's laws of obedience, how one should obey and rule in life, an interpretation with the belief that the Church twisted scripture to its benefit.[24] The book was banned in England, but many copies circulated, although it was difficult to purchase an imported copy. The book itself was not radical in any way but did question why people still read and prayed in Latin, not understanding their own words. It questioned how the Church believed itself above kings and laid out ways a person could better understand God. All Tyndale books were banned as King Henry hated the man and his perceived attack on Catholicism.[25] In evangelical circles, the book was widely well-read and owned, and many at court could have offered a king's mistress a copy for her pleasure. Tales of Henry stumbling across the book in Anne's rooms, or Anne offering the book to cheer Henry after his failed annulment aside, Louth told a slightly more complex tale.[26]

Anne Boleyn had this book and loaned it to one of her ladies, Anne Gainsford. The book was snatched from her by George Zouche, a young man at court who was wooing Mistress Gainsford at the time (a slightly unusual game suitors played, stealing items from their intended). Zouche did not return the book, wishing to read it himself, and was caught with it by Richard Sampson, then the Dean of Windsor, who confiscated the heretical text. The book was handed to Cardinal Wolsey, and Anne Boleyn petitioned Wolsey to return her book, either before or after the cardinal told his king of its existence. Henry became interested in the short read, which believed in the divine rights of kings. As far as Tyndale's books went, this was not extremist ideology, and the idea that a king ruled a country over God's authority quickly became a popular idea. While William Louth suggested Henry talked of his love for the book, that may have been wishful thinking recorded later in life, as Henry never loosened his stance on William Tyndale.[27] Thomas Cromwell and his secretary, Stephen Vaughan, were charged with bringing in reformist books from the Low Countries to give to King Henry until May 1531, when Henry decided he could stomach no more Tyndale, and would never allow the man to return to England.[28] Reports that Stephen Vaughan had been in Antwerp to coax Tyndale home to England at the king's request appear to have no basis. Cromwell's panicked letter to Vaughan telling him not to bring the king any more books, lest Vaughan be imprisoned, shows the king's continued hatred for Tyndale.[29] Tyndale remained overseas, exiled with other fine English reformists who could not safely return throughout their lives. However, Cromwell did manage to keep all the reformist books sent over without being punished, and he and Henry bonded over their identical book collections.

Anne Boleyn's book falling into King Henry's lap is often taken either as a symbol of her desire for reformation or as slander against her trying to turn a king away from his wife, depending on opinion. No one person can take such credit or receive such an accusation. There can be no doubt that Anne was well aware of the king's plans to annul his marriage to his wife, but in May 1528, when Edward Foxe returned from Rome after proposing a legatine court to the Pope, he went to Henry and Anne at Greenwich. Anne, tending to her ladies who were suffering smallpox, spoke with Edward Foxe and thanked him for his help with Rome, confusing him with Stephen Gardiner several times.[30] Had she been instigating the divorce, she would have known these men well. It was not Anne trying to foist divorce upon Henry and England, it was Henry himself. Anne was trying to help people on a smaller scale at the time, aiding her brother-in-law, William Carey, to petition the king to grant the position of abbess of Wilton to Carey's sister, Eleanor. Carey died of sweating sickness in June 1528, but Anne still pushed against Wolsey's decision over the new abbess at Wilton and petitioned for Eleanor. It soon became clear that the nun had two children by two different priests, and she was tossed from the convent.[31] It was not a good look, but it did not put Anne off trying to help people.

Anne was no fool, neither was she a homewrecker pushing the king to divorce or destroy the Church. As Nicholas Hawkins, Archdeacon of Ely, noted in 1532, 'all the lady does is by the king's order', after hearing that Anne had requested a copy of *De Potestate Papæ*[32] (*On the Power of the Pope*). Henry had requested the book, not Anne, who was prudent in all she did, never stepping outside the king's wishes. There was simply no benefit to doing so; Anne did not push Henry into reformation, he was a willing participant in anything that would remove him from Queen Katharine.

The lingering issue was that Anne Boleyn was the best person to take the blame for the religious changes in England. Not many wished to skirt around treason and blame the king but blaming his 'lowly' second wife did not bother people so much. Thomas Cromwell monitored ill-talk about the royal couple as much as he could and altered laws to punish people spreading lies and cruelty about Anne and Henry. Incidents such as the execution of Sir Thomas More and Bishop John Fisher were laid at Anne's feet when it was Henry alone who wanted them killed for refusing his supremacy within the Church. More, in particular, did not argue with Henry and Anne's marriage, only with Henry as the Head of the Church, and yet Anne was still blamed by the general public for More's death, which More easily could have prevented himself. Anne was blamed for so many changes to England and religion that chronicler George Cavendish even drafted a poem about it, claiming Anne knew the people of England blamed her, writing Anne, 'reigned in joy and now in endless pain, the world universal hath me in disdain, the slander of my name will aye be green, and called of each man the most vicious queen'.[33] In June 1535, King Francis in France wrote:

> 'Three days ago of the new queen of England, how little virtuously she has always lived and now lives, and how she and her brother and adherents suspect the Duke of Norfolk of wishing to make his son King and marry him to the King's legitimate daughter [Princess Elizabeth], though they are near relations. It seems to him there can be little friendship between the two kingdoms.'[34]

Anne could not seemingly get peace anywhere. Another issue for her was that she could not make changes on behalf of the Reformation on a large scale. She had no political power, unable to write or present laws to parliament, and once Princess Elizabeth was born in 1533, she was expected to be the subservient wife and mother rather than the exciting mistress Henry had wanted before their marriage. Why Henry believed Anne would simply get to the business of making sons and nothing else remains one of the mysteries of the male mind. Having a son was Anne's number one priority as Henry's new wife, but that did not interfere with her beliefs and her ambitions for religion. The relationship between Henry and Anne always had its ups and downs, they would argue, have lovers' quarrels, and then Henry would be back to proclaiming his love, saying he would rather beg door to door than give up Anne. Henry had taken up mistresses again by 1534 while Anne managed pregnancies, and one Venetian ambassador wrote in June 1535 that Henry seemed sick of Anne, yet two weeks later wrote of how all was well again, and Anne was 'back in charge'.

But now, in 1536, Anne felt the need to take more charge of religion and the wellbeing of England's people, not simply sit by while her husband threw her fate into the wind. It is a fine idea to see Anne Boleyn as the catalyst for the Church of England, but nothing is ever that simple. Anne, with all her beliefs, and her determination to never sit silently, certainly had ideas for religion and the people of England. But throughout the 1520s, as Anne either lived at Hever Castle, or at court, and always at the whims of the king, others were also seeing out their beliefs, which had formed the basis of the English Reformation through the 1530s. Anne had been certainly involved in the new religion, even if she was never publicly identified as an evangelical or a Lutheran in her lifetime. But she did not have the power to make substantial changes to the Church, nor legislative power. She could make minor changes in favour of reform, such as promoting certain men to the king or elevating individuals into power, to help those she believed needed advancement. Anne had read and owned all the banned books; the George Joye translation of the New Testament, the Tyndale English Bible of 1534, and Miles Coverdale's English Bible of 1535. Anne had the same protection as others in Henry's favour, able to defy English printing and reading laws. Thomas Boleyn's godson, Thomas Theobald, was the Boleyns' man in Antwerp, who reported back on the arrest and persecution of William Tyndale in 1536, while Stephen Vaughan was doing the same for Cromwell, showing the Boleyns' concern for the English reformist's safety. Anne regularly wrote to Cromwell, asking him for his help in advancing or assisting people in need.[35] Anne had visited Syon Abbey in London in December 1535, where her nephew Henry Carey lived,[36] and questioned the nuns about why they were still reading Latin primers, as she looked to give them the word of God in English. Syon Abbey had owned copies of *Mirror of Our Lady* written in English for 100 years, but Anne believed they were not doing enough to advance King Henry's wishes for an English Church.[37] Vicegerent Cromwell himself had visited the abbey a week earlier, to check on how reforming the religious house was advancing, as it was one of the houses he wished to preserve from dissolution. Reports of behaviour within Syon suggested it would be a challenge to reform, given the amount of corruption, most relating to the use of fake relics. But it shows Anne wanting to follow a similar path to others in power, by looking to fix the Church. Anne wanted more; she wanted to be proactive in the Church, not simply be the king's wife, and she certainly had the knowledge to assist the Reformation.

Within the Church, Anne had attempted to promote as many reformers as she could with her limited power. She had a strong group of supporters, either at court or in the Church. Her short reign achieved more in diminishing the old power holders in the Church, either sweeping aside those with conservative views (even as Henry flip-flopped in his religious opinion) or working to promote her favourites when a Catholic power died and needed a reformist replacement. Anne may have felt this would be a route to achieving influence, as those she believed in would grow in power over time. But by April 1536, Anne may have known time was no longer on her side.

Had Anne lived longer, she could have seen her efforts pay off. She was a promoter of Hugh Latimer, who became Bishop of Worcester in 1535, which would have felt like a victory, though she could not take credit for Latimer's advancement.[38] Latimer respected Anne but was Vicegerent Cromwell and Archbishop Cranmer's man through and through. He was one of the initial early reformers of England, alongside Cranmer, Robert Barnes, Thomas Bilney, Miles Coverdale, Matthew Parker, William Tyndale, Nicholas Shaxton, John Rogers, George Joye, John Clerk and John Bale.[39]

Chief among England's most prominent reformist men were the Thomases, Cromwell and Cranmer, who had been clandestinely discussing the Reformation in England well before Anne had any position with the king, as early as 1526. The men were part of a group that has been dubbed, 'the stubborn legend of the White Horse Inn'. In this 'little Germany', the key early Cambridge reformers would regularly meet at the White Horse Tavern and discuss the change of religion.[40] Sadly, evidence to suggest they were all there together all the time is severely lacking. Thomas Cranmer was holding secret evangelical meetings in 1526 and 1527 around sites in Cambridge, hidden away by Thomas Cromwell, who had access to closed buildings while working for Cardinal Wolsey. Once Wolsey found out that Cromwell had been setting up these secret meetings, the group was disbanded and many were imprisoned or forced from England forever, men like Tyndale, Coverdale, Joye, and Barnes in particular, who had only just got out of the Tower and placed under house arrest at Austin Friars where Cromwell lived.[41] Having a man like Hugh Latimer, one of the early reformers, as a supporter would have done Anne much good, and she would have felt like her voice was being heard with him on her side. Latimer had seen his friend, Thomas Bilney, burned alive as a heretic by Sir Thomas More, though Latimer had managed to gain much of Bilney's reformist knowledge before the horrific act. John Bale and George Joye remained eternally in trouble for their heretical speeches and translations in England but were safe under Cromwell's patronage, meaning Anne could have had access to their advanced reformist writings. William Tyndale and Miles Coverdale were good friends of Cromwell but were in exile, [42] and with Tyndale in prison in Brussels in 1536, Anne never got the chance to meet him. These men supported Anne on the throne, though as King Henry did not want any of these men in England, they provided Anne no regular support. John Rogers was in Antwerp, and Robert Barnes had newly come home from living with Martin Luther in Germany and was safe under Cromwell's protection.[43] Frustratingly for Anne, these powerful religious men were Cromwell and Cranmer's men, not hers.

But Anne was not completely alone in her beliefs. Others from the White Horse Tavern actively supported Anne alongside Bishop Latimer. Nicholas Shaxton, while a difficult man who was constantly in trouble, was an Anne supporter.[44] Sir Thomas More feared it was Shaxton who should have been put to the stake as a heretic in 1531, instead of Bilney.[45] Anne heard of Shaxton and arranged for him to have the position of treasurer at Salisbury Cathedral and appointed him her almoner in 1533. By 1535, he was Bishop of Salisbury, and protected from heresy charges by Cromwell and Cranmer. Another of the strong reformists, John Clerk, had become Bishop of Bath and Wells but was also a Cromwell and Cranmer man over Anne. Clerk also worked as a diplomat across Europe, alongside Edward Foxe, who became Bishop of Hereford in 1535.[46] Foxe too supported Anne but was Cromwell and Cranmer's man as well. Another strong reformist was Bishop John Hilsey of Rochester, but he wrote reformist translation material for Cromwell and would side with his powerful patron over the queen any day.[47] Thomas Goodricke, Bishop of Ely was certainly an Anne supporter, a reformist writer who gave Anne access to his teachings and translations.[48] Another who believed in Anne as queen was theologian Matthew Parker, who had been one of the White Horse Tavern men. Anne called Parker to court in 1533, made him her chaplain and saw that he was given a licence to preach.[49] In 1535, Anne ensured Parker became Dean of the College of Secular Canons at Stoke-by-Clare in Suffolk,[50] and he was high in her favour, as she trusted his preaching and advice.

Anne had Hugh Latimer, Nicholas Shaxton and Matthew Parker on her side and plenty of other men in varying degrees of power all over England.

The Barlow brothers, John, William, Roger, and Thomas were all Boleyn supporters and William Barlow was appointed Bishop of St Asaph's and St David's, with his brother John also given high-ranking positions thanks to Anne's involvement. There were men on their way to high-powered positions in the Church after Anne's death; Nicholas Heath was the Archdeacon of Stafford, a favourite of Anne who travelled to Germany with Bishop Foxe on Reformation matters. Archdeacon Thomas Thirlby was a strong believer in Henry as the Head of the Church of England and Anne's right to be queen and held the post of Dean of the Royal Chapel.[51] This position meant Thirlby held sway with the king and could help Anne's desire for reform. Another permitted to preach before the king was Anne's almoner, John Skipp, Vicar of Newington, Essex. He spent much time in Anne's company, giving his thoughts on the Reformation and the dissolution of the monasteries. Skipp was a biblical scholar and interpreter, selected by Anne herself to provide religious guidance. As much as Anne could be influenced by Skipp, she could likewise guide him with her needs, which was exactly what she planned to do. It would soon be time for the men of the Reformation to pick sides — Anne or Cromwell.

CHAPTER 10

Battle for the Pulpit

Archbishop of Canterbury, Thomas Cranmer, was by far Anne Boleyn's biggest supporter. John Fox did not believe it was Anne who ensured Cranmer's rise to power, though chronicler, William Latimer, thought she deserved some credit. Cranmer had been studying at Cambridge since the age of 14, as a master of humanist scholars. Not ordained, he married a woman named Joan in around 1517 and had to leave Cambridge as a result. Joan died in childbirth and Cambridge brought Cranmer back into the Church, ordaining him as a priest in 1520.[1] His humanist studies brought him close to the world of Martin Luther and the advent of reform, and by 1526 he was holding private meetings around Cambridge, preaching heretical writings with like-minded men.[2] Undeterred by the anger of Cardinal Wolsey over these private meetings, Cranmer remained in England, lucky to fly under the radar while other reformist scholars were killed or in exile.[3] While hiding from the plague in 1529, Cranmer stayed with friends, spending time with Stephen Gardiner, then secretary to the king, and Edward Foxe, later Bishop of Hereford. They discussed the possibility of going to Europe, to seek out scholarly opinion on whether a king could annul his marriage under the new religion. Cranmer's idea to speak to European scholars was put to King Henry and Anne Boleyn, who liked the idea immediately. Cranmer and Foxe set off to Europe, spending years travelling through Italy, Switzerland and Germany. While there, Cranmer married, believing it permitted under the new religion, despite King Henry's intense belief this was untrue. Cranmer married Margarete, niece of a new friend and Swiss reformer, Andreas Osiander, and his wife Katharina Preu.[4]

In November 1532, William Warham, Archbishop of Canterbury died while on a trip to visit his nephew in Kent.[5] This was what King Henry needed, as Warham had been one of the strongest opponents of Henry's annulment from Queen Katharine. Thomas Cromwell's legal avenues had only managed to break the Church as far as making Henry the head of religion, but it was not enough to rule the king's marriage invalid without ecclesiastical approval. A new Archbishop of Canterbury was the answer, and Cranmer's name was soon on the table. The Boleyns supported Cranmer; Thomas Boleyn had known Cranmer for some time. Edward Foxe spoke well of him, and Stephen Gardiner, despite being against reform and the royal divorce, had previously sung Cranmer's praises. Cranmer had sent home much reading for Henry and Anne on the new religion and the power it would give the king. Cromwell suggested they promote Cranmer at once,[6] as the Pope would agree to the appointment and sign off the paperwork needed to make it official.

Cranmer was seen as a no-one; Rome would fall for the plan to install a 'nobody' in their eyes. Cromwell sent his closest friend, Stephen Vaughan, on horseback to find Cranmer in France, and the pair returned after a harsh wintry trek to England in January 1533, with Cranmer's wife Margarete hidden away at the first opportunity. The Archbishop of Canterbury could not have a wife, at least not one the king knew about.[7]

Cromwell and Cranmer worked together to break the Church's hold over England. Cromwell changed laws that meant Queen Katharine could not appeal to Rome and Cranmer held a religious synod which decided, using the new religion, that the marriage was not valid in England.[8] Anne was crowned as fast as Cromwell and Cranmer could arrange it, as Anne's belly was far too big to hide, and news of the secret marriage had travelled far and wide. Cromwell had seen out his king's wishes, but Cranmer had genuinely believed Anne was the right person to be queen. Cranmer wholeheartedly believed and supported Anne and felt that the new religion was safe with her at Henry's side.[9]

But the new religion and marriage was no easy task for Cranmer to handle. He was not a strong, imposing man. He needed Cromwell at his side to take the criticism and offer support for Cranmer's changes. The pair worked in unison, meaning those clergymen who believed in the Church were firmly Cranmer and Cromwell's men. Those who did not believe in the new religion, those who were prepared to die instead of turning their back on the Catholic faith, poured scorn on Cromwell, Cranmer, and by association, Anne. By 1536, Cranmer may have been the Archbishop of Canterbury, but he did not have control of the Church and its clergy.[10] The added upset from the dissolution of the monasteries only made more people angry and unlikely to be supportive of change. At a time when all those in charge needed support, and to know where others stood on matters of religion, there was no consensus at all. If Anne was to keep her seat beside the king, she needed support more than ever, and while Cranmer loved his queen, he was often away at Lambeth Palace on the other side of the Thames, or at Knole Palace in Kent.

The whispers in the halls of Greenwich Palace would not have escaped Anne's ears on the first weekend of April 1536. While Jane Seymour was making her feelings known with her choreographed rejection of being a mistress, Chapuys was sharing that juicy gossip all over the place, and more was coming his way.[11] On 1 April, he wrote about a dinner he had held in previous weeks; among the distinguished guests were Henry Pole, Lord Montagu, Elizabeth Fitzgerald, Countess of Kildare, and her nephew, Henry Grey, 3rd Marquis of Dorset. The Grey family, being staunchly against Anne Boleyn and the new religion, spoke of the sad state of affairs in England. Henry Pole spoke of the Greys' favourite, Thomas Cromwell. Pole felt no love for Anne, even if Anne was doing favours for his sister Ursula, Baroness Stafford. The event and exact nature of the conversation went unexplained, but Pole spoke of Cromwell and Anne Boleyn in the worst of terms, suggesting they had openly argued sometime in March 1536.[12] No such event is recorded, though that was the same time that monastery closures and Poor Laws were completed in parliament. Anne made no secret of her desire to keep religious houses open and to help the poor. Cromwell had no power over whether the monasteries were dissolved or not; that power lay with the king. Perhaps Anne knew she could not fight Henry on the issue, especially with mild Jane Seymour so close by, and Cromwell was an easier target on which Anne could unleash her anger at the situation.[13] Gossip at Chapuys' event suggested King Henry could marry the noticeably young French Princess Madeline who was betrothed to King James of Scotland.[14] Chapuys reported that he often skipped visiting Cromwell at home, as he did not wish Anne Boleyn to know of their collusion on a possible treaty between Henry and the Emperor.[15] Chapuys told his dinner guests of how Cromwell had laughed off Anne's threats of wanting to cut off his head in the past, but Chapuys was no longer sure the threats were idle. Chapuys wrote:

> 'Such a threat, I said, was constantly before my eyes, causing me great care and anxiety, and I sincerely wished [Cromwell] a more gracious mistress than [Anne] was, one more grateful

> for the immense services [Cromwell] had rendered the King. He ought to take care not to offend or over-irritate [Anne], or else he must renounce all hope of that perfect reconciliation we both were trying to bring about. I therefore begged and entreated [Cromwell], in such an event, to guard against her attacks more effectually than the cardinal [Wolsey] had done, which I hoped his dexterity and prudence would be able to accomplish… yet the love and affection I bore the King, and [Cromwell] in particular, as well as my earnest desire for the peace, honour, and prosperity of England, made me wish that [Cromwell] should have another royal mistress, not out of hatred of Anne Boleyn, for she had never done me any harm, but for [Cromwell's] own sake.'[16]

The ambassador was dining with some of the most noble people in the country, those exalted in the king's favour and were unlikely to ever be brought to harm. The stories of the royal marriage had travelled and were reduced to gossip over dinner. But the mood at the court, and with Anne being so angry at Cromwell, was coming to a head. Blowing up in anger at the king was not an option, and seemingly Cromwell was the next best person for Anne to rally against. Unfortunately for Anne, all those beholden to her, loyal to her, were equally loyal to Cromwell and his power over England and religion. While she had spent years carefully trying to help and support people where she could, Cromwell had been making far larger gains in support and patronage. He had friends in every corner, spies in every household, and much older, far-reaching associations with everyone at court and in parliament. While Cromwell could not, and would not, ever fire back at Anne Boleyn over anything she said, lest he risk Henry's wrath, it was not a smart time for Anne to be angering the king's chief minister. Still, Chapuys took his concerns over Cromwell's safety to the man himself, reporting back to Emperor Charles that:

> 'Cromwell seemed to take my words in good part, and thanked me for the affection I professed to him, saying that he was well aware of the precarious nature of human affairs, to say nothing of those appertaining to royal courts… [Cromwell], however, admitted to himself that the day might come when fate would

> strike him as it had struck his predecessors in office: then he would arm himself with patience and place himself for the rest in the hands of God.'[17]

By this time, Anne was so angry at Cromwell that Chapuys believed Cromwell would need God's help if he were to escape Anne's wrath. Cromwell admitted to Chapuys that he had been the one to promote Henry's marriage to Anne, the one who had made it possible, but only because the king had been so determined to be with Anne. Cromwell told Chapuys that, while Henry continued to play the game of courtly love with other women, the king wanted a chaste and marital life with Anne. Cromwell's voice was so cold in these words that Chapuys did not believe a word of it and saw through Cromwell's unhidden lie. Chapuys pressed Cromwell on what he meant, and Cromwell tried to hide his grin, leaning back on a window with his hand over his smile, and told Chapuys, 'you may be sure, namely, that should the King, my master, want another wife, it is certainly not among the French that he will look for one'.[18]

It was obvious that Vicegerent Cromwell knew exactly how far the king's interest in Jane Seymour had developed when he spoke with Chapuys. Cromwell had an unfortunate ringside seat near the new romance, which was happening in the rooms he gave to the Seymours. Cromwell also seemingly had no problem with the king romancing Catholic Jane, though Edward Seymour was a quiet reformist himself. Cromwell was determined to continue with negotiations with Ambassador Chapuys on behalf of their leaders to create an Anglo-Imperial alliance. The alliance could see Anne accepted as queen of England, yet Cromwell did not seem to care one way or another if Anne remained the queen. Cromwell ended the meeting by insisting Chapuys take a gift of a new horse.[19] Chapuys refused the gift, an effective way of ensuring Anne did not hear about the Cromwell-Chapuys meetings, but Cromwell insisted this time that it would be a slight for the ambassador to turn down the horse (which Cromwell was regifting, having received it himself from the steadfast Catholic Robert Radcliffe, Earl of Sussex only a day earlier). Cromwell no longer seemed to care if this luxurious gift was noticed at court. The man was happy to go to battle against Anne Boleyn.

The feeling was mutual. On Passion Sunday, 2 April, the court sat down to their sermon in the Royal Chapel at Greenwich, and the speaker was John Skipp, Anne's almoner. He had been well prepared by Anne for a sermon that would go down in history. It started simply, with Skipp explaining that when he said 'you', he meant the audience, when he said 'me', he meant the Church and clergy. The theme chosen was John 8:46, 'Quis ex vobis arguet me de peccato?' or 'Which of you can convict me of sin? If I speak the truth, why do you not believe me?' Here was a committed evangelical attacking the changes to the Church and the clergy. There was no doubt over the barely hidden agenda of John Skipp's words; he was attacking the dissolution of the monasteries and the effect many policy changes were having on clergy members, on behalf of his patron Anne Boleyn. Skipp called the king's councillors sycophants and wished that:

> 'Men would therein use a more temperance and first amend their own lives before they taxed other men's … nowadays, many men take upon [themselves] to rebuke the clergy very sore, far otherwise moved by their malicious mind, or because they would have from the clergy their possessions, rebuking them at every place at the table and elsewhere very sure, so much that if they spy a great or notable vice or fault in one priest, or any of the clergy, then they will defame and rebuke all the clergy for the same.'[20]

Skipp defended the clergy, their ways, their beliefs, and their work, and then swerved into the story of King Solomon, who Skipp recalled as a wise king who was gentle in his governance of his people, who at the end of his reign became, 'very unnoble and he defamed himself with his sensual and carnal appetites by taking too many wives and concubines … and also by an avaricious mind in levying too greater sore burdens and yokes [constraints] upon his subjects'.[21]

Even the most foolish in the court could see what Skipp was saying to King Henry. Then Skipp spoke of King Nebuchadnezzar, who sent a minister of God to punish the Jews and was punished in return, giving allusions to how King Henry needed to be criticised for his punishment of the clergy with the dissolutions. But Skipp was far from finished; Anne had used him to highlight Henry and Jane, and the greed of the dissolutions, and now wanted to take a swipe at Cromwell too. Skipp told the story of King Ahasuerus and Queen Esther, who was Jewish. Gentle King Ahasuerus had an evil councillor, Haman, who had deceived the king into killing all the Jews in the land. Skipp warned of the tale, that a good king:

> 'To be well wary what he does, after the counsel of his counsellors, for some time, for the malice that they bear toward many men, or towards one man as of a multitude, they would see the multitude destroyed.'[22]

Of course, Ahasuerus did not kill all the Jews, and his wife Esther, the king's ever-good friend and counsel, swooped in to save the day, and evil Haman was executed instead. The story was not recounted the way it had been told for centuries; Skipp made it so 'Haman' was evil and greedy, taking money for himself.[23] The sermon went on for some time, and was mostly Skipp justifying images, ceremonies, relics, worshipping of saints, all things that were to be changed under new religious laws. It was odd for Skipp to defend such Catholic positions, but even if Skipp was unusually conservative with the remainder of his speech, the damage had been done.

Anne had needed to speak out and used Skipp perfectly. This was far from the only time people spoke out against the dissolution of the monasteries. Cromwell was certainly the target, being the man who wanted to reform the monasteries, particularly the larger houses while amalgamating the smaller ones, and Anne was picking a fight with a man who could have agreed with her stance on using the land and buildings for the benefit of the people. Anne and Cromwell were not so fundamentally different in their beliefs. If Anne wanted the dissolutions stopped, she needed to talk to her husband, something that seemingly did not happen. The dissolution legislation was days away from receiving royal assent as parliament was due to finish its session. Cromwell's *Compendium compertorum,* a summary of findings on monastery inspections, had already been submitted to parliament, and the state of corrupt houses in England could not be ignored. Allowing monastic houses to remain as they were could not continue. Cromwell wanted reform, he wanted houses tidied up, and their teachings updated to the new religion. Anne wanted the same and feared that the mass sell-off of land and buildings would benefit no one except a few. Henry wanted to gain the power and money of owning the monasteries. Archbishop Cranmer even entered the fray (possibly even on Anne's behalf), despite being away at Knole in Kent, writing to Cromwell with concerns about how the dissolutions would be handled, but the project had largely left Cromwell's hands in favour of the new parliament plans. But the potential for all those involved to come together and agree on a way forward no longer mattered;

Anne and Cromwell's opposition to each other was now fully exposed to the court, along with Anne's thoughts about Henry romancing Jane Seymour. There would be no going back now, including for Skipp who was arrested and interrogated for his speech.

Anne had been brave by standing up to Henry against the dissolutions. Cromwell had tried to stop Henry, without success. Cranmer had spoken with Cromwell and completed a Lent sermon on using monastic lands for the poor, but seemingly never spoke directly to the king. Hugh Latimer, Bishop of Hereford, had preached on the subject of using monasteries to help the poor, probably under Anne's instruction. But King Henry would not be placated, and as parliament closed in Westminster, the *Act of the Dissolution of the Lesser Monasteries*, all houses with less than twelve inhabitants or a yearly income of less than 200*l*, were to be dissolved, the people moved and given a pension. The law bore none of the provisions for the needy and poor that Anne wanted and did not adhere to Cromwell's early dissolution style of reforming houses. All small houses were to be seized for the king and:

> 'Shall have to him and to his heirs all and singular such monasteries, abbeys, and priories, which, at any time within one year next before the making of this Act, have been given and granted to his majesty by any abbot, prior, abbess, or prioress, under their convent seals, or that otherwise have been suppressed or dissolved ... to have and to hold all and singular the premises, with all their rights, profits, jurisdictions, and commodities, unto the king's majesty, and his heirs and assigns forever, to do and use therewith his and their own wills, to the pleasure of Almighty God, and to the honour and profit of this realm.'[24]

Even with the relationship between Anne and Cromwell now laid bare for all to see, there could be no benefit for either of them. Cromwell was a man who tended to his work and retreated from court life with his friends and family. He had no desire to have an open quarrel with Anne. Anne was still the queen and could still petition her husband to exempt religious houses from dissolution if she desired. The situation would never stop; any noble could still petition Henry to stop any particular dissolution. But with Easter fast approaching, Cromwell and Anne would again be in close quarters for the celebrations, and secret plans and old rivalries would ignite even more hatred, leaving a trail of destruction Jane Seymour could use as a path to victory.

This particularly inflammatory sermon by Skipp seemingly lit a fire under Thomas Cromwell. The entire speech would have been sanctioned by Anne Boleyn, and aside from the personal attack on Cromwell himself and his king, the speech on the protection of Catholic rituals would have set off a major concern. The day may not have been just one of humiliation before the court, but one which triggered a memory of something far more abstract.

Despite claims made by those at court, the idea of prophecy and divination intrigued the so-called higher-educated men and women of the Tudor court. The whole fatal calamity of the Elizabeth Barton case was a classic example of the fear of fortune telling and prophesising.[25] Countless times Cromwell was asked to investigate various cases of prophesy,[26] and while investigations always proved that fortune telling was just wishful thinking, Cromwell was likely as fascinated as everyone else. After all, the vast majority of prophesiers believed they spoke with God and were led by God, an incredible stretch of the truth. Cardinal Wolsey had investigated many such reports in his time, and had people come to him with stories of his own life and fate. Wolsey was told he would die in Kingston,[27] which was a town in Surrey, between his homes of Hampton Court and Esher Place. Wolsey avoided the town, only to die in Sir William Kingston's custody at Leicester Abbey. Cromwell knew of Wolsey's various investigations into prophecies, though whether he believed any of them was another matter.

While almost everything written by Cromwell in 1536 was carefully and deliberately destroyed, he received a report of a prophecy from Flanders, that King Henry was in danger.[28] Whether Cromwell shared this with Henry is unlikely; Cromwell was already the one to investigate claims and stamp out the treason surrounding them. Who made the prognostics and how they got to Cromwell's desk is unknown,[29] though secretary, Stephen Vaughan, spent much time in Flanders on Cromwell's behalf, and Vaughan had much to do with William Tyndale at the time.[30] Likewise, Miles Coverdale was in Antwerp, having just finished printing his first complete English Bible, which both Cromwell and Anne Boleyn had in their libraries. Coverdale read of this prophecy and translated it in 1536 and it became part of the English Short Title Catalogue.[31] The seven-chapter prophecy is like most prophecies, generalised and making claims around various ailments such as future illnesses and droughts. But it also spoke of the 'trouble and strife of this year' and that Satan would, 'by the children of unbelief (especially by the shaven Madianites) stir up trouble, including instigating secret treason'. Shaven Madianites refers to the Roman Catholic clergy, named so due to their use of incense and adornment of gold and jewels.[32] The prophecy spoke of King Henry and mentioned 'threatening the king with a conspiracy of those who were nearest his person',[33] though, like all prophecies, it was vague and ripe for misinterpretation.

A conspiracy, which spoke against King Henry and his reforms would certainly be treason, but the Catholic faction at court were not conspiring against the king. Nor would they have sided with Anne Boleyn to save monasteries. Certainly, the Catholic faction was looking to undermine Henry's authority of the succession, and elevate Princess Mary to her 'rightful' place, but this created no threat to the king. Cromwell could have seen this threat as Anne Boleyn and her faction, such as it was, but Cromwell could easily manipulate anyone at court or the clergymen who promoted Anne. The only people Cromwell did not have control over was Anne herself, and her brother George. Yet George Boleyn, Lord Rochford had no business in the monastery reforms, though surely he had strong opinions on the topic. Perhaps it was Anne Boleyn who was the prophesied threat to the king and his power, by looking to undermine the changes to the monasteries. Again, this seems unlikely as Anne was a promoter of the Reformation; she would have been too shrewd to push and upset the changes being made. The idea that Cromwell needed Anne out of the way so he could destroy the monasteries holds no weight, as he wanted to reform monasteries into colleges much like Anne and pushed to continue that until the end of his life.[34]

What is documented is that Cromwell kept this Flanders prophecy, like all small details he came across, in the back of his mind,[35] and events over the next few weeks of April 1536 showed that he was suspicious of Anne and saw how she remained an impediment to his Imperial alliance plans. If anything, the prophecy could have simply added to Cromwell's growing concerns that Anne was a threat to him, far more than just her simple dislike of him, but instead a powerful adversary who could lash out if provoked. Whether Cromwell believed in such prophecies can only remain conjecture, though with the benefit of hindsight, Cromwell should perhaps have paid more attention to the prophecy, as his own fall from grace came through a Catholic coup at court only four years later.

CHAPTER 11

The Dinner

On 14 April, parliament was officially closed by the speaker, Richard Rich. While the simpler laws that needed to be passed went through with no issues, the larger concerns were hit-and-miss for Anne Boleyn and Thomas Cromwell. Anne's fiery attack on King Henry and Cromwell at mass had done her no good; whether she had spoken to her husband over the next two weeks is unknown. Jane Seymour occupied most of Henry's attention now, and Anne had taken a huge risk that did not pay off. The *Suppression of Religious Houses Act* was not a win for Cromwell either; it was a mutilated version of his plans, reconfigured to make the king richer. But at least Cromwell could maintain control over the new plan and potentially reform larger houses. Cromwell would have been similarly disappointed with his watered-down *Act for Punishment of Sturdy Vagabonds and Beggars,* with most of his Poor Law stripped away. How Anne felt about the tepid new regulations went unrecorded. Anne did have some success: she had supported the campaign to ensure universities and colleges were exempt from First Fruits and Tenths taxes, which went into law.[1] Cromwell got his tax reforms through: the *Statute of Uses* and *Statute of Enrolments* were passed, which overhauled taxes on land sales and transfers.[2] This made Cromwell especially unpopular among the people, though it was for Henry's benefit, and no one would dare be mad at the king. Cromwell also got both his *Jurisdiction in Liberties Act* and *Laws in Wales Act* through, bringing Wales into line with English laws, in a bid to get the area's crime under control.[3] This took the power over Wales from the Welsh people, which only ever led to anger, but the king's will was done. This was to be the final quiet two weeks at court all year, and the final few of Anne's life.

Europe was in a state of flux; the Emperor and the Pope were meeting in Rome to discuss peace, while there were rumblings in the Low Countries and Germany, and the threat of war with the Turks always loomed. King

Henry's romantic behaviours were not important in such context, and writers shared more concern about Princess Mary's wellbeing over anything else in England.[4] Martin Luther wrote to Cromwell from Wittenburg, pleased to hear the Reformation was still going well in England,[5] while Stephen Vaughan wrote from Antwerp, fearing William Tyndale would soon be executed if Cromwell and the Privy Council did not immediately send a letter in his defence.[6] Cromwell, seemingly eager to escape his troubles, told Vaughan he wished he was in Antwerp instead of London, while Vaughan wished the opposite. But the most pressing matter was whether England and the Emperor could finally renew their alliance after almost a decade at loggerheads over Queen Katharine's treatment. Ambassador Chapuys in London and Ambassador Richard Pate in Rome wrote back and forth to Emperor Charles and King Henry respectively, explaining the situation, and Emperor Charles seemed eager to push ahead and have peace with England.[7] Pate told Henry that the Emperor was not afraid to go to war with England, if necessary, but preferred to avoid it, and making Princess Mary England's legitimate heir was the way to make peace.[8] Chapuys was eagerly discussing similar terms, and Cromwell had spent months, years even, discussing the possible amity between the nations. At this stage, Anne remaining queen over any other was still part of the deal.

On Thursday, 13 April, ahead of going to court for Good Friday celebrations, Vicegerent Cromwell and Ambassador Chapuys met at one of Cromwell's new homes, a manor leased to him by King Henry in Hackney. Cromwell had spent an enormous sum on making this new home one of the finest homes in England, marvelling Chapuys with its incredible makeover.[9] The pair were at the house alone; Cromwell had not moved a household into the manor, with renovations still to be completed. The men were to discuss the initial plan for peace they proposed outside Austin Friars back on 24 February. Cromwell, ever hating the French, denounced any suggestion England would pay favour to King Francis and proved this with letters to that effect, and kissed Emperor Charles' letters on the matter as a sign of reverence.[10] There were four points of discussion over peace, none of which related to Anne as queen. Emperor Charles still wanted King Henry to return to the Catholic faith and had convinced Pope Paul to hold off on King Henry's official excommunication so Henry could return religion in England back to its original state. But the Reformation was advancing in England, and simply reverting everything was not as simple now as it had been just months earlier. Reinstating Princess

Mary as the heir-apparent of England was the second point to consider. This was no small feat. Princess Elizabeth needed to be removed as heir in the succession for her older sister to take her place. Cromwell had created the law which stated Anne's marriage to Henry was legal and that Elizabeth was the legitimate heir to the king. Reinstating Mary as heir meant voiding Anne's marriage to Henry, which was not presented as an option. This outcome could be achieved with legal changes saying Henry could choose his heir, and altering the Act of Succession, which only Henry could agree upon, also no small feat. The third point was about England aiding Emperor Charles in the war against the Turks, not something that would be too much to ask for, as backing out would be easy, and the fourth point was England going to war with France over Milan, backing the Emperor's claim to the republic.[11] Again, fighting against France was not an impossible task. England had been on friendlier terms with France for the entire term of Anne's marriage to the king. But multiple embassies to France yielded no formal alliances nor a betrothal for Princess Elizabeth. King Francis talked of amity between the nations, but in reality, had never shown any outward support for Henry or Anne. France's own treaty with the Empire was looking shaky, and even the ardent French supporters at court like the Boleyns knew it was time to support Emperor Charles and ease away from France. Yet, King Henry decided he would make a trip to Dover, with an eye to travelling to Calais, as close to France as possible without actually standing on French soil, and Anne was to accompany her husband, their first trip in four years. Anne had managed to politely put off the meeting between Henry and King Francis for several years using her friendship with Margaret of Angouleme, but this time, there needed to be a royal visit.

The trip to Dover to inspect port defences with a view to visiting France, was not seen as a threat to a possible alliance with the Emperor. The last seven years at the English court had been fraught with emotion and hostility, but now without Katharine of Aragon, all could calm down; England and the Emperor could be allies again and tempers could finally cool. Easter held at Greenwich was a reasonably quiet affair given the fireworks of previous months. Henry and Anne appeared as king and queen, side by side as if nothing was wrong with the world.[12] The Boleyns were out in force — George Lord Rochford and his wife Lady Jane were both at court, and Thomas and Elizabeth Boleyn, the Earl and Countess of Wiltshire attended, though Anne was concerned for her mother, who had a nasty cough.[13]

On Monday, 17 April, Cromwell had a private dawn meeting with King Henry and relayed the four points of discussion for an alliance with Emperor Charles. At once, Henry was interested in the terms of the arrangement and Cromwell sent a panicked message to Chapuys; they were getting their longed-for alliance. The entire affair and coming debacle survives in Chapuys' long recollection of events.[14] Before dawn on Tuesday, 18 April, Vicegerent Cromwell met Chapuys near Chapuys' country lodgings, placed between London and Greenwich, and together they travelled to the king for a 6 a.m. meeting. Chapuys wanted Cromwell with him, and together they discussed how best to speak with the king to get their plans approved.

Ambassador Chapuys found all the men of the court there to congratulate him on his fine work in preparing a peace deal, including Lord Rochford, who spent some time with Chapuys, and offered to help any way he could. Chapuys noted that Lord Rochford could not refrain from making 'Lutheran remarks'. Cromwell informed Chapuys that King Henry had invited Chapuys to meet with Anne and kiss her hand. Ambassador Chapuys had been at court since late 1529 and yet had never met Anne Boleyn. Calling her 'the concubine' in correspondence, and no doubt when speaking of her, Chapuys had always failed to pay favour to Anne, a mark of respect for his patron the Emperor, Queen Katharine and Princess Mary. But now, if England and the Empire were to be allied again, and Princess Mary was to ever be the successor to the throne, Chapuys had to swallow his pride and bow down to Anne. Chapuys could not do it; and Cromwell made Chapuys apologise to the king. The court went to mass, with Lord Rochford accompanying the ambassador, though afterwards, as Chapuys stopped behind a door to the chapel, Henry and Anne passed through, and Anne deliberately stopped and turned, coming eye to eye with Chapuys. Anne silently bowed in reverence to the ambassador, and he returned the favour, the moment over in an instant.

That same day, many at court were accompanying the king and queen to dine, but Chapuys excused himself and instead dined with Lord Rochford in a presence chamber, where many of the court awaited. Chapuys overheard Anne speak poorly of King Francis and how he made war against his uncle, the Duke of Savoy, to gain Milan. Anne had enquired why Ambassador Chapuys was not presented to her like the other ambassadors that day, but Henry brushed it all away, and Anne continued her public criticism of France, to show she was keen on an Imperial alliance. All was going perfectly to plan, or so everyone thought. Not Chapuys, not Cromwell, not even Anne could foresee Henry's erratic behaviour to come.

King Henry knew the terms of the agreement Chapuys and Cromwell had put together, had heard them a day earlier and wanted to discuss the matter. After dinner, Henry took Chapuys by the hand, and led him to a private chamber space where only Cromwell and Lord Chancellor Audley waited. Henry and Chapuys stood at a window away from the others to discuss matters. Chapuys spoke at length of his meetings with Cromwell, and also their letters with John Wallop, who worked with Stephen Gardiner as the ambassador in Paris. Chapuys reiterated the four points of an alliance; pull back on the Reformation, make Mary the heir, go to war against the Turks and help take Milan from the French. Chapuys was painstaking in his delivery, speaking gently and carefully, so as not to provoke Henry's whimsical moods. Henry listened to Chapuys but then mentioned that Milan belonged to France by right, not to the Emperor. Henry believed that when the Emperor had renounced his right to Burgundy, he had also lost all rights to Milan and Savoy. The republics were now all French and the king believed a new war would make the Emperor simply an invader. The king of England would not support a war that did not have a rightful claim as its basis. Chapuys politely tried to tell Henry that he was wrong, that the Treaty of Cambrai did not prevent Charles' claim to Milan, but Henry was not interested.

Something was horribly wrong, and Ambassador Chapuys could sense it in Henry's demeanour. What had suddenly changed? Chapuys felt that Henry was not sincere in his interest in an alliance anymore. Was it the refusal to kiss Anne's hand that morning? Had Henry expected to hear something about the Emperor publicly acknowledging Anne as queen? Emperor Charles saw Anne as nothing more than a mistress, a handy placeholder preventing a French princess from being on the English throne. Henry did not mention the requests to return to the Catholic faith or for Mary to be England's heir again. Instead, King Henry bit back at Chapuys when the ambassador mentioned whether England would support a strike against the German States if the Emperor needed support in the area. Henry grumbled that Emperor Charles only had his throne because of Henry's help and needed to be more agreeable. Seeing all their arduous work starting to unravel, Chapuys could barely say anymore before Henry called Cromwell and Audley to the window, where Chapuys was expected to repeat everything to the pair. Chapuys then returned to the party, and stood with Sir Edward Seymour, making light conversation as the group watched the king and Cromwell discuss the alliance. The conversation became ever more heated, Cromwell seemingly refusing to back down to the king's increasing anger. The body language and raised voices told everyone something was seriously wrong, before Cromwell stalked away from the king, and went and sat down out of sight, calling for a stiff drink. Chapuys watched Cromwell, visibly exhausted 'with pure vexation' before the king came back and pulled Chapuys aside again. Henry was angry that it was Cromwell, not himself, who had been entering into these serious discussions. Cromwell knew he did not have the authority to negotiate an alliance, which was only for rulers and their ambassadors. Chapuys and Cromwell had put nothing in writing because it was for Henry to decide on matters before anything was official and put to the Privy Council for discussion. Matters had not progressed too far, but Henry had hurt feelings over men managing a good deal without his input. Henry's ego was blocking any alliance plan. Chapuys assured Henry nothing had been approved without his agreement and this seemed to calm the king, but Henry refused to discuss an alliance further. Henry insisted that his poor relationship with the Pope had nothing to do with Emperor Charles, and he was wise to stay out of the matter. Henry also insisted that Princess Mary was his daughter, and he would treat her however he wished, and no one could interfere in such matters. England would not fight the Turks, as Henry's relationship with Emperor Charles was weak, and then Henry began to mimic an adult calling over a child in kindness and said that no one could treat a king like a child, being kind, 'give them the stick', and then beg forgiveness again. Henry wanted old favours acknowledged and started bringing up arguments between himself and Emperor Charles that were more than ten years old. Henry wanted Charles to write to him personally, to beg forgiveness for past wrongs before any more could be done. Chapuys used King Henry's expression when recalling the discussion, that 'delay was the ruin of all good works'.

Vicegerent Cromwell and Chancellor Audley overheard the second part of the conversation, though Cromwell was brave to stand that close to the king after arguing with him just minutes earlier. There was nothing to be done; Henry was not expecting any domestic conditions to a treaty; Anne was queen and Mary was a bastard, and Henry had no intention of changing those things for anyone. Plus, Henry could not simply back a war against France; King Francis had a copy of the papal decree written by Pope Paul, stating Henry could be deprived of his throne due to the break with Rome.

Three rulers were bargaining against one another with the threat of war and Henry was not going to be the one to back away. Cromwell, Chapuys and Audley were left speechless, and the night ended abruptly.[15]

Vicegerent Cromwell and Ambassador Chapuys met up the following morning; Chapuys never divulged the location, but it was certainly away from court, near one of their respective homes on the edges of London. The pair were equally as regretful over the whole affair and Cromwell was so disappointed that he, 'was hardly able to speak for sorrow and had never been so mortified in his life'.[16] Chapuys suggested they stop their plans, their meetings, their deals, and focus on getting Princess Mary married and out of the country. Then they could maybe work on the biggest issue; how to resolve King Henry's feelings about past slights from Emperor Charles. At once, Cromwell snapped out of his melancholy and said he still thought they could achieve a good result. He did not elaborate to Chapuys, but Cromwell had a plan.

Wednesday, 19 April had a scheduled Privy Council meeting, and the potential alliance criteria were discussed among all the men present: Thomas Howard, Duke of Norfolk; Lord Chancellor Thomas Audley; Sir Nicholas Carew; Sir William Fitzwilliam; Thomas Boleyn, Earl of Wiltshire; Sir Richard Rich; Sir John Russell; Robert Radcliffe, Earl of Sussex; and of course, Thomas Cromwell. Not all members attended regularly, and others were out of London at the time, but Cromwell reported that all in the meeting ended up on their knees begging King Henry to take the alliance deal Chapuys offered.[17] That may have been Cromwell's exaggeration or Chapuys' wishful thinking, but everyone in London knew the deal was a good one; there had not been a deal between England and the Emperor since the Treaty of Windsor had been broken in 1523, and the Treaty of Bruges that failed to be secured by Cardinal Wolsey.[18] But King Henry's pride had been hurt and he stated that, 'he would sooner suffer all the ills in the world than confess tacitly or expressly that he had done [Charles] any injury, or that he desired this friendship'.[19] On Thursday, 20 April, Cromwell visited Chapuys again and told him the king was not angry at the ambassador for all his troubles but would only consider alliance talks with letters that came written by Emperor Charles himself. Cromwell told Chapuys how King Henry was acting strangely and had also suffered an outburst at the French ambassador, Antoine de Castelnau, who had limped away equally degraded as Chapuys days earlier, after a fight over French ships in English waters.[20]

Cromwell told Chapuys not to lose hope and then departed, but on Thursday night, Chapuys received a letter from Cromwell, saying he had proof from France of a secret alliance between Emperor Charles and King Francis, but Chapuys knew nothing of such an alliance. The Imperial ambassador thought all was lost, but Cromwell urged him again not to lose all hope.[21] He had a plan but was not about to share it with Chapuys.

Vicegerent Cromwell's next step is murky, as Cromwell and his attendants were excellent at destroying paperwork. Whenever Cromwell had a particularly secretive issue going on, he fell silent. Almost all of 1536 is missing from Cromwell's extensive archive, except for a few letters Cromwell sent to Paris in the second half of the year. Destroyed either at the time or after Cromwell died in 1540, to help preserve his memory, what Cromwell planned — to destroy a queen — has been lost. The plan and those involved can be seen by finding who is missing from the paperwork of others. From Thursday, 21 April onwards, Chapuys wrote that Cromwell was so upset by the affair with the king that he took to his bed with sorrow.[22] It was a plausible tale, as Cromwell regularly disappeared inside his manors and refused to see people when he was busy. The trouble was, this time, Cromwell was busy planning against Anne Boleyn.

CHAPTER 12

An Affair to Invent

Thursday, 20 April

Vicegerent Thomas Cromwell had picked a side — Princess Mary over Anne Boleyn. King Henry had been continuing his leisure time with Jane Seymour rather than Anne, but Jane Seymour's group, those who supported Princess Mary as heir, were not the strongest group at court or had much to offer Cromwell. Jane Seymour as queen instead of Anne Boleyn would have the backing of the noblest families in England: the Grey family, the Pole family, the Courtenays, the Duke of Suffolk, and probably even the Duke of Norfolk, despite him being Anne Boleyn's uncle. However, Jane Seymour as a Catholic queen by Henry's side, threatened to undo all of Cromwell's work on the Reformation. But largely, the nobility, the gentry, the clergy, and the general population would have no qualms about having a conservative like Jane Seymour as queen. This could clear a path for Princess Mary to be named heir-apparent. The problem with the conservative faction was that they underestimated how much King Henry enjoyed royal supremacy. He was never going to return to the control of Rome and renounce being Head of the Church. Henry knew it and Cromwell knew it. But Cromwell could have a lot of powerful people on his side if they believed Princess Mary could come out with a favourable position when Anne Boleyn was toppled.

The Boleyn faction was a different story. Thomas and Elizabeth Boleyn as Earl and Countess of Wiltshire and Ormond were nothing but loyal, trustworthy courtiers. Sir Thomas Boleyn had succeeded in his work repeatedly throughout his royal career and maintained a good relationship with most people, despite the elevation of his daughter to queen rubbing many the wrong way. George Boleyn, Lord Rochford was a restrained man who had a career as a diplomat in France and was trusted by the king. He had a quiet disposition, and no one spoke ill of him. His wife Jane, Lady Rochford, was the daughter of a beloved noble family, and whose father was one of Cromwell's close personal friends. Archbishop Cranmer would be apoplectic when he discovered Cromwell had turned against Anne, the queen he and Cromwell had created together, but Cranmer was hiding out in Knole, twenty-five miles from London. Thomas Cromwell was not a noble man; he had his personal friends, and his many administrative posts, but Henry had not elevated Cromwell to any title. He was an outsider and always would be, and just maybe, that was about to come in handy.

Ambassador Chapuys believed Cromwell was in bed with sorrow, but Cromwell was nowhere to be found. Many men of court were still in London after the closing of parliament, and the king was busy planning a trip to Dover to see the harbour work he and Cromwell had spent so much time planning. Anne planned to travel with the king, the pair stopping for a visit at Rochester before reaching Dover.[1] Lord Rochford assisted the king in his planning, while Margery Horsman readied the queen's household. Cromwell, away from court after his public fight with the king, would easily go unnoticed.

At first glance, destroying Anne Boleyn would not be the answer to Cromwell's problems. It was King Henry's petulant behaviour that soured the Imperial alliance plans, not Anne's existence, though it was her place as the king's wife that caused the rift between England and Europe in the first place. No more Anne would certainly smooth the waters for an alliance and given how much vitriol Anne had spread publicly about Cromwell, she surely had spoken to the king about her hatred for the man in private. Now, after the awkward alliance dinner, Cromwell could not have felt safe in his position. Simply removing Anne was not enough to save Cromwell, for someone else could simply appear and remove him from power; he was not noble, with no family ties to save or assist him. The risk was incalculable; removing Anne could see him killed, either by her when she outsmarted him, or by the conservatives furious at his religious and taxation changes to England. What Cromwell needed, as much as Anne Boleyn was a threat, was actually for Princess Mary to agree to the Royal Supremacy and her illegitimacy. If Mary was back in favour with her father, the conservatives would be more supportive of Cromwell, and he could tackle Anne with more confidence. Nothing about his plan was certain, and Cromwell was about to spend weeks wondering if he would either succeed or be destroyed.

Friday, 21 — Saturday, 22 April

International affairs were dominating the court at a time when it would be easy to assume the downfall of Anne Boleyn was more important. Henry was not spending any time with Anne, but whether that was because of the king's sudden panic about international alliances, or because Henry was more interested in Jane Seymour is impossible to tell. Vicegerent Cromwell had plenty to juggle and spent up to four days with Richard Sampson, Dean of Windsor, and one of Cromwell's long-time colleagues, the pair having both been close to Cardinal Wolsey. There was no certainty of Cromwell's private meetings with Sampson; the dean had been consulted frequently (as many had) about Henry's marriage to Queen Katharine and was a canon law expert available to discuss any future annulments.[2] The official story was that Sampson was being considered as an ambassador to travel to the Emperor and meet with others there on behalf of England. Ambassador Chapuys did not believe the report but had no proof to the contrary.[3] Whatever Cromwell spent days discussing with Sampson, it was fruitful; Cromwell soon ensured that Sampson was promoted to the exalted position of Bishop of Chichester within six weeks, and the pair remained loyal for the rest of their days. Ambassador Chapuys still believed Cromwell had:

> 'Taken to his bed from pure sorrow. He has certainly shown himself, in this, an honest man; for although he knew it displeased his master, and that he incurred some danger, he would not retract anything he had said to me.'[4]

Sunday, 23 April

A great many members of the nobility were at court at Greenwich on Sunday, 23 April. For St George's Day, the present members of the Most Noble Order of the Garter were called to the King's Chapel to cast their votes for a new member. Only twenty-four people could be admitted at any one time, and with the death of George Nevill, 5th Baron Bergavenny in June 1535, the position Nevill held since 1513 was finally vacant.[5] King Henry left the running of the voting process to Henry Percy, Earl of Northumberland, who was extremely ill, and there were fears he could not even stand long enough for the ceremony to take place.[6] Voting alongside Northumberland were the Earls of Sussex (Robert Radcliffe), Rutland (Thomas Manners), Oxford (John de Vere), Westmorland (Ralph Neville), and Wiltshire (Thomas Boleyn), the Dukes of Norfolk (Thomas Howard), and Richmond and Somerset (Henry Fitzroy), plus the Lord Chamberlain, William Lord Sandys, and Treasurer of the Household, Sir William Fitzwilliam. They were a group of men who could be seen as the old guard; each man had been in the Garter for ten to twenty years; twenty-five years in the case of the Duke of Norfolk. Norfolk, like the king's son Fitzroy, was Catholic and not especially impressed with the ways of the court in 1536. Sussex, Rutland, Oxford, Westmorland, and Northumberland spent little time at court, and were only in London due to parliament sitting. They were career courtiers who supported their king regardless of the queen. Even Northumberland, who had once wished to marry Anne Boleyn, was Catholic, living in the north as part of one of the most influential families who controlled the border with Scotland. Lord Sandys was unhappy with Anne on the throne and spent little time at court, and Sir William Fitzwilliam, despite being a long-time friend of Cromwell, Wolsey's protege, and having his sister in Anne's household, was loyal to the king over anyone. Only Thomas Boleyn was the voice of Anne and the Reformation on this particular day.

Each member voted for nine different people of their choice, a first, second and third choice in three distinct categories: three 'princes' (men ranked an earl or higher) in preferred order, then three barons ranked in preferred order, and then three knights ranked in preferred order.[7] Of the twenty names which appeared in various orders of preferment, Sir Nicholas Carew got ten votes, a significant majority, and was the first choice knight for all but two men. Interestingly, Thomas Boleyn did not vote for his son George (who got five votes); perhaps he felt it inappropriate to vote for his son, though such manners did not bother William Fitzwilliam, who happily voted for his brother. This vote of the Garter is often seen as a slight against the Boleyns when Lord Rochford was not elected, but among the names which came up in voting, Carew was the only man each Garter member chose as a knight. King Henry had once promised King Francis that he would promote Nicholas Carew for his fine diplomatic work, and now, a position was available for Carew, a man liked by all. It was not a majority rule vote; King Henry could decide the new member based on the selections and chose to go with Sir Nicholas Carew, who fell to his knees before the king to give thanks ahead of a banquet celebration in his honour on 21 May. Gossip that the decision was deliberately against Lord Rochford did whisper through the court, alongside rumours that Anne was upset her husband did not promote her brother.[8] Whether this was true, or Anne's detractors imagined her upset about this event is open to interpretation.

With everyone at Greenwich, it was an opportunity for men who did not see each other often to meet. If talk was about the king setting aside his unliked queen, it would have been a difficult weekend for Anne Boleyn. It also gave time for men like Nicholas Carew to speak with men like Thomas Cromwell. Carew and his wife were Princess Mary's main backers, and their Catholic faction was large but quiet, serving their king as loyally as they could. Cromwell and Carew must have spoken about Princess Mary on the day of the Garter, as Cromwell had just reappeared from his four days of skulking outside of court.[9] Chapuys likely spoke with Carew too, being the man most often sending letters to Mary. Meanwhile, Anne was present and visible at court as queen, yet no mention of her presence or behaviour has survived. The king was caught up in international negotiations, and none of them hinged on Anne's presence or removal.[10] Yet in the final hours of Sunday, 23 April or the following Monday morning, hidden among an administrative flurry, hid a decision to end a queen.

Monday, 24 April

The Vicegerent was a busy man at the start of a new week on Monday, 24 April. The new Court of Augmentations needed to have its leaders formally appointed. They would oversee the dissolution of the monasteries and the distribution of their people and wealth.[11] This would have been an issue Anne Boleyn would have been most interested in; having people sympathetic to her cause of saving monasteries would have worked in her favour. Yet Anne was nowhere to be seen among the projects. Clergymen had begun returning their papal licences to preach and having them replaced with licences awarded by the king as Head of the Church.[12] Meanwhile, Jane Seymour had some paperwork of her own; she received a life grant of one hundred marks a year (about 15*l* or £6,000 today), the details unspecified.[13] It was not unusual for King Henry to give out odd little gifts; lands or annuities would land on Henry's desk, and he would see fit to give them away as gifts, in this case, to his current mistress. Hopefully, Anne did not hear of this gift, though gossip seemed to spread like wildfire. Ambassador Chapuys wrote that news of his fleeting interaction with Anne Boleyn a week earlier reached Princess Mary at Hunsdon, where his acknowledgement of Anne, 'the concubine,' did not sit well, and noted:

> 'Although I would not kiss or speak to the Concubine, the Princess and other good persons have been somewhat jealous at the mutual reverences required by politeness which were done at the church. I refused to visit [Mary] until I had spoken to the King. If I had seen any hope from the King's answer [about permission to visit]. I would have offered not two but 100 candles to the she-devil [Anne], although another thing made me unwilling, that I was told [Anne] was not in favour with the King; besides, Cromwell was quite of my opinion that I should do well to wait till I had spoken to the King.'[14]

Who told Chapuys that Anne was still not in favour with the king? Any of the gossips of the court could have said that, but Cromwell was the one who spoke most often with the ambassador, and Cromwell had been with the king that day. Henry was working on his plans for international alliances, and Henry's notes were written in Cromwell's secretary's handwriting.[15] But the most important piece of paperwork to be created on Monday, 24 April were two oyer and terminer (to hear and to determine) commissions, one relating to crimes committed in Middlesex and another for crimes in Kent. Oyer and terminer commissions were set up after someone was arrested and a panel of judges was needed to hear evidence before deciding if a trial was necessary. They were not typical; oyer and terminer commissions were for serious cases only, such as murder, treason, and heresy. The Privy Council were meeting every day, and so everyone was distracted from these papers being drawn up, as most people, including the men who would be listed on the papers to act as commissioners, would not be aware of anything until they received a summons.

Only two people could draw up oyer and terminer papers — King Henry, and Lord Chancellor Audley. However, another person could request such papers — Thomas Cromwell. Without doubt, Cromwell went to Audley for these papers, for the king was not one to do tasks himself, but whether the king knew of the papers being created was another matter. No crimes had been committed that needed a commission. No arrests had been made over any incident. No people were named in the indictment and no charges had been laid. All these things were needed when drawing up an oyer and terminer. During King Henry's reign, seventeen cases were placed into the Baga de Secretis, twelve top-secret files kept in bundles, and fifteen times the papers were drawn up after arrests were made (with two others not being treason cases, but accessories to crimes). Oyer and terminer papers were not produced blank for future crimes, except in this case.

For Cromwell to do this and not tell the king would have been a risk that would cost him his head if it did not play out in his favour. Cromwell was not a man who took risks; until the Imperial alliance over-reach, he had never done anything without full royal approval. There is no way to tell if Cromwell asked Audley to draw up these papers on his behalf but given how the next several weeks were to play out, it shows that Cromwell did not need these advance papers. Other cases would need at least ten days to prepare an oyer and terminer, assemble the commissioners and prepare a trial. Time shows Anne Boleyn's arrest and time to execution would have allowed everything to have been prepared after the fact. A key detail is that oyer and terminers were not needed to arrest Anne Boleyn or her brother George. As peers they could not be tried by a commission, which would be overseen by the High Steward (who was coincidentally, their uncle the Duke of Norfolk[16]). When Cromwell had these papers prepared, he was looking at someone lower ranked than Anne Boleyn and had a plan. He wanted an arrest to play out quickly and neatly and utilise Henry's predictable rage to destroy those arrested before the king had a chance to calm down and be rational. After all, Henry's inconstancy which had blown up at the Easter alliance talks was a classic example of the king's erratic moods.

The oyer and terminer papers being drawn up were almost certainly done with the king's knowledge. It may have been to aid with punishment for those murmuring of the queen's adultery, which had been whispered about for months without a hint of proof.[17] The papers could have been used to punish those who were continuing to believe in the Pope's authority in England, as many were dragging their feet in returning their papal bulls to be reinstated with English replacements. It could have been that Cromwell's discussion with the Dean of Windsor, Richard Sampson, about the possibility of annulment between Henry and Anne was fruitful, so Henry was interested in the possibility of arresting people to gain information for an annulment proceeding. There is simply no way to tell what day Henry turned against Anne, after all, he was about to do something so cruel no one could have suspected such a calamity. But between Cromwell returning to court on Sunday, 23 April, and the morning of Monday, 24 April, the king realised there were possible arrests to be made.

What can be certain is that these papers were not drawn up to ensnare Anne Boleyn; they were of no use against a queen. King Henry and Vicegerent Cromwell were looking for someone. This may have been where Elizabeth Somerset, Countess of Worcester and her brothers Anthony Browne and William Fitzwilliam came into play. Sir William Fitzwilliam was another, like Sir Nicholas Carew, who was largely untouchable at court. He never did anything out of step with the king's wishes, never had his name dragged into scandal, never criticised, or denounced anyone or any of the king's plans. He had grown up alongside the king, a lucky break for the son of Lady Lucy Neville.[18] Lady Neville was one of the white rose families, and she fought for Yorkist power after her father (a brother of Richard Neville, The Kingmaker) was killed in the Battle of Barnet, fighting for King Edward IV.[19] Lady Neville had married Sir Thomas Fitzwilliam, and under the reign of King Henry VII, she was still considered suspicious despite the end of the War of the Roses, as she supported her cousin, Edmund de la Pole, 3rd Duke of Suffolk's rival claim to the throne.[20] The couple had eight children, one being William, only for Lady Neville to lose her husband around 1497. She quickly remarried Sir Anthony Browne, Constable of Calais, who was a descendant of the powerful FitzAlan/Arundel/Le Despenser families through his mother.[21] Being across the sea from England did not stop Lady Neville from promoting Yorkist claims for the throne. In addition to heavy fines for trying to topple a king, Henry VII took young William Fitzwilliam from his mother and placed him in Henry VIII's household, so he could grow up a loyal Tudor ally.[22]

Sir William Fitzwilliam fought in battle with his young new king in 1513 and was Vice Admiral for twelve years, involved mostly in naval battles and keeping pirates out of the English Channel.[23] Cardinal Wolsey took a shine to Fitzwilliam and his intelligence, ensuring Fitzwilliam became a French diplomat and treasurer of the Royal Household, which elevated him to the Privy Council. Fitzwilliam was a loyal servant to his king and had been working on legal cases with Thomas Cromwell since at least 1524.[24] The pair spent time together professionally and socially, and it was no surprise that Fitzwilliam would go to Cromwell when potentially devastating news became known; after all, no one would have wanted to tell the king of whispers about his wife's alleged poor behaviour. Only Cromwell was likely to come away from such an audience with his head still on his shoulders.

Fitzwilliam used his time at court to promote two of his four half-siblings; his sister Lady Elizabeth Somerset who was one of Anne's ladies, and Sir Anthony Browne, who had joined his elder brother in battle and French embassies and was working in the king's privy chamber by 1520.[25] Browne had married Alice Gage, the daughter of one of Cromwell's closest friends, Sir John Gage, who was on a sabbatical living in a monastery in 1536.[26] Cromwell would have been the first person for Lady Browne to contact if she needed anything, and in turn, her husband could have done the same. Fitzwilliam, and the Browne and Gage families were all still Catholics, though had supported the king's changes without complaint and remained friendly with Cromwell. But Elizabeth Somerset, the Countess of Worcester, had been friends with Anne Boleyn since at least 1530 when Anne paid for one of Lady Worcester's midwives[27] (common for a godmother), though the child did not survive. By 1536, Lady Worcester had been suffering regular pregnancies thanks to her husband Charles Somerset, Earl of Worcester (a son of the illustrious Beaufort and Woodville families). But the earl did not feature heavily in his wife's story. In 1536, Lady Worcester was pregnant, and she later confided to Cromwell that Anne Boleyn had given her 100*l* (around £44,000 today), and she had never paid back the money. Why the undocumented loan was made, and where the money went was never shared, or if Cromwell knew, he did not make the mistake of writing down the details and he told Lady Worcester she would not have to repay the funds.[28] She was immediately grateful, as Lady Worcester told Cromwell, 'I am very loath it should come to my husband's knowledge. I am in doubt how he will take it'.

One theory is that this money to Lady Worcester was a bribe to stay quiet, but this bears no truth or evidence. By all accounts, Anne Boleyn's lady-in-waiting needed a large sum in a short time and could not dare to have her husband find out. Lady Worcester would have needed regular gowns and jewellery made to be befitting of her rank, but that could not have been a need that would anger a noble husband. Anne had been Lady Worcester's long-time friend and gave her this money from her private purse; she knew who or what her friend was paying for. This kind of large assistance was not unusual for someone like Anne; she was aiding Lady Bridgewater in her divorce case at the same time.[29] Anne had also just petitioned King Henry for the Prioress of Catesby in the matter of somewhere to live post-dissolution.[30] Countless other men and women aided by Anne Boleyn likely go unrecorded; many of the nobility had their favourites and gave them friendships and assistance, a way to install goodwill in any community.

But more detail lies in the sixty-four-page poem *Épistre Contenant le Procès Criminel Faict à l'Encontre de la Royne Anne Boullant d'Angleterre*, written by Lancelot de Carles, who at the time was the secretary to the French ambassador in London, Antoine de Castelnau. The 1,813-line tale tells the story of Anne's demise and tells of a privy councillor admonishing his sister, a lady in Anne's court. Of the thirteen copies of the poem that survive, only one names the councillor: Antoine Brun.[31]

While Sir Anthony Browne was not a privy councillor, he was in the privy chamber and his brother, William Fitzwilliam, was a councillor. De Carles wrote that the councillor spoke with his sister, angry that she had, 'd'aymer aucuns par amour deshonette' (loved someone with dishonourable love). De Carles wrote that the brother was aware that his sister's behaviour was 'damaging her reputation' by, presumably, sleeping around. Lady Worcester was pregnant at the time, and we can only assume her baby came about by her visiting her husband, but it could have just as easily been another man's child. If Lady Worcester needed 100*l* to ensure a secret was kept, she had acquired it. It is important to note that everything in de Carles' poem cannot be proven by other sources, and what the 100*l* was used for can never be known. By the time Lady Worcester wrote to Cromwell in 1538 regarding the outstanding debt, all of the debts relating to Anne Boleyn had long been written off in the accounts, and Cromwell was not the type to press a wronged woman for anything, let alone money.

The de Carles' poem continued with Lady Worcester's involvement, saying that the sister did not deny her brother's accusations of being promiscuous at court, telling her brother:

> 'But you see a small fault in me while overlooking a much higher fault that is much more damaging … if you do not believe me, find out from Mark [Smeaton] … I must not forget

> to tell you what seems to me to be the worst thing, which is that often her brother has carnal knowledge of her in bed'.[32]

With the benefit of hindsight, the tale of Lady Worcester telling her brother this story is convenient for how the saga would later unravel. De Carles authored his poem on 2 June 1536, two weeks after Anne's death, the facts of the case travelling across Europe. The other issue is that de Carles may have embellished what he knew in 1536, as he did not publish until 1545 and was high-ranked enough to avoid any kind of criticism for his work. The third issue is that the poem has been republished, rewritten, and retranslated multiple times since 1545, with its most recent English translation in 1927.[33] Whether Lady Worcester threw Anne Boleyn to the wolves to save herself is a matter of guesswork, but the words of de Carles' poem have been largely believed for almost 500 years, as there are almost no other contemporary accounts to compare.

The de Carles poem says that Browne told two others about his sister's tale, one of which is almost certainly their brother Fitzwilliam and the other probably Vicegerent Cromwell. If anyone was to uncover such news, it had to be shared with Cromwell before it went to the king. Everything the king heard, saw, and read went through Cromwell. The poem claims that Cromwell and Fitzwilliam told the king plainly of these rumours, adding that Sir Henry Norris was another of Anne Boleyn's lovers, presumably hearing this from Lady Worcester. Henry took this news calmly and wanted a further investigation. That is precisely where oyer and terminer papers would have come in handy. Not to ensnare a queen, but to arrest and punish a fool committing treason by slandering Anne and her husband by association. But Cromwell was no fool, and an exceptional lawyer, and he surely knew rumours from a lewd lady-in-waiting were not enough to make any arrest.

CHAPTER 13

Indecision of a King

Tuesday, 25 April

International relations dominated the council meetings yet again. Discussions between England and the Emperor remained at a standstill, while King Henry was desperate to interfere with any possible peace treaty between France and the Emperor, and possibly make a treaty with France for England.[1] Cromwell got word from his long-time Italian friend, Antonio Bonvisi, that the mood in Lyon, where he was travelling with the Emperor's court, was that no peace could be achieved between the Empire and France.[2] King Henry, with Cromwell at his side, wrote letters to Ambassador Pate who was with the Emperor, and Bishop Gardiner and John Wallop at the French court, making it clear that the Emperor's terms for an alliance were not suitable, and one letter mentioned Anne as, 'our most dear and entirely beloved wife, the queen', who could still give him a male heir.[3] Whether Henry still believed any of that was not important; he wanted to give the Emperor and the French king the impression all was under control in England.

A French alliance with England hinged on one demand from King Henry — that King Francis assist in ensuring that the Pope stop all sanctions and excommunications against England.[4] Henry wanted Anne recognised as queen, and for the Royal Supremacy to be respected. France needed to support Henry's demands, and Anne was firmly at the centre of his requests.

At the same time, a potential alliance between Scotland and France was also falling apart, as King Henry's nephew, King James V of Scotland, had called off a potential French marriage. His mother, Henry's sister, Dowager Queen Margaret, was much upset.[5] King James also called off any intention of travelling over the English border to meet with his uncle, further irritating his mother.[6] A potential split between Scotland and France could only be good for England, meaning one less hostile border in the quest for peace in Europe.

The Dover trip for Henry and Anne was currently still going ahead, planning to leave Greenwich for Rochester on 2 May. If Lord Rochford and Margery

Horsman, who were in charge of preparing the king and queen's households, suspected anything was wrong, they certainly did not show it. Sir Richard Page was also assisting in organising the trip to Dover but was possibly also involved in some subterfuge at the same time.[7] Sir Nicholas Carew sent a letter to Princess Mary, and it was mentioned that others in the privy chamber did the same, and this was likely to have been Page. As Edward Seymour's father-in-law, and long-time Katharine and Mary supporter, Page was most likely the senior member of the privy chamber alongside Carew assisting the princess and the possible new queen of England. It was Ambassador Chapuys who shared details of these secret letters being sent, writing that:

> '[Carew] and some persons of the chamber sent to tell the Princess to be of good cheer, for shortly the opposite party would put water in their wine, for the King was already as sick and tired of the concubine as could be.'[8]

This was entirely at odds with what Henry was writing to his ambassadors on the same day. Whether Henry even believed in his own words or wished to look entirely innocent of any potential investigation into Anne, cannot be certain. What is certain is that King Henry loved to play one favourite off another, as seen in the Cromwell vs. Gardiner battle of 1540 and the Gardiner vs. Cranmer battle in 1543, openly supporting neither and letting his ministers destroy one another.[9] Henry may have been acting one way and thinking another entirely. At this point in the plan, there are no further hints towards the truth. Whispers at court of Anne being an adulterer were not proof enough that Carew could feel confident telling Princess Mary she was safe, but he seemingly knew something was happening if he made the bold claim to the princess. Just rumours of someone committing treason with their words and rumours of oyer and terminer papers already drawn up would have been enough to send the court into a spin. Anyone with a secret suddenly felt nervous.

Wednesday, 26 April

> 'I am persuaded that the true and chief cause of the hatred, the treachery, and the false accusations laid to the charge of that most holy Queen, your most pious mother, was this, that she persuaded the King to send an embassy into Germany to the

> Princes who had embraced the Gospel. If other arguments of the truth of this were wanting, a single one would be sufficient, namely that before the embassy had returned, the Queen had been executed.'[10]

Whatever the rumours swirling around the royal court on 26 April, the likelihood of them being that Anne Boleyn was in trouble for supporting an embassy to Germany is incredibly unlikely. While Alexander Alesius told this story to Queen Elizabeth in 1559, proof is something he never produced. But Alesius did believe the notion and wrote about it in detail for Anne's daughter, although he also tried to inject himself into the story; a case of vanity triumphing over truth.

In August 1535, King Henry and Thomas Cromwell agreed to send several ambassadors to Germany, and Cromwell's paperwork on the plan still survives.[11] Before Katharine of Aragon's death, international relations were frayed, and Sir John Wallop had been sent to France to 'renovate the communications' between King Francis and his chancellor, Anne de Montmorency.[12] Wallop needed to request Francis' support on Henry and Anne's marriage, and justify the executions of More and Fisher and the changes to the Church in England. Naturally, he had little success, and Stephen Gardiner took over the position months later. There had been, for several years, the notion that Philip Melanchthon, a theologian as influential as Martin Luther, could visit England so King Henry could discuss the Reformation and how it would aid Henry's takeover of religion. Melanchthon wrote polite messages to Cromwell and others but never took the request seriously.[13] It was not safe to travel; the Holy Roman Emperor and King Francis hated Melanchthon and the Reformation, and his safety could never be assured. The German reformers also believed King Henry was not a true reformer, simply a greedy man using their cause to feather his own nest (a sentiment that frequently turned out to be true). Sir John Wallop had gone to France to locate Melanchthon and again ask him to England, but Melanchthon fled to the safety of home in Wittenburg, safe under the authority of Fredrick and Sybilla, the Duke and Duchess of Saxony. Cromwell oversaw the issue of getting Melanchthon to divert from France and visit England instead, as he had already suggested his long-time friend and German translator, Christopher Mont, and Cambridge scholar, Simon Haynes, go to France and persuade the French to leave Melanchthon alone so he might be persuaded to travel to England.[14] Mont had been in Germany twice already in two years collecting German books and teachings for Cromwell and would be the best man to find Melanchthon. Whether Anne Boleyn had any opinion on the matter of Melanchthon goes unacknowledged but given her intelligence and constant interest in reformist beliefs, she surely knew of these plans and likely would have been most interested in the chance to speak with a man like Melanchthon.

Within a week, it was clear this plan was not enough. Charles Booth, Bishop of Hereford, had died in May 1535, and by September, Edward Foxe, Henry's almoner, was chosen as Booth's successor.[15] Foxe was a man invested in the Reformation and would be an ally of Anne Boleyn as queen, as her place beside the king ensured the continuation of reform in England. Henry and Cromwell decided that Foxe would be the best man to send into Germany, taking with him Cromwell's ally and fervent reformer, Robert Barnes, alongside Princess Mary's ally, Nicholas Heath, and recent theology graduate, John Croke, the son of one of Cromwell's late personal friends. The group were to meet Christopher Mont in Germany and go to visit the Duke of Saxony. It was an odd, unofficial visit to Germany. Multiple embassies from both nations had travelled back and forth over several years, each as disappointing as the last. King Henry wanted to create goodwill between England and Saxony, to show off England's gains in repelling the Pope, and see signs that the reformist northern German States were allies of England. Naturally, wanting a sign they supported Henry and Anne's marriage was included in the paperwork Cromwell wrote to Foxe when he prepared their trip, itinerary and passports.[16] The German States were in the process of holding diets surrounding the Augsburg Confession, allowing states to join the military Schmalkaldic League, which was headed by the Duke of Saxony and Philip, Landgrave of Hesse. The Confession was to ensure unity in the beliefs of Lutheran religion. By 1535, six nations had joined this league, which was big enough to form an army to repel the King of Hungary, who had not argued against this alliance forming in the Catholic northern area of the Holy Roman Empire, in return for the Schmalkaldic League remaining at peace. By 1535, many states were interested in joining the Augsburg Confession,[17] which had the blessing of Lutheran leaders, and the Scandinavian countries were likewise looking to join the group, their royal houses all converted to reformist beliefs.

Anne Boleyn would have undoubtedly been interested in the Augsburg Confession and the theological arguments being agreed upon in Germany, which consisted of twenty parts, with eighteen articles on the change of religion; the largest articles concerning monastic vows and ecclesiastical power.[18] While she was never labelled a Lutheran, Anne was more than capable of interpreting these changes to religion. Had Henry sent someone like Edward Foxe, whom Anne Boleyn knew, she would have been able to speak with both Foxe and the king on the subject. But Alexander Alesius went further, claiming that Anne was the one to promote the embassy to Germany. Alesius may have given Anne more praise than was due, and the claim does Anne no credit.

Despite the huge amount of planning and cost Cromwell laid out for this embassy, there were no signs of success. Christopher Mont moved to Germany to meet the men and spent time with Philip Melanchthon, and the English scholars travelled around the German States as the Confession diets took place. But they had no official capacity in which to sit in on signings or negotiations, and the German scholars present constantly remarked that the English had outstayed their welcome. English diplomats simply stood on the edges of important moments surrounding the Augsburg Confession, hoping to gain scraps of information and favour. While this was not the worst embassy meeting between the countries (one German delegation had been two men, mostly drunk, slurring at King Henry for thirty minutes and then disappearing forever[19]), the entire affair came to nothing. If Anne Boleyn was planning a delegation to garner support for her position as queen, she surely had the plans and ideas to make it more successful than the lukewarm embassy King Henry sent to Europe.[20]

But in the initial stages of this mission in late 1535, there were hopes of success, enough to make Catholics concerned. Alesius reported that Stephen Gardiner, in Paris with King Francis, was worried about the German embassy's potential success and spoke with other bishops back in England about the problem. Alesius believed this became a collusion of bishops against Anne.[21] Many of the most influential bishops did not like Anne and had not forgotten their loyalty to the Pope or Queen Katharine; men such as Cuthbert Tunstall, Bishop of Durham, John Stokesley, Bishop of London, John Longland, Bishop of Lincoln, Richard Sampson, new Bishop of Chichester, and Richard Nix, Bishop of Norwich. Neither Thomas Cranmer nor Thomas Cromwell could manage most of these men either.[22] Alexander

Alesius believed men like these who were the ones who began the rumours of Anne's adultery, the same whispers that made it into Stephen Gardiner's letters in December 1535, sparking off the whole adultery idea in the first place. All these men hated Anne and hated her support of the Reformation and made up lies to discredit her. None of this is hard to believe, but also there is no way to prove exactly who told Stephen Gardiner of adultery rumours in the first place. Either way, by April 1536, these rumours were again spreading.

The rumours eventually spread as far as Anne Boleyn's ears. Whether she heard something, spoke to her husband, or her ladies were sharing details, Anne knew something was happening around the court. The last four months had been hard enough for Anne, so she may not have felt any more concerned or upset than usual about the malicious whisperings behind her back. She had certainly developed a thick skin in her time beside the king. On 26 April, Anne spoke with her chaplain, Matthew Parker, which in itself is not unusual, but the conversation stayed with Parker for the rest of his life.[23] But rumours had advanced beyond the usual gossip of the king's new mistress and arguments with his wife, and Anne asked Parker to swear he would take care of Princess Elizabeth in the event Anne was no longer able to do so. Anne may have been genuinely frightened for her safety or scared she would be banished and exiled from Elizabeth, as Katharine and Mary had suffered for five years. It showed Anne still had people around her she could trust, and if Anne wanted a scholar to oversee her daughter's safety, she had certainly made an excellent choice, as Parker was one of the wisest reformers in the country. The tale often goes that Parker cared for Elizabeth for the rest of his life, which is not quite true. Parker remained Dean of the College of Secular Canons at Stoke-by-Clare in Suffolk, a role Anne petitioned for him,[24] and then became Dean of Corpus Christi College in Cambridge in 1545 and helped King Henry close other colleges around the country.[25] Parker then served King Edward VI and the Duke of Northumberland. But throughout Queen Mary's reign, Parker remained hidden away, deprived of all offices, but did not flee in exile which led to him being brandished as something of a coward. He was selected as Queen Elizabeth's Archbishop of Canterbury in 1559, but was extremely reluctant to take the role, only doing so because he remembered Anne Boleyn's words from twenty-three years earlier.[26] He had done nothing to aid Elizabeth up until that point. Parker did serve as archbishop for sixteen years under Elizabeth, but achieved little, though he was a man of morals and authority. Queen Elizabeth hated Parker's wife, Margaret, to the point she was openly cruel to their faces,[27] and despite many desperate attempts to never serve Queen Elizabeth in the first place, Parker did manage to finally honour Anne Boleyn's request and served Elizabeth as archbishop until his death, leaving a manuscript collection that has given him a respectable lasting legacy.[28]

Thursday, 27 April

Vicegerent Cromwell surprised everyone on 27 April, when he sent out summons to Thomas Cranmer as Archbishop of Canterbury, Sir Richard Rich as the king's attorney, and even Sir John Gage as the Chancellor of Lancaster, plus all bishops, abbots, lords, judges, serjeants-at-law, and the sheriffs of each county, that parliament would be reopened, only two weeks after closing the previous session.[29] As much as Cromwell loved parliament, this was an extreme measure and unless he and the king had pressing matters to attend, there would be no need to do such a thing. Under Cardinal Wolsey as Lord Chancellor, he only ever called parliament once, in 1523. King Henry had Sir Thomas More summon parliament in 1529, and then Cromwell had ensured a sitting every year since. There were to be fresh faces in parliament this time, and Cromwell had a lot of work to do to set everything up for a sitting on 8 June.[30] Much has been made of Thomas Cranmer's specific summons to appear, but it does not need scrutiny, as Cranmer always appeared in parliament, regardless of his travels or workload. He and Cromwell made sure they always attended, and if one had to be away on a day, the other would make double sure to be there to be eyes and ears for them both. Summoning Cranmer was not unusual, though he was away from London at the time, staying at his favourite palace of Knole, twenty-five miles south-west of London.[31] Many of those who had travelled to London may have not even arrived home again after the last session. Six weeks to prepare a new parliament was a big task for Cromwell, whose in-tray was already overflowing with requests for closing monasteries. In addition, friends like Lady Mary Guildford were in need of help, Henry and Anne's supposed trip to Dover was not ready, the imminent return of the failed embassy into Germany was upon them, and meetings with the French ambassador were due on 30 April.[32] There were thirty-five

Anne Boleyn, artist unknown. (National Portrait Gallery, London, NPG 668)

Anne Boleyn, by Hans Holbein. (The Queen's Gallery, Buckingham Palace, London, RCIN 912189)

Possibly George Boleyn, by Hans Holbein. (The Royal Collection, London, RCIN 912260)

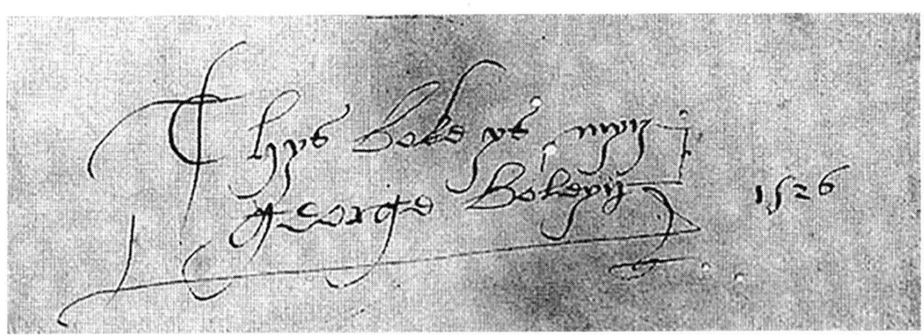

Signature of George Boleyn, Lord Rochford. (Adrienne Dillard)

Signature of Jane Boleyn (née Parker), Lady Rochford. (Julia Fox)

Jane Seymour, by Hans Holbein. (Kunsthistorisches Museum, Vienna, 881)

Elizabeth Seymour, by Hans Holbein. (Toledo Museum of Art, Ohio, 1926.57)

Margaret Wyatt, by Hans Holbein. (Metropolitan Museum of Art, New York, 14.40.637)

Possibly Anne Gainsford, by Hans Holbein. (Pennethorne Gallery, The Queen's Gallery, Buckingham Palace, London RCIN 912252)

Above left: Mary Fitzroy née Howard, by Hans Holbein. (Nash Gallery, The Queen's Gallery, Buckingham Palace, London, RCIN 912212)

Above right: Mary Shelton by Hans Holbein. (Royal Collection, London, RCIN 912227)

Right: Jane/Joan Astley, Hans Holbein. (Royal Collection, London, RCIN 912222)

Above left: Princess Mary by Master John. (National Portrait Gallery, London, NPG 428)

Above right: Katharine of Aragon, artist unknown. (National Portrait Gallery, London, NPG163)

Left: Henry VIII, by Hans Holbein. (Thyssen-Bornemisza Museum, Madrid, 191 (1934.39))

Thomas Cromwell
by Hans Holbein.
(Frick Museum,
New York, 1915.1.76)

William Fitzwilliam, artist unknown.
(Fitzwilliam Museum, Cambridge, 164)

Anthony Browne, artist unknown. (National Portrait Gallery, London, NPG5186)

George Brooke, Lord Cobham, by Hans Holbein. (The Royal Collection, London, RCIN 912195)

Above: Nicholas Carew, by Hans Holbein. (Drumlanrig Castle, Scotland)

Right: Thomas Wyatt, by Hans Holbein. (Pennethorne Gallery, The Queen's Gallery, Buckingham Palace, RCIN 912250)

Hugh Latimer, artist unknown. (National Portrait Gallery, London, NPG 295)

Thomas Goodricke, artist unknown. (National Portrait Gallery, London, NPG D24830)

Matthew Parker, artist unknown. (Lambeth Palace, London, 50)

Thomas Cranmer, by Gerlach Flicke. (National Portrait Gallery, London, NPG 535)

Stephen Gardiner, by Quinten Metsys. (Liechtenstein Museum, Vienna, GE928)

Thomas Howard, 3rd Duke of Norfolk. (The Queen's Gallery, Buckingham Palace RCIN 404439)

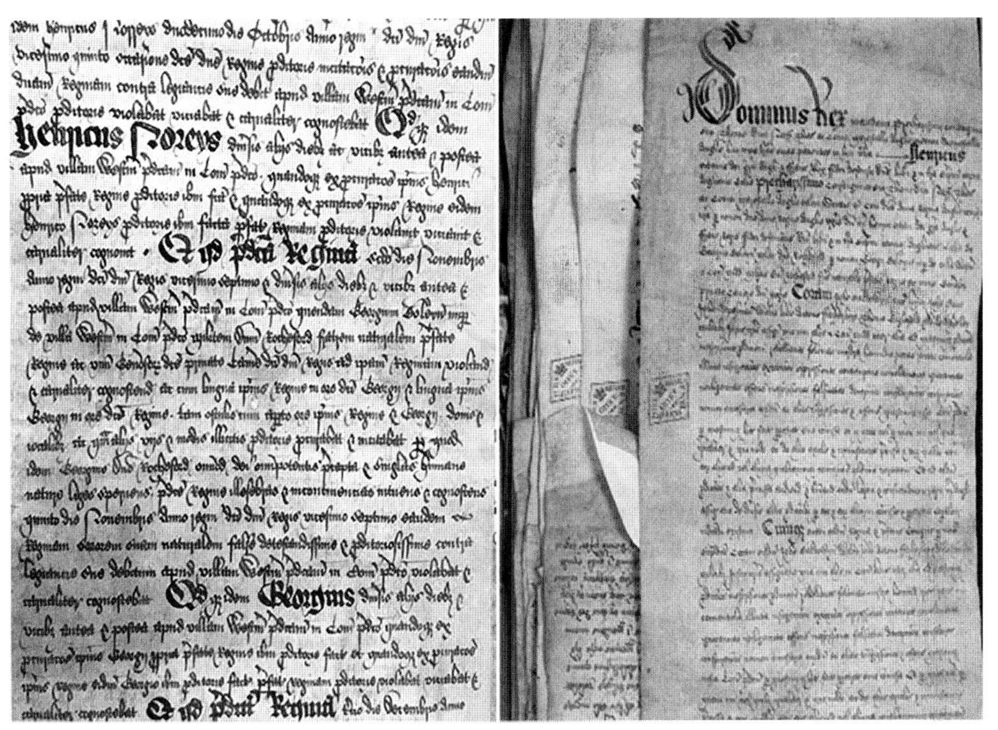

Trial papers against Anne Boleyn from the Baga Secretis. (The National Archives, Kew, KB 8/9, f. 9v)

Trial papers against George Boleyn from the Baga Secretis. (The National Archives, Kew, 8/9, f. 9v)

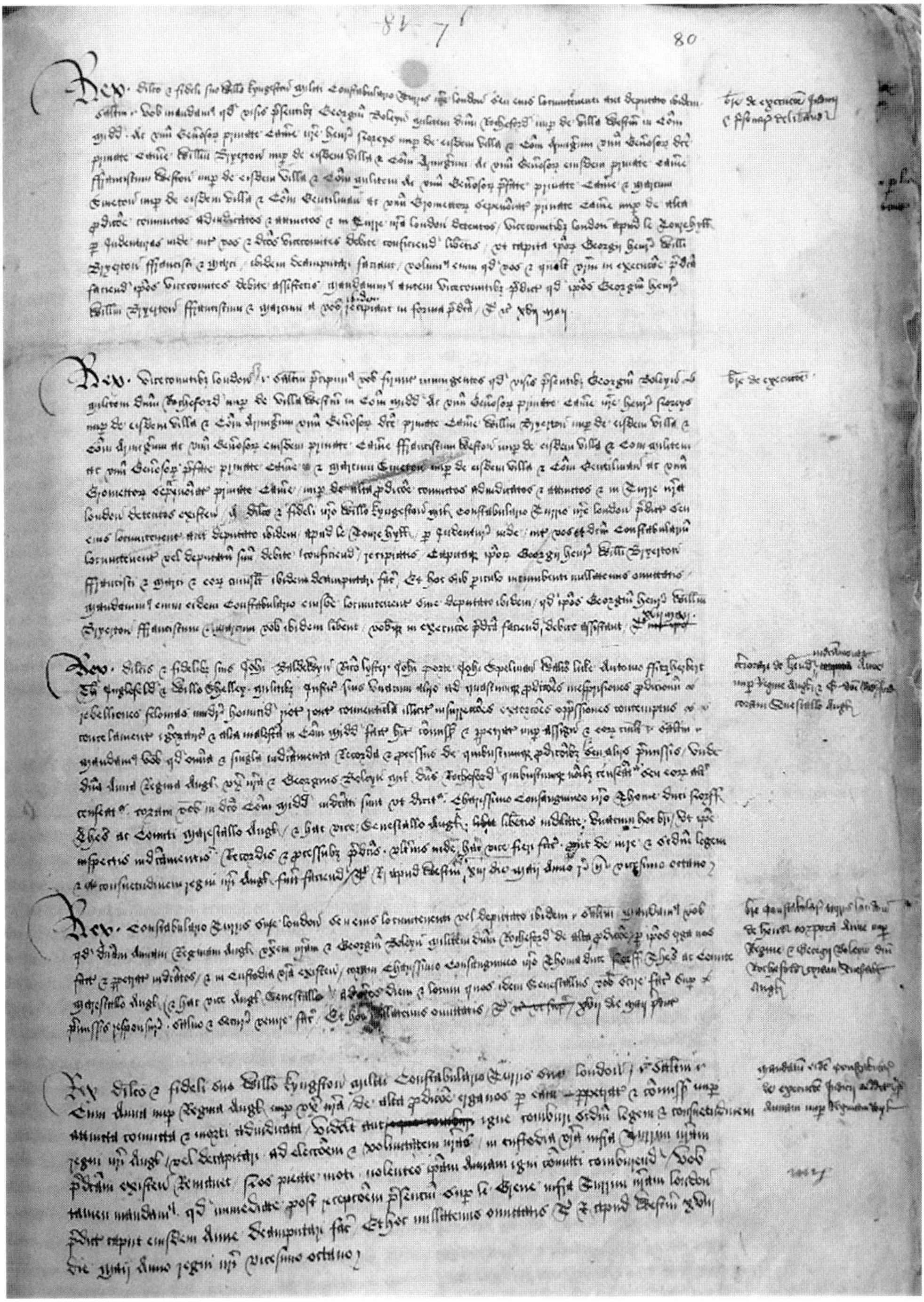

Writs discussing executions, clerk of the crown's Precedent book. (The National Archives, Kew, C 193/3, fol. 80)

King Henry's decision on Anne's execution method. (The National Archives, Kew, C 193/3, fol. 80) private acts to go through, mostly lands changing hands around the country, much arising from the monasteries who were surrendering lands to the king, many were in need of new homes, and many widows were receiving their inheritances.[33] Among these private acts sat the attainder of Thomas Lord Howard (one of Anne Boleyn's many Howard uncles, not to be confused with his brother Thomas Howard, Duke of Norfolk). He had been having an affair with the king's niece, Lady Margaret Douglas, who sat too high in the line of succession for secret marriage pre-contracts to be occurring. Both ended up in the Tower.[34] Again, a call to parliament would not suggest the king intended to destroy his wife; the session oversaw the heavy-handed See of Rome Act pass, destroying anyone who continued to bow to the authority of the Pope rather than King Henry.[35] Calling parliament for this law specifically could have been enough justification for needing an extra session, but Cromwell would have spent a long time on the paperwork and should have simply put it through the recent session. Also voted into law was the Ecclesiastical Licences Act, invalidating licences and dispensations created by Rome, another essential law in imposing Henry's new heavy-handed religious demands on the public. The Tithe Act also passed the Commons and Lords, tidying up loopholes on taxes by religious houses. All of these laws were essential for ensuring the dissolution of the monasteries and Henry's control over his people.[36] Small laws were also passed, and things that likely did not fit into the last sitting could now be voted on, such as laws about apprentices and wine customs duties. It was a good time to tidy up small and large laws; parliament would not sit again until 1539, not that anyone knew this at the time. But if a plan to destroy Anne Boleyn was forming, everyone involved had an excellent cover story. King Henry just needed a reason to leave his wife.

Friday, 28 April

When King Henry and Vicegerent Cromwell summoned Bishop John Stokesley to court on 27 April, surely something had changed.[37] Calling a bishop at short notice for a private audience with the king while Cromwell was preparing parliament was surely something to garner attention from the gossip of the court. Given Stokesley's history, this definitely would have rattled the Boleyn camp. John Stokesley was like many religious men of his age; born in 1475, he rose through the educational ranks to become the Vice President of Magdalen College, Oxford by 1506. When King Henry came to the throne in 1509, Stokesley was one of the younger generations to be taken in by the new king, put on the royal council and became Henry's chaplain and almoner.[38]

Stokesley was equally faithful to Catholicism as to the king, and his life ticked past quietly until 1529 when he was asked to travel to France and Italy to find international favour over Henry and Katharine's divorce. Despite being a strong Catholic, Stokesley supported the divorce, and though he found little support for said divorce, he returned home in 1530 and became Bishop of London and Lord Almoner.[39]

Like many clergy of the period, Stokesley bit his tongue as Henry left Katharine and married Anne, but those who sat idly by were less impressed once Henry wanted authority over the Church which directly impacted the lives of men like Stokesley. Despite his Catholic stance, the king had Stokesley perform the christening for Princess Elizabeth, a cross-faith affair in every sense.[40] Stokesley rallied against Thomas Cranmer's reforms and would have been an agitated man in 1536 as the dissolutions began.[41] Being called to see the king at short notice would have made him nervous, but the discussions in the meeting were kept strictly secret. Everyone had their theories; after all, Stokesley had spent much time with the king in the past, discussing how to annul a royal wife. The strength and longevity of Henry and Katharine's marriage had been an obstacle on the path to annulment, but Henry and Anne's marriage did not have the stability or backing of Katharine of Aragon's royal connections. With Henry as the Head of the Church in 1536, he could get Archbishop Cranmer to annul a marriage, but that did not stop Henry from reaching out for Catholic opinion, with men such as Stokesley, and with Sampson meeting Cromwell a week earlier.

There were several options on the table if Henry wanted to end his marriage. First was the undeniable fact that Henry was married to Katharine when he married Anne. While the first royal marriage was annulled by Archbishop Cranmer, the Pope and the Catholic Church did not agree. Henry and Katharine had been married under the Catholic Church's rules and they had received a dispensation from Pope Julius to marry (and importantly, the dispensation did not require Katharine to be a virgin on marriage, despite Henry and Wolsey's assertions[42]). Henry did not believe in the power of the Catholic Church over him any longer but that did not mean their previous rulings were suddenly void. Archbishop Cranmer may have had the authority to legitimise Henry and Anne's marriage, but in this messy changeover during the Reformation, many did not believe he had the power to undo what the Catholics had already done. Now, with Katharine dead, Henry did not face the threat of having to return to Katharine if he left Anne.

King Henry's already intensely mercurial moods must have been teetering on the edge of detonation. He was not a man to make bold choices. He had dithered for years on the matter of his marriage, talking the talk, but ultimately towing the Catholic line until he got Anne Boleyn pregnant. Even with the sluggish start of the Church of England and the Reformation, Henry personally lived a largely Catholic existence. Now, the Reformation had taken a new turn, being enforced on a larger scale, coupled with Henry's foolish idea to close all monasteries. The king had suffered a backlash from many corners since he had tried to divorce Katharine, but the English people were now being directly impacted in their everyday lives thanks to Henry's choices, and they were getting restless. Internationally, Henry had lost all credibility. The man with no sense of responsibility was facing the consequences of his actions, and that could not have created a safe atmosphere for anyone.

The proposed treaty with Emperor Charles did dangle the possibility of King Henry's official excommunication by the Pope being suspended.[43] But Henry would also be expected to fall back into line with Catholic doctrine, weakening his domestic power and financial plans of confiscating Church wealth. Even when Emperor Charles did sign treaties with other nations, he usually reneged on all conditions soon after, which did not make a new treaty particularly appealing. The German delegation was returning to London, with letters from Reformation leaders showing they had the measure of the English king and his weakness.[44] Philip Melanchthon had stated he was not planning on visiting England. The Duke of Saxony praised the English ambassadors Foxe, Heath, and Barnes, wished goodwill to England without any suggestion of alliance, and said he was too busy to worry about England (though Saxony believed Henry and Anne's marriage was valid[45]).

But what did the king and Cromwell need to discuss with the likes of John Stokesley? Opinion on the royal marriage, or more on the relationship between Catholicism and England? Cromwell and Stokesley were not friends, though at least Cromwell was happy to concede reform measures to appease his king and make international alliances. Stokesley had pandered to the king's changes without adopting them in his own life. England had been losing face for several years, at home and abroad, and the pressures stemming from Henry's legal and ecclesiastical changes were mounting. Someone had to face the king's wrath.

As always, Ambassador Chapuys had the gossip to share. He immediately wrote of developments after having dinner with Sir Geoffrey Pole, and likely others, who favoured Princess Mary.[46] Pole reported that Jane Seymour was the woman taking up all of the king's time and that Stokesley shared that the meeting was about removing Anne from Henry's life.[47] The king may have wished to escape the past few years of his life, but he still had no legal reason to do so.

CHAPTER 14

Creating One's Own Proof

Saturday, 29 April

In many ways, the royal court was no different to the hallways of a high school. Notes were passed, gossip whispered behind hands, and factions sprung up. The only difference was the biggest bully could sanction your execution if you looked at him the wrong way. On Saturday, 29 April, while preparing for the annual May Day celebrations and readying for a trip to Dover, Anne Boleyn was not indulging in any of her interests or managing her affairs. She was the subject of the court gossip, her future discussed as if it were a light-hearted subject of conjecture. Outwardly, things had not changed; there was to be a ball on Sunday, 30 April, followed by the traditional 1 May celebrations and jousting tournaments. Everything was in place and ready to go, and the royal trip to Dover would head away from Greenwich to Rochester on Tuesday, 2 May.[1] Lord Lisle had received his paperwork permitting him to sail from Calais to Dover to meet the king and queen. Cromwell had cleared his schedule (or so he claimed) so that he could travel as well, meaning his administrative behemoth had to be carefully scheduled and balanced, with his couriers in place to get news to London and back every day.[2] The king and queen's households were fully prepared for the trip. But with the king spending his time with Jane Seymour and Anne Boleyn fearing the worst, it was only a matter of time before the façade of peace slipped away.

In no mood for games, Anne came upon Mark Smeaton in her presence chamber at Greenwich Palace. Smeaton was a man separated from all others at court. Possibly Flemish, Smeaton was only around 23 years old in 1536. A talented musician picked up to play for Cardinal Wolsey as a teen, Smeaton lived at court firstly in King Henry's household before transferring to Anne. Smeaton was a common-born man, who had no family or allies to call upon, but had been welcome at court, and had played games of courtly love with the queen as much as the noblemen around him. As queen, Anne needed to be flirtatious and witty, but also pious and submissive at the same time. It was easy to cross the line with these messy expectations, and likely everyone had made comments or jokes in the past that may have inadvertently overstepped at some stage. Smeaton, playing and singing for the queen, may have been seen as 'overly familiar' by others at court. But there had seemingly been nothing suspicious to mention until 29 April. Anne came across Smeaton in her chamber looking unhappy. She stopped to ask about his problem, and Smeaton was seemingly in a mood as bad as Anne's, as he simply replied, 'it was no matter'.[3] Anne, either thanks to having little patience or simply making a joke, remarked, 'you may not look to have me speak to you as I should do to a noble man, because you be an inferior person'. Smeaton replied to Anne that all he needed from Anne was a look.[4] A comment such as this, to suggest that just being noticed by the queen would make a man happy, was not any sign of a relationship, or that Smeaton was interested in a queen. It appears a simple compliment from a man to a queen.

While Smeaton may have felt himself on par with the noblemen who could visit Anne's court as much as he could, Anne likely thought of him as a lesser man.[5] Rank was always important, and Anne understood the need to be appropriate at all times. Anne's mistake of saying this to Smeaton was made bigger by the fact she allowed others to overhear the conversation. Who else heard these words went unrecorded, but the following events showed that Smeaton's 'involvement' with Anne was suspected before her ramblings in the Tower the following week. Was it her ladies who whispered of the occasion? A court event such as the May Day celebrations would have been well attended and a great many of Anne's ladies would have been seeing to her in her chambers. Most notable was Margery Horsman, who would be attending her queen in Dover. Anne's regular attendants, Nan Cobham and Elizabeth Somerset, were at court, as were Jane Boleyn, Margaret Lee, a full array of Howard women, the Shelton sisters, and course the king's niece, Lady Margaret Douglas. A great many servants would have been at court as well, including men like cloth importer, William Lok, who had been delivering fine clothing to Anne all year long,[6] and had been a close friend of Thomas Cromwell for almost twenty years.[7] The whole affair may have been more in jest than anger, but someone felt the need to share the news with Cromwell and William Fitzwilliam. Why Anne chose to share this information later also, and the later chat with Norris, has never been explained; Anne likely thought at least Smeaton's encounter to be innocent.

Sunday, 30 April

It was the following morning that the incident with Norris occurred. Sir Henry Norris was the king's most trusted man in the privy chamber. Both Henry and his brother, John Norris, worked in Henry VIII's chamber, though Henry Norris had gone on to become one of the king's best friends. Norris was in Henry's chamber when they were young, with Norris a decade older than the king, and he had served in the royal privy chamber since at least 1517.[8] By 1526, Norris was the Groom of the Stool, the closest personal daily servant to the king, a position given only to someone the king trusted with absolutely everything (including, obviously, his toilet habits). Norris was the grandson of Sir William Norris and Jane de Vere, daughter of the 12th Earl of Oxford, both Lancastrian families in the Wars of the Roses. William Norris was exiled for his Lancastrian defiance against King Richard III and fought alongside Henry VII in the Battle of Bosworth, earning the king's unending support.[9] William and Jane Norris went on to have five children, the eldest being Edward, who was Henry Norris' father.[10] Edward Norris married Lady Frideswide Lovell, sister of infamous Sir Francis Lovell, (the loyal Yorkist friend of King Richard III), who disappeared after the Battle of Stoke Field, the same battle in which Edward Norris lost his life fighting for Henry VII under his father's command.[11] Edward and Frideswide Norris' five children were raised in Lancastrian households, leading to John Norris' close relationship with Henry VII and Henry Norris' close personal relationship with Henry VIII.

In 1531, Sir Henry Norris lost his wife, Mary Fiennes, daughter of Thomas Fiennes, 8th Baron Dacre and Anne Bourchier.[12] Anne Bourchier was one of Anne Boleyn's aunts by marriage, had served Queen Katharine of Aragon, and her sister was Margaret Bryan, who ran the royal nursery. The Norris family were considered impeccable courtiers, trusted completely by kings, and awarded gifts and offices to illustrate that trust.

Henry Norris was probably the closest thing to a friend that King Henry VIII ever had.

After losing his wife in 1531, Henry Norris was slowly on the lookout for another. Many courtiers remarried quickly, sometimes within weeks or months, but Norris had taken his time. He had two surviving children in 1536, Henry Norris the younger, aged around 10, who lived with Mary Boleyn's son Henry Carey in 1536[13] (though was moved after 1536, and was raised by Sir John Williams, a relative of Thomas Cromwell), and a daughter Mary Norris, in her early teens (who went on to marry Sir George Carew in 1540, and lived at court with Anna of Cleves and Katheryn Howard[14]). An audit of Norris' household showed his combined personal and court yearly incomes came to almost 2600*l* (or £1.1 million today[15]). Most of the nobility did not have this kind of money, and only Thomas Cromwell's income could have been any higher than what Norris earned in a year. Suggestions of discord between Norris and Cromwell are simply that; while the pair were both with the king daily, they had completely different roles and business. Norris likely was no fan of the dissolution of the monasteries, but Cromwell was not pleased with the project either. But only one of them was a commoner and had to keep his mouth shut.

Sir Henry Norris had amassed many offices throughout the 1530s and had been friendly towards Anne Boleyn, showing no religious differences or loyalties. Norris was widely liked at court and had been betrothed to Lady Margaret Shelton for an undetermined length of time in 1536.[16] Margaret Shelton and her sister Mary (the pair often confused with one another, thanks to Mary and Madge looking identical in manuscripts) were Anne Boleyn's cousins and in Anne's privy chamber, and Henry Norris would often come to visit the queen. Sunday, 30 April was one of those days, when Anne snapped at Norris about taking too long to marry Margaret Shelton, and Norris replied that he 'looked to tarry' and take his time.[17] Norris would have undoubtedly joked and flirted with Anne Boleyn in the past, as was expected, but this time, Anne was having none of the court games and told Norris (recorded in an unfortunately mutilated manuscript):

> 'You look for dead men's shoes, for if aught came to the King but good, you would look to have me'... and [Norris] said if he should have any such thought, he would his head were off

> … and then [Anne] said she could undo him if she would … and there with they fell out…'[18]

This was a catastrophically stupid thing for Anne to say, especially before a group of people. It had always been treason to harm the king, but Cromwell's 1534 update of the Treason Law made mentioning or even thinking about the king's death a treasonable offence.[19] Anne knew instantly she had made a mistake in snapping at Norris in such a way, and sent Norris from her rooms, to see her almoner, Bishop Nicholas Shaxton, to swear that Anne 'was a good woman'.[20] Norris did as the queen asked, but if Anne thought that Norris swearing to Shaxton would somehow erase the argument, she was sorely mistaken. Whether it was Norris himself who took Anne's words down to Henry's rooms, or Anne's ladies discussing the skirmish (or Shaxton telling Cromwell, which would not have been a surprise), the outburst soon reached many ears around Greenwich. Norris would have known that Henry and Anne were not on good terms, and despite his support for Anne, would have always sided with Henry. Regardless, as soon as Cromwell and Fitzwilliam heard these words, they would have known they had cause to tell Henry. The king was not known for his loyalty and could smile at a friend and simultaneously be planning their destruction only five minutes later.

The May Day celebrations at Greenwich were one of the most attended events of the year. The arrival of the warmer weather brought out the finest jousters to entertain the king, and many years had seen lavish pageantry, events and games performed for Henry and Katharine. But the exquisite events of the earlier years of Henry's reign were long over, and 1536 had the standard fare on offer, albeit an occasion for everyone with invitations to court to enjoy themselves at the palace. Sunday, 30 April was the date of the ball and would have been attended by all the major players, including those Anne probably did not want to see. Jane Seymour certainly would have been seen in attendance, alongside her brother Edward and his wife Anne. Sir Nicholas Carew would have attended, and possibly his wife Lady Elizabeth too. Sir Francis Bryan, who had been dipping in and out of court throughout April (in negotiations with Cromwell over getting the money owed to him from the king) likely attended. The strong pro-Princess Mary families were all in London: Henry Courtenay, Marquis of Exeter; Henry Pole, Lord Montagu, and his brother Sir Geoffrey Pole; Sir Henry Grey,

Marquis of Dorset and his wife Lady Frances had been in London; and of course, the Privy Council, all foreign ambassadors and the Cromwellian entourage.

Henry and Anne were well known as a couple who would fight and make up with alarming regularity.[21] So when the court witnessed another outburst between the royal couple at the end of the ball, it should not have come as a huge surprise, especially given the tumultuous months they had suffered. Surviving only in the tale told to Queen Elizabeth by Alexander Alesius, he recorded:

> 'Never shall I forget the sorrow which I felt when I saw the most serene Queen, your most religious mother, carrying you, still a baby, in her arms and entreating the most serene King, your father, in Greenwich Palace, from the open window, of which he was looking into the courtyard, when she brought you to him…. I did not perfectly understand what had been going on, but the faces and gestures of the speakers plainly showed that the King was angry, although he could conceal his anger wonderfully well. Yet from the protracted conference of the Council, (for whom the crowd was waiting until it was quite dark, expecting that they would return to London,) it was most obvious to everyone that some deep and tricky question was being discussed.'[22]

How accurate Alesius was with his letter to Queen Elizabeth is hard to say. The letter is marked with inaccuracies, likely a by-product of the thirty-three years passing between the event and the eventual recording. There is no record that the young Princess Elizabeth travelled to Greenwich for the May Day celebrations, and her household and its movements are not hard to track. At this time, both Elizabeth and Mary were living at Hunsdon, though it could be possible that Elizabeth travelled the twenty-eight-mile journey to Greenwich for a quick visit and was then spirited away again. Elizabeth did not travel anywhere in the months before or after her mother's death according to records.[23]

So many of the court had stood and watched the king and queen argue, their words hidden from all but themselves. Alesius may have remembered the wrong day, or they could have easily been arguing about Henry Norris.

At 11 p.m., Henry postponed the trip to Dover, which ended up only going ahead in July.[24] When Anne was told about this development went unmentioned.

Like so much surrounding Anne's destruction, it was a case of looking for who was not present rather than who did witness the fight. No one person is specifically mentioned in Alesius' story of the royal argument, and thus, no mention of Thomas Cromwell's attendance, which could come in handy in establishing the moves against Anne Boleyn. The one eyewitness account of the whole sordid case against Anne was the recollection of George Constantine, who wrote his account three years after Anne's death. Constantine was a servant to Henry Norris, who wrote to Cromwell in 1540, talking about discussions he had with John Barlow, then Dean of Westbury, one of the most fervent Boleyn supporters, who had been deep in the ecclesiastical arguments during Henry and Katharine's divorce hearings years earlier.[25] Constantine told Barlow about how he had written to his master when he was in the Tower. Recalling the events around Anne's destruction, Constantine told Barlow that Mark Smeaton was the first man to be arrested, on the eve of the May Day celebrations and taken to Stepney.[26] There is no other proof that this happened, other than Constantine's account. However, Constantine's conversation with Barlow was written to Cromwell, so lying would have been pointless.

Stepney was the location of Great Place, an extraordinary two-level wooden manor home owned by Thomas Cromwell. Cromwell rarely took anyone to his home in Stepney; it was his retreat outside of the city, and other than Ambassador Chapuys, few ever got to visit. The court was never invited to Great Place, which was across the road from St Dunstan's church on Stepney Way. But in a pinch, it was likely the closest place where Mark Smeaton could be taken for interrogation without anyone realising he was missing. It was only four miles up the Thames to the inlet of Salmon Lane, a small river that led from the Thames, a half a mile north to the farmland that sat next to Great Place. Nobody noticed Smeaton was missing from court, which in itself was not surprising, given the busy nature of the celebrations. But for Cromwell to take Smeaton to his private home does suggest it was a spontaneous event, rather than a planned attack, and spontaneity was not a characteristic usually associated with Cromwell, a man who had paperwork sometimes ready years in advance.

George Constantine wrote that he thought Mark Smeaton was tortured, though admitted he relied on hearsay about Smeaton being put to the rack in the Tower.[27] Suggestions Cromwell tortured Smeaton at his home bear no proof and are more likely confusion and suspicion around the whole affair. But Cromwell himself may have been with Smeaton when he was quietly removed from court, or already at Stepney when the party arrived. Cromwell leaving court for London would not have aroused any suspicion, as Cromwell regularly left the king's side to attend to his work and was not contactable by anyone other than the king's messengers. Whether Cromwell took Smeaton away himself or had close attendants like Thomas Wriothesley, Ralph Sadler and Richard Cromwell do the task, it would have been a terrifying prospect. Cromwell tended to tread lightly with people and gave out second chances for even serious offences, so for Cromwell to interrogate a man rather than simply send a letter with a servant spelled disaster for Smeaton from the start. Alexander Alesius wrote that he recalled the sound of a canon blasting at the Tower on the night of Sunday, 30 April or the early hours of 1 May, which denoted someone entering its confines.[28] This would not have been done for Smeaton's arrival (not being a nobleman), so this is likely confusion in Alesius statement. The *Cronica del Rey Enrico*, written in 1874, suggested that Cromwell lured Smeaton to Stepney and then had him tortured with a cudgel wrapped around his head, but this suggestion is totally at odds with Cromwell's usual private behaviour. There was no reason for Cromwell or his men to commit such an act. Smeaton may have been kept in irons, unlike the noble suspects in this infamous 'crime', and Smeaton surely knew that there would be no escape.

Smeaton proved to be a useful target, one that could have flown under Cromwell's radar if Anne had not snapped at him the day before. Norris, however, would have been in Cromwell's sights from the beginning, given his immense power at court, lack of support for reform, and the convenience of him sending much time in the queen's apartments. If Cromwell wanted Anne Boleyn to be found guilty of adultery, the more men involved increased the odds of the plan to topple a queen.

Who Cromwell chose to be guilty was less important than who he did not choose to be condemned. There was a list of dozens of men who worked in the king's privy chamber, rotating in and out as they managed their lives and the king's business. Many of the lower-ranked attendants were friends with Cromwell, or old Wolsey allies, and MPs who could help vote through Cromwell's bills in parliament. This meant quiet but diligent men such as Sir Thomas Heneage and Sir William Fitzwilliam were safe, as Cromwell respected both men. Sir Francis Bryan joined his brother-in-law, Sir Nicholas Carew, who was staying with Jane Seymour at Chelsea, and neither were at court often enough to be credible adulterers. Edward Seymour was safe, being prepared as a new brother-in-law to the king, while William Fitzwilliam's brother, Sir Anthony Browne, was married to Alice Gage, adored daughter of Cromwell's long-time personal friend, Sir John Gage.

Sir Thomas Wyatt was harder to deal with; Sir Henry Wyatt was one of Cromwell's dearest friends, but if Anne were to be accused of adultery, past affection from Wyatt would undoubtedly come up in conversation. Wyatt was not a rake like more boisterous courtiers like Carew or Bryan, but even his own father openly admitted that his son perhaps needed punishment for his general behaviour.[29]

If such a plan could bring down a man as powerful as Norris, it could also bring down a man like William Brereton, a man beloved by the king, but hated by so many others, Cromwell included. Significant courtiers who had not secured Cromwell's friendship were about realise their mistake.

But the clergymen who flitted around Anne Boleyn were in a unique position; while they were seen with her regularly, Cromwell supported each man, as they were keen reformists, and each had Cromwell's personal backing for their place in the Church and at court.

As always, the whims of the king, and how far he wanted to push the narrative would decide guilt or innocence. Would Henry require any proof at all, or was he simply ready to play the victim regardless of the situation?

CHAPTER 15

Planning the Murder of Anne Boleyn

Monday, 1 May

The 1536 May Day celebrations went ahead as scheduled, despite Henry and Anne's outburst after the evening ball. How much contact the king and queen had that day goes unrecorded, likely forgotten in the melee about to come. Jousting was the highlight of the event at Greenwich, an event the king was now too old and too unfit to personally enjoy. One of the biggest signs of masculinity at court, Henry now had to watch the jousting and competitions while other men of the court took all the glory.[1] Everyone was at court, and most of Henry's men were competing, among them Henry Norris, who was now in the king's sights. The king allowed Norris his chance to compete, seemingly letting much of the day run as expected, and no account exists of Henry looking as if anything was untoward. Many of the men who would soon be in the Tower were still jousting, and life outwardly looked as expected by all at court. Anne waited to see her brother George perform, and Cromwell had his nephew Richard competing. When the king decided he was suddenly leaving the event at 6 p.m., it caught everyone by surprise. This may have been the time when they received word that Smeaton had confessed to adultery with Anne.[2]

The event came to a halt when Henry walked off without any word, taking six men with him, according to multiple accounts.[3] Who those men were goes omitted, except for Sir Henry Norris. The only information shared was that the king needed to go to Westminster, so Cromwell accompanying Henry would not have looked unusual, nor Richard Cromwell, a man high in the king's esteem. Sir William Fitzwilliam would be another likely candidate to follow his king, likewise his brother Sir Anthony Browne. Sir Thomas Heneage, another of Henry's close privy chamber men, and one of the few never implicated in any wrongdoing, could have been a likely attendant that Henry could trust on the fateful ride.

Constantine recalled his master, Norris, was interrogated personally by the king.[4] Had he ever slept with Anne Boleyn? A confession would save Norris from execution for such treason, so Constantine claimed. But Norris was blindsided by the questioning and put in the Tower the same day (this may have been the cannon firing at the Tower that Alesius recalled hearing). Most of the court remained at Greenwich to continue their May Day celebrations without the king, and if Anne was suspicious, there was absolutely nothing she could do. But Lady Jane Seymour was quietly removed from court and travelled the twenty-five miles southeast of London to Carew Manor at Beddington. Anne Boleyn had made the prudent decision to stay away from London when Katharine of Aragon was on trial for her marriage, and now Jane Seymour could make the same choice for the trial of Anne Boleyn.

Tuesday, 2 May

It is difficult to say when the news of Norris and Smeaton's arrests made it downstream to Greenwich, but George Boleyn, Lord Rochford was sufficiently worried on the morning of Tuesday, 2 May.[5] Rochford left his sister at Greenwich and headed for Westminster, presumably to speak with the king. The trouble was that Henry had made up his mind; either Anne was an adulterer, or another excuse would be made so Anne could be removed. All those late-night barge trips to Beddington or Chelsea to spend time with Jane Seymour were more enticing than having Anne as a wife. Ambassador Chapuys already reported that an excuse, that Anne had been pre-contracted to the Earl of Northumberland as late as 1525, could be a way for the king to dispense with his wife.[6]

Lord Rochford was not able to see the king; restricting access to Henry would be a certain way of ensuring Henry did not suffer an attack of guilt for supporting such a chaotic and ill-thought-out plan against a queen. By two o'clock, Rochford too was in the Tower, though whether incest had been suggested, or Rochford's vocal support for his sister ensured the arrest is yet another unknown. Rochford's desire to support his sister came much too late, as by the time he was entering the Tower, Anne had already been questioned at Greenwich and would have been preparing for her own trip up the river. Anne would have known how serious the charges were, as she was accompanied on the ride by Vicegerent Cromwell, Chancellor Audley, the Duke of Norfolk, Constable of the Tower, William Kingston, Treasurer, William Fitzwilliam and Comptroller of the Household, William Paulet. The most powerful men in government all rode the barge with the queen.[7] There was no escape.

Anne arrived at the Tower at around five o'clock, through the 'court gate' and barely it made up the wharf before begging those around her to tell the king to be good to her, unsurprisingly overwhelmed by the fact she was accused of adultery with three men.[8] Across the drawbridge and through the Byward postern gate into the outer ward of the Tower, Anne would have been accompanied by Kingston and the Lieutenant of the Tower, Sir Edmund Walsingham.[9] Anne asked Kingston if she would go to the dungeon, but Kingston had the queen's apartments ready for her. Anne collapsed, telling Kingston, 'it is too good for me … Jesu, have mercy on me,' before alternating between crying and laughing in panic.[10]

It was hardly a surprise that Anne was in a panic; the plan to have her arrested was haphazard, to say the least. If Anne had not argued with Norris or snapped at Smeaton the previous weekend, they may not have been implicated at all. Norris supported Anne as queen, and was liked by the Boleyn family, but ultimately would have always done the king's bidding. The man had done little more than have cosy chats with a few of the ladies in Anne's chambers, something entirely permitted at Anne's court. Smeaton was merely a musician, little more than a decoration in the background and carried zero importance. The men were probably sitting in cells in the Tower feeling as blindsided as Anne was, as she was taken to the queen's apartments in total confusion.

It had been planned, probably by Cromwell, to have Anne separated from her loyal ladies, but still with people of trust around her. The ladies to stay in the Tower were well-picked for their roles. Sir William Kingston had his wife Lady Mary put in the apartments. Lady Mary Kingston had served Queen Katharine on and off for almost twenty years and was a member of the Scrope family, long friendly with Cromwell.[11] Another was Lady Margaret Coffin (née Dymocke), wife of Anne's Master of the Horse, Sir William Coffin. Lady Coffin was not part of Anne's regular entourage of ladies, but someone happy to comply with Cromwell's plans.[12] Also appointed to the Tower was Elizabeth Stonor (née Chamber), the Mother of the Maids. Lady Stonor held the court position of being in charge of all ladies in the royal court for all of King Henry's wives and was married to Sir Walter Stonor, the king's trusted serjeant-at-arms. Two of Anne's aunts were also placed in her rooms, firstly Lady Anne Shelton (sister of Thomas Boleyn) who had been running Princess Elizabeth's household. The fact Lady Shelton was in London at the time, and not at Hunsdon does hint that Princess Elizabeth was possibly at court at the time of her mother's arrest. Whether Sir John Shelton, Princess Elizabeth's Comptroller of the household, was also in London goes unmentioned, though Lady Shelton's sister, Lady Alice Clere, could have been in charge at Hunsdon when the Sheltons were away. Lady Clere was known to be far more sympathetic to Princess Mary than Lady Shelton, but in this precarious time, Princess Mary needed to be watched. Also placed with Anne was Lady Elizabeth Boleyn (née Wood), wife of Sir James Boleyn (brother to Thomas Boleyn, Anne Shelton and Alice Clere). Unfortunately for Anne, both James and Elizabeth Boleyn were not supportive of her or the Reformation. Even Anne Shelton, with her own daughters Mary and Margaret in Anne's royal rooms, had become increasingly sympathetic to Princess Mary and her plight, even allowing visitors and letters to Mary in recent months, and accepting small bribes from Ambassador Chapuys.

Sir William Kingston was a man who had seen many nobles in the Tower and was no stranger to seeing innocents being locked away thanks to the king's whims. Despite the widespread destruction of all records around Anne's downfall, letters written by Kingston to Vicegerent Cromwell have survived, giving an insight into how Anne coped in the Tower, and it appears as if Kingston did have some sympathy for the panicking queen. He reported to Cromwell on Anne's movements after her arrest, and asked to have the sacrament moved into her closet so she could pray for mercy, as she told Kingston, 'for I am as clear from the company of man as for sin as I am clear from you and am the Kynges true wedded wife'.[13]

Anne had no idea what was going on beyond rumours, and pleaded with Kingston for answers, asking about the king, where her father was, and where her brother was, believing Rochford was still at court with Henry.[14] Anne knew she was accused of adultery with three men, and asked about Norris and Smeaton in the Tower. She was worried her mother would die of sorrow, and worried about Elizabeth Somerset, Lady Worcester, fearing for her lady's unborn baby.[15] Anne feared for herself too, asking Kingston, 'shall I die without justice?' Kingston assured her that even, 'the poorest subject the King hath, hath justice,' and Anne just laughed at him. She knew better.

Margaret Coffin and Mary Kingston were to be Cromwell's spies in Anne's rooms. Lady Coffin slept on the pallet bed with Lady Boleyn in Anne's rooms, while Lady Kingston slept at the door with her husband. No one was meant to speak with Anne without Mary Kingston present, but this being impractical, Margaret Coffin assured Kingston she could be a fine spy. It was these women who overheard the words that would come to destroy Anne and others at court. Sitting quietly on the evening of her arrest, Anne spoke of what worried her, talking of her fight with Norris the previous Sunday and how he had gone to Anne's almoner, Nicholas Shaxton, to swear on Anne's good name. Anne knew her argument with Norris had come back to haunt her. But then she went on to speak about Sir Francis Weston, a member of the privy chamber that had not been mentioned in any discussion. All was reported to Kingston, who told Cromwell in a letter:

> '… the Queen spoke of Weston, saying that she had spoken to him because he did love her kinswoman, Mary Shelton, and [Anne] said [Weston] loved not his wife, and he made answer to [Anne] again that he loved one in her house better than them both. And the Queen said, "Who is that?" "It is yourself." And then she defied him…'[16]

Anne accidentally implicated Francis Weston in discussing his love for the queen. It was likely only a game, a tease, a joke, but it was useful information, so Cromwell could use that anyway he liked. The careless manner of the arrests screams of a plan not made by Cromwell, as he was always methodical in his behaviour. It would not be wise for any man to be in control of such an audacious plan; everything had to come from the king. Ambassador Chapuys wrote on the day of Anne's arrest, that he knew that Henry wanted to annul his marriage, and Anne's contract with Henry Percy (and possibly even consummation) would be the way to undo the marriage.[17] King Henry already had made up his mind about ruining Anne, and now was simply using hearsay as an excuse to highlight Anne's 'poor' behaviour and make himself look like the victim. If Henry wanted to end his marriage to Anne, he could simply get rid of her. All Cromwell needed to do was follow the king's whims. Henry loved to be the wronged victim, the innocent. If he wanted Anne to be an adulterer, he could easily convince himself. On the night of Anne's arrest, Henry cried at Whitehall to his son Henry Fitzroy, who 'owed a great debt for having escaped from the hands of that cursed and poisoning whore'.[18] Henry said the same of Princess Mary having narrowly escaped Anne's clutches. Henry would believe anything he wanted, and people were more than happy to discredit Anne to ease Henry's conscience. There were never any suggestions that Anne ever wanted to harm Henry Fitzroy. Anne had spoken ill of Princess Mary in the past, but to suggest Anne planned to kill her is more of Henry's fantasies, playing into his victim complex. Why else would a king be so happy to be a cuckold, if not to look like an innocent caught up in a web of a temptress?

The news of Anne's arrest spread domestically and internationally from 2 May. Chapuys fired off letters to Europe, talking of Henry annulling his marriage while Anne and Lord Rochford languished in the Tower.[19] The words of Rodolfo Pio da Carpi, the Italian ambassador in France, imagined the entire Boleyn family arrested over Anne's affair with Mark Smeaton.[20] Sir Richard Bulkeley, Chamberlain of North Wales, received a letter from his brother Robert, who worked in London as a lawyer, who said Anne, her father and brother, plus Smeaton, Norris, 'one other' and 'sundry ladies' were all imprisoned. Bulkeley lamented, 'that Master Norris should have a do with the Queen, and Mark and the other accessory to the same. They are like to suffer, all the more is the pity'.[21] One of the Bulkeley sisters had married into the Norris family, and they all knew Henry Norris, as he had once been Chamberlain of North Wales himself. There was nothing supporters could do or say in the matter.

Those less supportive spoke up right away; a man named Richard Staverton, who had been given a job by Cromwell at Windsor, wrote on 2 May to the Vicegerent, wondering if he could have Norris' room of the Black Rod at Windsor so he could house his fourteen children.[22] Cromwell was busy with his usual workload, combined with an urgent letter about Alice Hymond, a 12-year-old who was attacked, viciously raped, stabbed and beaten, and left for dead in a ditch just four miles from Hampton Court Palace. The young girl managed to survive multiple stab wounds and identified her attacker out of a group of one hundred townspeople in Walton, and Cromwell was the man to ensure the arrest and imprisonment of the attacker.[23] A crime against a woman was not going to go unpunished by a man like Cromwell, which may be why he specifically made sure none of Anne's ladies were arrested or questioned.

He knew Anne was not guilty, but Henry's moods needed to be placated, and Anne's character needed to be discredited. But none of the other ladies of the queen's chambers would come to harm.

Wednesday, 3 May

Sir Henry Norris' clothes were already being redistributed on 3 May, which made it clear that he was never going to be released from the Tower. Thomas Draper, John Dorsett, and Thomas Frere went through an inventory of Norris' items at Greenwich and Richmond, mostly wall hangings, curtains, feather beds, all items made of quality fabrics.[24] Sir William Kingston spoke with Norris in his cell when delivering his dinner, and Norris was not in a good state of mind, seemingly aware that 'his grace's pleasure' would decide on his fate, rather than any facts.[25]

Lord Rochford fared slightly better than Norris. His wife, Jane Boleyn, spoke with William Kingston, trying to see how her husband was coping, and said she would go to the king in search of mercy. Lady Rochford was probably surprised that no one from the king's council had spoken with her, and Lady Rochford wanted to petition both Henry and Cromwell. Lord Rochford was pleased to hear his wife was looking out for him, and wept before Kingston, seeking how he would receive judgement in front of the king's council.[26] Anne herself was surprised not to have been questioned during her stay in the Tower.[27]

Lord Rochford's feelings on the entire affair have been lost in the whole sordid mess. While Anne's arrest and subsequent words are recorded, her brother's arrest and reaction have been wiped from the record. Given King Henry's penchant for overreacting, anything could have happened when Rochford arrived at Westminster to see the king. Perhaps Henry interrogated Rochford over what he knew about alleged adultery in the queen's rooms. Perhaps Rochford was accused of covering up his sister's affairs. Who exactly came up with the idea that Rochford slept with his own sister seems to be muddied by a combination of affidavit destruction and time. Regardless of Henry's reasoning behind having Rochford arrested, it would have felt like a deep betrayal. As George Boleyn, he first appeared at court for the Christmas mummery on 25 December 1514 alongside his father, to dance in the masked entertainment for the festive season.[28] But while Mary and Anne Boleyn were off to France and elsewhere furthering their educations, George Boleyn likely stayed close to his father, a diplomat of the highest order with the king's total faith. His mother, Elizabeth Boleyn, likewise was at court serving Queen Katharine, but George Boleyn does not appear in records again until 1522 when he received a joint grant with his father for land in Kent. It was likely his eighteenth birthday. Two years later, he received Grimston Manor in Kent from the king,[29] and was already a favourite at court participating in the king's various pastimes while his father continued with the hard work of serving the king. This opportunity to be close to the king may have come through his sister, Mary, who had been the king's mistress. Or perhaps Henry simply liked Thomas Boleyn's young son for company. George Boleyn soon after married Jane Parker, quite a coup for them both, and he was taken into the privy chamber in 1525, only to lose the position six months later due to Cardinal Wolsey's Eltham Ordinance, a mixture of budget cuts and nepotism hires. George Boleyn became a Royal Cupbearer and received payment for his lack of position.[30] But it was not long before he was back in favour when his sister Anne became the target of King Henry's affections. By 1529, George Boleyn was knighted, given many titles and offices, in the king's privy chamber and became Lord Rochford when his father was elevated to Earl of Wiltshire and Ormond. Despite his young age,[31] Rochford became an ambassador to France like his father before him, travelling between London and France for the rest of his life.

Lord Rochford was well known as Anne Boleyn's brother and the son of Thomas Boleyn, one of King Henry's loyal attendants. Anne's ascendancy meant Rochford's ascendancy, and as brother of the new queen, he was virtually untouchable. Rochford was known as intelligent and talented, a fine poet and translator, and well-versed in matters of religion as King Henry oversaw changes to his country.[32] While Rochford was also known as a something of a womaniser,[33] and a bit too arrogant,[34] there was never any suggestion of impropriety on his part. Poor Lord Rochford likely travelled to Westminster on 2 May looking for answers to rumours about his sister and never saw daylight again.

Kingston also made note of Sir Richard Page and Sir Thomas Wyatt. The date of their arrests goes unrecorded, but it may have been on Wednesday, 3 May, or possibly the day after. Why these two men were arrested goes wholly unmentioned. Thomas Wyatt had once been interested in Anne, and much has been made of the pair growing up near one another in Kent, but suggestions of being childhood friends or romantically involved as adults bears little fruit. Wyatt had been working for the king since 1515, first at court and then as an ambassador, promoted by his father's constant good work in royal service. Wyatt's sister, Margaret Lee, did work in Anne's household, and the families were well known to one another, but no one mentioned any long-past romance between Anne and Wyatt beyond reading into Wyatt's lauded poetry. He may have been arrested on suspicion of what had happened in their past, but aside from a few rumours and Wyatt's poetry, there was no proof.

Why Sir Richard Page was arrested made even less sense. Page was a long-time courtier to the king; his stepdaughter was married to Sir Edward Seymour. Page had worked in Henry Fitzroy's household and was trusted by King Henry. At least two decades older than Anne Boleyn, Page was a quiet career courtier, a tradition that ran in his family. His father, Henry Page, had been a soldier and died when his son was very young, while his grandfather, also Sir Richard Page, was Receiver for King Edward IV.[35] The Page family could trace its roots back through royal service for hundreds of years through Page's grandmother, Lady Beatrice Burgh, who came from the illustrious de Warrene family. The de Warrene and de Burgh families had a colourful history, but by 1536, Sir Richard Page was a quiet man in his fifties simply serving his king. It was likely that Page, like Wyatt, was being interrogated for what he knew about Anne and the court, rather than for having any kind of inappropriate relationship with her.

Sir Edward Baynton, Anne's chamberlain, wrote to his old friend Sir William Fitzwilliam on 3 May, perplexed by the whole business. Still at Greenwich with Anne's household, Baynton told Fitzwilliam:

> 'There is much communication that no man will confess anything against her, but only Mark of any actual thing. It would, in my foolish conceit, much touch the King's honour if it should no further appear. I cannot believe but that the other two [Norris and Weston] are as fully culpable as he, but they keep each other's counsel. I think much of the communication which took place on the last occasion between the Queen and Master Norris. Mr. Almoner [Shaxton] told me that I might speak with Master Secretary [Shaxton] and you, and more

> plainly express my opinion in case they have confessed… I have mused much at the conduct of Mrs. Margery, who has used herself strangely toward me of late, being her friend as I have been. There has been great friendship of late between the Queen and her. I hear further that the Queen stands stiffly in her opinion, that she will not be convicted, which I think is in the trust that she has in the other two.'[36]

Information leaked like a sieve from the Tower. Anne's behaviour was being shared, and she felt positive Norris and Weston would not say anything to implicate her or themselves in an affair. Smeaton's movements go unrecorded, but his confession on either Sunday or Monday was surely extracted from him, something that could not be tried on noblemen like Norris and Weston. Baynton's opinion of Margery Horsman is unusual. The pair knew each other well and had worked in Anne's household for the entire time Anne had been married to the king. Margery Horsman had probably spoken to Cromwell or his men, but there could be no harm coming to her, or any of the other ladies. The fact Mistress Horsman no longer trusted Baynton, a man she knew to be loyal to Anne, speaks volumes about how the ladies of her privy chamber felt. Surely if Anne had been having affairs, all the ladies would have known, and yet they were not interrogated or arrested. There is not a single mention from anyone that Anne had done anything wrong. No one suggested she might be guilty, and all the ladies knew this. Those from Anne's household all had their freedom, and no way to help their mistress. And not a single member of the nobility had spoken up in Anne's favour, despite her vast familial links at court.

On 3 May, Archbishop Thomas Cranmer was back in London, making the hasty twenty-five-mile journey from his manor at Knole. Cromwell had sent for Cranmer with urgency and must have done so as early as Sunday to allow time for Cranmer to arrive. Cranmer wrote to the king at once after hearing what happened to Anne. In his naivety, not knowing Henry was constructing the destruction of his wife, Cranmer wrote a letter to the king, carefully hedging his bets:

> 'I cannot deny that you have great causes of heaviness and that your honour is highly touched. God never sent you a like trial; but if He find you no less patient and thankful than when all

> things succeeded to your wish… If the reports of the Queen be true, they are only to her dishonour, not yours. I am clean amazed, for I had never better opinion of woman; but I think your Highness would not have gone so far if she had not been culpable. I was most bound to her of all creatures living, and therefore beg that I may, with your Grace's favour, wish and pray that she may declare herself innocent. Yet if she be found guilty, I repute him not a faithful subject who would not wish her punished without mercy… I loved her not a little for the love which I judged her to bear towards God and His Gospel, so if she be proved culpable there is not one that loveth God and His Gospel that ever will favour her but must hate her above all other'.[37]

Cranmer was in panic mode, not necessarily for Anne, but also for himself and the Reformation. Having Anne on the throne was the backbone of everything Cranmer and Cromwell had built. A reformist queen was what they needed to establish the new religion in England. Using the rules of the new religion was how Cranmer and Cromwell broke the Catholic Church. The king would not have looked to the new religion had he been able to divorce Queen Katharine any other way, and they knew it. Cranmer signed off his letter to the king, 'I trust, therefore, you will bear no less zeal to the Gospel than you did before, as your favour to the Gospel was not led by affection to her'.[38] Cranmer's letter to the king has long been discussed as something borne out of his affection and respect for Anne. That may have been true, as Cranmer admired Anne, but he was making sure he looked like a neutral party in the whole affair, and that his position, and the Reformation were at least safe in this time. The letter has a postscript stating that Cranmer had visited the Star Chamber after he wrote the note, with Chancellor Thomas Audley, John de Vere, Earl of Oxford, Robert Radcliffe, Earl of Sussex, and Lord Chamberlain, William Lord Sandys. They summoned the archbishop to 'tell' him that Anne was guilty and that the plan to remove the queen was going ahead. Cranmer told the king they, 'declared to me such things as you wished to make me privy to. For this, I am much bounden to your Grace. They will report our conference. I am sorry such faults can be proved against the Queen as they report'.[39] Cranmer had made a huge mistake in suggesting Anne may have been innocent, because in Henry's mind, she was guilty, and facts no longer mattered. The king busied himself with other matters, such as the possible meeting between himself and his nephew, King James of Scotland,[40] and Cranmer did not risk his reputation by mentioning Anne again.

Thursday, 4 May

Another arrest came on 4 May, the strange accusations thrown at Sir William Brereton. Brereton, a man around a decade older than Anne, worked with his brothers Urian, Randle, and Roger at court, with William and Urian (Brereton sons, numbers six and eight of nine, respectively) both in Henry VIII's privy chamber. Originally from Cheshire, Brereton's father Sir Randolph/Randle Brereton served in Henry VII's chamber and fought alongside Henry VIII in France, gaining accolades and building successful lives for his thirteen children.[41] John, Thomas and Peter Brereton all became priests. Eleanor, Jane, Anne, and Elizabeth Brereton were all married off to landed gentry in the Cheshire area, while Randle, Roger, William, and Urian were set up for a life in the royal household as knighted landed gentry (son Richard was born with a mental disability and was provided for, while remaining son Robert was something of a black sheep, the only son never to be knighted[42]). William Brereton entered Henry VIII's privy chamber by 1521, with his brother Urian joining him in approximately 1527. William Brereton gained the king's confidence and friendship, and Brereton's landholdings in Cheshire, which had been small due to his father's lands being split between so many sons, became enormous in 1530, giving him one of the largest incomes at court at 10,000*l* (£4.5 million today) a year.[43] Cheshire and the Welsh Marshes, largely all under Brereton's control by this time, had no position in the House of Commons, as it remained a county palatine, with its own legal system and parliament. Sir William Brereton had almost total control over the region thanks to his gifts of land from the king and had a list of lands and preferments longer than most at court. He married Elizabeth Somerset, Lady Savage in 1530, and gained control of her late husband's (Sir John Savage) lands in Cheshire. The Savage lands had been forfeited to the crown to recover debts when Savage died in the Tower after being arrested for murder of a justice.[44] The Savage family had been powerful Lancastrian supporters who helped Henry VII onto the throne and taking over these western lands, and John Savage's widow elevated Brereton even further than his already prime position close to the king. Lady Savage was born Elizabeth Somerset, daughter of Charles Somerset (the illegitimate son of Henry Beaufort, thus cousin of Henry VII) and Elizabeth Herbert (daughter of Mary Woodville, sister of Queen Elizabeth Woodville).[45] This made Elizabeth Somerset, Lady Savage a second cousin of Henry VIII on both sides of her family. (Elizabeth Somerset can be easily confused with her sister-in-law Elizabeth Somerset (née Browne), Lady Worcester, who became the focus of investigation about Anne Boleyn's adultery.)

In terms of power and influence, Sir William Brereton was almost untouchable by 1530 when he became Chamberlain of Cheshire and travelled his lands to gain support for his king's annulment quest.[46] Brereton was one of the few who witnessed Henry and Anne's marriage in 1533, and dispensed justice with a heavy hand in Cheshire and Wales, making him well noted as an ally or adversary to many.

What Brereton had failed to achieve in his long career was winning the support of Thomas Cromwell and had no want or need of the Vicegerent's company. Cromwell was loathed by so many of the powerful and wealthy court, their disdain evident for the secretive common newcomer the king kept in his offices. Cromwell was old friends with Rowland Lee,[47] Bishop of Coventry and Lichfield and Lord President of the Council of Wales and the Marches, who held total control over northwest England and Wales in ecclesiastical matters. The Reformation was taking shape far slower than Cromwell and Lee liked, and the lawlessness in Wales was a constant headache for Cromwell as he sought to get the country functioning under England's laws.[48] Brereton seemingly did not care for dispensing justice, nor obeying laws, and was accused of multiple murders, theft, releasing guilty criminals, and much more in the Welsh areas.[49] As early as 1518, Brereton had been investigated for covering up a murder committed by one of his relatives and a servant, who killed a Master Swettenham during a bowls match. Brereton had developed a habit of letting murderers go free in Wales and Cheshire and let lawlessness run wild on Henry Fitzroy's estates when he was meant to be running them on behalf of the king's son. Instead of investigating corruption in Welsh monasteries, Brereton was participating in corruption in Welsh monasteries.[50]

But in 1534, Brereton pushed his luck too far. One of Brereton's men, John ap Griffith Eyton, accused Brereton of multiple crimes in the Star

Chamber in London, including the murder of two of Eyton's relatives, and the deaths of two servants, one named William Hamner in Bromfield west of Ludlow.[51] In return, Brereton accused Eyton himself of the murder of Hamner, but Eyton was acquitted in a trial in London and released. Brereton took Eyton for a walk through London, where they crossed a judicial line into Brereton's city property, and Eyton was rearrested and shipped back to Holt Castle in Wexham, where he was immediately tried and convicted by a jury of Brereton's allies and hanged by 9 a.m. the morning after he arrived.[52]

Getting away with crimes far from London was one thing, but this time, Brereton had heard a not guilty verdict in the Star Chamber of London, on Cromwell's turf, and then committed kidnapping and murder anyway. Cromwell was never going to forgive Brereton for what happened to John ap Griffith Eyton, but there was also not much Cromwell could do to have Brereton pay for any of his many crimes. Brereton had a reputation for corruption, which seemingly did not bother Brereton or the king. Power over the Welsh Marshes sat entirely in Brereton's hands, which was stifling the people and the advancements Cromwell needed to make in the region at the king's command. Already a rumoured womaniser and adulterer, an accusation of adultery with the queen was the perfect way to remove the dictator from his region, and no one was in a position to complain, lest they fall under the king's suddenly paranoid eye. As George Constantine wrote in 1540 of Brereton, 'if any of them was innocent, it was he'.[53] But no one was going to miss Brereton when he was gone, and his brother, Sir Urian Brereton, took much of his brother's lands and power, alongside Cromwell allies Sir Piers Dutton, Sir Rhys Mansell, and Hugh Starkey.[54]

Coincidentally, a letter landed on Cromwell's desk after Brereton's arrest, written by Brereton himself before he was sent to the Tower, asking to be given multiple religious houses which were being closed under the dissolution of the monasteries. Until the very end, Brereton looked after only himself.[55]

Friday, 5 May

Three days on from Anne Boleyn's arrest, rumours were travelling far and wide, and it was immediately obvious there would be no coming back from the charges. Once someone was in the Tower for an offence against the king, there could be no backtracking. Among the high-profile arrests of powerful men like Norris and Brereton, the shocking news about Lord Rochford, and the puzzling arrests of Page and Wyatt, Francis, Weston's name was thrown in as a possible lover to Anne, and yet was not high profile, shocking or puzzling. Yet young Weston was about to throw his family's quiet name towards infamy. Yet, if Anne had not mentioned Weston when she was arrested, he may have been spared entirely, not considered a suspicious courtier, nor had he angered the king or Cromwell enough to be arrested.

Sir Francis Weston was only about 25 years old in 1536 but had been at court for ten years. His father, Sir Richard Weston, was a quiet man himself, coming from a relatively unknown family with small landholdings, with a father and uncle in royal service and the Church under Henry VII. Richard Weston likely started his royal service for Queen Elizabeth of York, listed in the queen's accounts from 1502, around the time he married Anne Sandys, one of the queen's ladies.[56] Richard Weston paired up with his wife's distant relation Sir William Sandys, also in the king's service in 1506, and Weston was named custodian of Castle Cornet, a role held by his father. By 1509, Richard Weston was in the privy chamber as Henry VII passed away, immortalised in the sketch made of the great king's passing. Weston went into Henry VIII's household, and his wife, Lady Anne Weston, went into Queen Katharine's household immediately after the coronation. Sir Richard Weston was always at the king's side, including in battle, working as an ambassador, accompanying Princess Mary Tudor to France for her wedding, and received a string of offices and awards for his loyal service.[57] In 1525, Weston was appointed Treasurer of Calais, and so his son Francis was placed in the king's household.

Young Francis Weston was decades younger than the king but was quiet and likeable. He was beating the king at bowls, cards, and tennis in no time.[58] Sir Richard Weston returned to England in 1529 to testify in Henry and Katharine's annulment trial, and in 1530 found a suitable wife for his son, Anne Pickering. Richard Weston had long been Master of the Wards and had the wardship of Anne Pickering since an early age, as she was the sole heiress of Sir Christopher Pickering and his wife Jane Lewkner, and set to inherit the Pickering and Moresby estates plus lands in Yorkshire, Middlesex, Cumberland, and Westmorland.[59] Francis Weston and Anne Pickering were only 19 and 14 respectively when they married, and seem to not have spent much time together, as Weston was at court, made a gentleman of the privy chamber in 1531, and then knighted and made a Knight of the Bath in 1533.

Sir Francis Weston, like his father, remained a quiet, likeable courtier in the 1530s. His son Henry was born in 1535,[60] and a daughter Anne born in 1536, and all was seemingly fine with the Weston family. But unlike his father, Francis Weston had not built a substantial income over his time at court, as his wife's estates were still in possession of her mother, and his generous father, Richard Weston, was still alive and well, living at the new Sutton Place in Surrey, a manor suitable for a king's visit.[61] Weston loved the fun and flashy life at court, and had racked up 925*l* (£400,000 today) in debts by 1536. Weston was a regular visitor in the queen's rooms, just like Norris; as Baynton wrote to William Kingston, Norris and Weston kept each other's counsel. How long the completely trusted long-time friend of the king and the young, energetic gentleman had both been visiting the queen's rooms is unknown, though much of their attention seems to have been showered on Anne's cousins the Shelton sisters. Norris' engagement to Margaret Shelton seems to have been a reasonably informal affair, and Anne Boleyn had chastised Weston for flirting with Lady Shelton as she was to marry Norris. This led to the infamous moment when Weston joked that Norris came to the queen's rooms for Anne Boleyn, not her cousins. Anne had accused Weston of neglecting his own wife, and Weston joked of loving Mary Shelton, but loved his queen over his wife and any others. Anne shut him down,[62] the courtly game gone too far, but all was harmless. Many such jokes about loving the sovereign's wife, which was almost expected, likely happened in many parts of court. Had Anne not mentioned this encounter on 2 or 3 May, Weston's name may not have ever come up in the scandal at all.

Given that Sir William Kingston's report to Vicegerent Cromwell after Anne Boleyn's arrest is the first mention of Weston, he was likely arrested around the same time as the incredulous Sir Richard Page and confused Sir Thomas Wyatt. The bombshell of Norris' arrest on 1 May and the surprising arrest of Brereton on 4 May have caused Weston's arrest to get lost in the panic, which was likely the same day as Brereton's arrest.[63] What became immediately clear was that Francis Weston was emphatic about his innocence, as were the others. Weston's parents and wife made an appeal for his life, to no avail. By the close of Friday, 5 May, King Henry had likely already decided on who he wanted painted as the co-conspirators in this imaginary crime.

CHAPTER 16

Some Force Other Than Reason

Saturday, 6 May

A letter which now rests in the British Library, dated 6 May, is claimed to have been written by Anne Boleyn to her husband. Sir William Kingston had mentioned to Vicegerent Cromwell days earlier that he had told Anne he would pass on a letter from Anne to Cromwell to be given to the king,[1] and she may have been given the chance to have her thoughts written by a scribe, as the letter does not bear Anne's handwriting. The letter, irreparably damaged by fire and time, has been long considered to be a forgery, because why would such a letter be allowed to survive when all other papers on the incident were destroyed? This letter would have been the first item to be destroyed if Cromwell planned to keep it a secret. More recent studies make arguments for the letter being real and place the blame on Cromwell for not passing the letter to the king.[2] An excellent recent study of the letter suggests it was written by a scribe for Anne in the Tower, given to Cromwell, who then did not show the king, and after Cromwell's death, his adopted son Ralph Sadler took the letter, eventually passing it to William Cecil, who kept an enormous archive of correspondence. Then it went into the Camden collection, then the Cotton collection before being burned in the fire of 1731, and only copies are now available to easily read.[3]

Vicegerent Cromwell was a fastidiously organised man, and all papers were carefully catalogued right down to his remembrances, daily to-do-lists he made himself. But the Cromwell archive was ripped apart in 1540, first by his supporters in an attempt to save him from a conspiracy, and then by the king's men after Cromwell's death as they struggled to run court and government without Cromwell.[4] He very rarely ever stepped out of line and had he got a letter from Anne and hidden it, there could have been dire consequences. Had Anne written a letter to her husband, it would not have been a secret; Kingston, along with the women staying within the Tower would have known, and Cromwell would have been caught hiding the letter. It is more likely if Anne did write a letter, that Henry either did not wish to see it, or he had Cromwell take the letter away. (In 1540, Cromwell wrote a Tower letter, and Sadler was made to read it aloud three times to a tearful king, who then had the letter taken away.[5] Henry could have done a similar thing in 1536).

The letter opens:

> 'Your grace's displeasure and my imprisonment are things so strange to me, that what to write, or what to excuse, I am altogether ignorant. Whereas you send to me (willing me to confess a truth and so obtain your favour), by such a one, whom you know to be mine ancient, professed enemy, I no sooner received this message by him, than I rightly conceived your meaning; and if, as you say, confessing a truth indeed may procure my safety, I shall with all willingness and duty, perform your duty. But let not your grace ever imagine that your poor wife will be brought to acknowledge a fault, where not so much as a thought ever proceeded. And to speak a truth, never a prince had wife more loyal in all duty, and in all true affection, than you have ever found in Anne Bulen — with which name and place I could willingly have contented myself, if God and your grace's pleasure had been so pleased. Neither did I at any time so far forget myself in my exaltation or received queenship, but that I always looked for such alteration as I now find; for the ground of my preferment being on no surer foundation than your grace's fancy, the least alteration was fit and sufficient (I knew) to draw that fancy to some other subject'.[6]

Anne went on to write that she wanted a fair trial so that she could show the world she was innocent of such crimes. But Anne was no fool; she would have known as much as anyone that those arrested were not going to be freed from the Tower. Anne knew herself to be innocent and wrote as such, and asked the king to be lenient on those who were also accused.[7] The king was now known as a cuckold at home and abroad and had done nothing to refute those claims. A man who needed to appear masculine and powerful at all times had gone along with this chaotic plan to blame anyone in a whirlwind of gossip and finger-pointing. People loved to talk of the drama, saying Anne would have men lined up to sleep with her at night, including her brother.[8] Lord Rochford had likely been thrown in the Tower for concealing his sister's affairs, or at least protesting her innocence, but it rapidly changed into a rumour that they too were sleeping together. Surely Anne knew that the king could not simply change his mind at this stage of his plan. There can be no way of knowing if Anne's letter is real or not, but if it is real, the Tower letter reveals the voice of a woman who knows she is innocent. There seemed no one, anywhere, who appeared confident of Anne's guilt, except King Henry.

Monday, 8 May

Sir Thomas Wyatt and Sir Richard Page were both still in the Tower, though 'without threat of life', and nothing surrounding their arrests survives, not even the date of their arrests, though it was likely within a day or so of Anne's arrest.[9] Both had been summoned to the court to answer questions and were stunned to find themselves implicated. Page's relationship with Cromwell never recovered from the betrayal and Wyatt complained about his arrest until his death in 1542. As no crimes had been committed by anyone, it was little wonder these men were flabbergasted by their summons to see the king himself to answer for what they knew about Anne. Sir Henry Wyatt wrote to his son, Sir Thomas, on 7 May, begging him to do whatever the king wanted. Sir Henry was in Allington, eighty-five miles northwest of London, and was too sick to travel to see his son. Sir Henry wrote, 'I pray to God, give him grace long to be with him, and about him, that hath found out this matter, which hath been given him of God, and the false traitors to be punished according to justice to the example of others'.[10] Sir Henry Wyatt could only hope his old friend Cromwell would watch over his son in the Tower.

There were others in Anne's rooms who were nervous. George Taylor, Anne's general receiver was seen visibly relieved that he was not among the men working for Anne who were hauled away.[11] Harry Webb, Sewer of the Chamber, was suspected, not unusual since Norris as Groom of the Stool had been taken away, and the men's jobs had similar privacy and responsibility in the king and queen's households.[12] Anne's almoner, Bishop Nicholas Shaxton, in his haste to ensure he was not implicated in any wrongdoing, wrote to Cromwell, honouring Cromwell's much earlier request for a chantership of Salisbury Cathedral. Shaxton thanked Cromwell for all he had done for him over the years, including making Shaxton a bishop, and offered a prebend to one of Cromwell's friends, as a little bribe.[13] Shaxton had already left London for Ramsbury in Wiltshire and was likely hoping that the whole sordid business would pass him by.

The arrests kept coming. William Latimer was one of Anne's chaplains, though he was arrested on charges of importing forbidden books from the Low Countries. Latimer had been in prison after being arrested in Sandwich and was transferred to London.[14] He was not touched by the affair scandal, but it was hardly a glowing review of Anne's household management or reading material. Latimer was released on 12 May and allowed to continue his studies, ignored by King Henry and Chancellor Audley, and unable to say anything in support of Anne. But his arrest in Sandwich and transfer to London only made for even more gossip; but like the arrests of Page and Wyatt, it was more about what Latimer knew, rather than being accused of any wrongdoing.

Sir Francis Bryan also arrived at court on Monday, 8 May, along with Sir Nicholas Carew, although Carew was never under any threat. Bryan was interrogated personally by the king, who had the man thrown in the Tower.[15] Bryan had been coming and going from the court for several months, seeing Cromwell each time, creating a paper trail about their dealings over money and lands Bryan needed help to gain.[16] Why the king suddenly felt the need to involve Bryan, such a strong Jane Seymour supporter, made no sense at all, but the king was grasping at any suggestions or rumours. Sir Francis Bryan's arrest and interrogation was prolonged, and he was placed in the Tower by the end of the day on 8 May. [17] He would only be in the Tower for four days, released at the same time as William Latimer, but these arrests at least gave the impression the king was doing a thorough investigation, and those set free were innocent, while those who remained in the Tower looked guilty.

Tuesday, 9 May

Vicegerent Cromwell needed nothing more to send Mark Smeaton, Henry Norris, Francis Weston, and William Brereton to trial. Anne Boleyn had not been interrogated, other than speaking to the Duke of Norfolk and Sir William Paulet when she was first arrested. Sir William Fitzwilliam claimed he had confessions from each of the men, but no one seemed to believe that. Smeaton had given up and admitted guilt to save himself without success, and no witnesses had come forward. None of this haphazard plan bears any resemblance to a Cromwell trial.[18] This case had all the hallmarks of an angry man grasping at any excuse to get rid of his wife.

Noblemen and gentlemen needed to be called to London, both to be the jury on the oyer and terminer cases of Norris, Weston, Smeaton and Brereton and as the jury of their peers for Anne and George Boleyn. Others were called to give information or evidence to the king.[19] The trial date for the accused men was set for 12 May; any evidence collected was to be done in haste, as Henry was not going to give himself time to change his mind about this entire mess.

Thursday, 11 May

Sir Henry Wyatt wrote to Vicegerent Cromwell from his home in Allington in Kent. Cromwell had sent Wyatt a letter the day before, assuring his old friend that his son, Sir Thomas Wyatt, was safe and in no danger. Cromwell and Wyatt had a friendship that spanned at least twelve years when Cromwell worked for Wyatt as a lawyer in several matters. Now, with Wyatt's son in the Tower, Cromwell was about to do his dear friend another favour and preserve Thomas Wyatt's safety.[20] Sir Henry was interested in when the king was going to release his son so that he could 'show [Thomas Wyatt] that this punishment, that he has for this matter, is more for the displeasure that he has done to God otherwise, and to admonish him to fly vice and serve God better'.[21] The letter shows that Henry Wyatt was not concerned for his son's life but rather just an angry father whose wayward son had got himself into trouble. Henry Wyatt had already retired from court, but no doubt knew of the difficulties his son had in his court position.

A letter on the same day shows how indiscriminately the whole arrangement had come together, when Sir William Paulet wrote from Hampton Court Palace with the king, where the Duke of Norfolk was also staying, stating that Norfolk was having trouble preparing the jury to oversee the trial of his niece and nephew. Norfolk could not understand who he was to place on the panel of judges, how many barons were needed and how many commissioners had to be appointed for the trials.[22] Norfolk was unlikely to know that many men had already been summoned and he could have the choice of those who were able to arrive in London in time. It illustrates how little preparation had gone into this plan. But who could blame anyone involved for wishing to make the case airtight; after all, Henry could still change his mind, and until Anne was convicted and the royal marriage annulled, the wrath of a king could have fallen on anyone.

CHAPTER 17

Dead Men Walking

Friday, 12 May

As 12 May dawned at Westminster, the juries for the oyer and terminers in Middlesex and Kent were brought forward before the judges' panel to deliver their rulings so the trials could go ahead.[1] The Duke of Norfolk sat as the Lord Steward of the judges' panel as expected, alongside the highest ranked men in the realm — Charles Brandon, Duke of Suffolk, John de Vere, the Earl of Oxford, Ralph Neville, Earl of Westmorland, Thomas Boleyn, Earl of Wiltshire, and Robert Radcliffe, Earl of Sussex. None of these men would dare do anything against the king, and expecting Thomas Boleyn to sit in judgement when his children's lives were on the line was an extraordinarily cruel move on the king's part, though as an earl, he had little choice. Boleyn may have offered to be part of the jury to gain whatever grace he could with Henry, in the hope of showing the Boleyns' support for the king. The jury, the same for both oyer and terminer cases, had met on 10 May and already determined that there was a case to answer for the Middlesex-based crimes committed at Westminster and Hampton Court. They had also met on 11 May and determined there was a case to answer regarding the Kent-based accusations relating to the crimes committed at Greenwich and Eltham.[3] These hearings had simply been formalities, decreeing that the trials of the men could take place on 12 May, as they claimed to have enough evidence and cause to move ahead.

The Panel

In addition to the nobles on the judges' panel sat many of the trusted legal minds of the realm, the finest being Thomas Cromwell, alongside Lord Chancellor Thomas Audley. William Lord Sandys, Sir William Fitzwilliam and Sir William Paulet, all high-level courtiers loyal to Henry sat on the panel.[4] Presiding over the case was Sir Giles Heron, whose wife, Lady Cecily Heron, was a daughter of Sir Thomas More. It was no secret they were deeply Catholic and pro-Princess Mary. The foreman of the trial was Edward Willoughby, uncle of Catherine Willoughby, the Duke of Suffolk's wife, another anti-Boleyn couple; the Duke of Suffolk had never supported Henry's second marriage but had kept quiet and away from court. Sir Walter Hungerford and William Musgrave were hostile debtors of Cromwell, the pair personally owing Cromwell over 3000*l* (£1.5 million today) and had to do as they were told. Sir Richard Tempest was another of Cromwell's debtors from Yorkshire, who hated the Boleyns.[5] Sir Anthony Hungerford was close with Sir Edward Seymour, and his aunt was Jane Seymour's grandmother. Sir John Hamden was a relative of Sir William Paulet, a strong Catholic, as was Sir Robert Dormer, while Sir John Fitz-James, Lord Chief Justice, was a man loyal to the king and Cromwell. William Askew (father of Anne Askew), was described as a personal friend to Princess Mary.[6] Sir William Sidney was close friends with the Duke of Suffolk, Sir Thomas Palmer was a lawyer and MP under Cromwell's patronage, and Sir John Baldwin, the judge who oversaw the oyer and terminer meetings for Middlesex on 10 May before the trial, was the Chief Justice of the Common Pleas and not a man prone to sympathy despite being Sir Henry Norris' brother-in-law.[7] Judge Sir John Spelman oversaw the oyer and terminer meetings for the Kent crimes and had overseen plenty of cases that resulted in handing out death sentences.

Catholics Sir Walter Luke, Sir Anthony Fitzherbert, Sir William Shelley, Sir Thomas Englefield, Sir John Porte, and Sir Richard Lyster served as Justices of the King's Bench and Justices of the Courts of Common Pleas, many of whom were members of Gray's Inn like Thomas Cromwell and had expressed their distaste for the Reformation. Still, they did their duty to Henry throughout the previous five years of trials against Catholics.

When Sir Henry Norris, Sir Francis Weston, Sir William Brereton, and Mark Smeaton were brought to trial, they likely knew their fate. After all, the oyer and terminer meetings had deliberated on the information and already made their determinations. The choices about the make-up of the jury would have told them their fates before any words had been uttered in court. But the reality was that there were no witnesses and no evidence. Vicegerent Cromwell had to fabricate the entire case, and surely it was hoped that no one was foolish enough to point out the glaring errors. It did not matter what anyone on the panel believed, or what the accused said; the king believed his wife had slept with one hundred men and wanted her punished. It was likely something Henry simply imagined to make himself feel better while enjoying himself with parties and ladies as his wife sat in the Tower. Many tales of Anne's sexual exploits have arisen since her death, yet none lean towards any kind of truth. As Ambassador Chapuys told his masters, 'you never saw a prince or husband show or wear his horns [be a cuckold] more patiently and lightly than this one does. I leave you to guess the cause of it'.[8] From the outset, it was clear Henry wanted rid of Anne.

The Evidence

The case had no witnesses, and the defendants had no way of arguing their innocence. There was of course the disagreement between Anne and Smeaton on 29 April (though no one came forward to recall the argument in court), followed by Smeaton's alleged 30 April confession. The Queen's words with Norris on 30 April were heard by many, including Sir Edward Baynton[9]; a mere mention of courtly love by Weston more than a year prior was repeated, and absolutely nothing surfaced about Brereton.

There were also the alleged reports of three of Anne's ladies, not officially interviewed or interrogated, having their words used as evidence. There was Elizabeth Somerset, Countess of Worcester's words after she argued with her brother, Anthony Browne, suggesting indiscreet behaviour in Anne's rooms, plus whispers from 'Nan Cobham', and 'another'. It is plausible Sir Anthony Browne and his sister Lady Worcester had words of some nature and the argument was twisted for convenience by their brother, Sir William Fitzwilliam. But Lady Worcester herself was not asked to give evidence, oral or written.

The identity of Nan Cobham has never been identified with certainty but is most likely Anne Brooke (née Bray), Lady Cobham, wife of Cromwell ally George Brooke, 9th Baron Cobham. The Cobham family was a huge one; George Brooke was of one of thirteen children, and all the multiple generations of the Cobham family lived and married around the court. Any number of Lady Cobhams could show up in records, and since George Brooke's grandmother was named Anne Boleyn (she was an aunt of Thomas Boleyn), many of them could have been close to the royal chambers. The Cobham couple and Cromwell had long been friends; Cromwell was godfather to their son Henry, Cromwell regularly loaned Lord Cobham money, and they regularly sent each other gifts.[10] Innocent talk between husband and wife or between friends could easily be made into innuendo needed for an arrest. After all, when it became time for the trials, neither Lady Cobham nor Lady Worcester needed to give evidence of any kind.

The one other lady who had been whispering could have easily been Margery Horsman. She had been close to Anne Boleyn in the lead up to the arrests, and Edward Baynton had remarked on the closeness between the women. While Margery Horsman did have extended familial connections to high profile pro-Princess Mary Catholics, and the fact the extended Horsman family owed much to Thomas Cromwell, there was no reason for Mistress Horsman to say anything against her mistress. Again, she was not interviewed or interrogated, nor expected to give evidence.

The fact that the third lady was only listed as 'another' leaves the window for speculation wide open, and any number of false allegations could be used by an unnamed witness. This could be where the theory that Jane Boleyn, Lady Rochford (by choice or accident) spoke against her husband. Lady Rochford never said anything negative about her husband or the other accused men; she was never even interrogated. Another possible 'other' could be Lady Margaret Lee (née Wyatt), who was a good friend of Anne Boleyn and the families had known one another for years. If there ever had been anything resembling a relationship between Anne and Sir Thomas Wyatt in the past, Margaret Lee would have most likely known about it. Sir Thomas Wyatt was also not questioned beyond his initial meeting with King Henry and was not accused of any wrongdoing. Margaret Lee also could have said something inadvertently that could be twisted to use in court. Her husband, Sir Anthony Lee, worked for Thomas Cromwell and despite the case against Anne Boleyn going ahead, Lady Margaret Lee remained close with Cromwell post-1536. But sadly, we lack as much concrete evidence today as was available in 1536.

Also mentioned was Bridget, Lady Wingfield (née Wiltshire), who had died in approximately January 1534 after giving birth to her eighteenth child.[11] John Spelman noted in court that Lady Wingfield had mentioned, on her deathbed, Anne's inappropriate behaviour in the past. Much of the paperwork is either destroyed or lost, and no detail is given. But why would a woman make such a comment on her deathbed? What did she know of Anne's past? A single letter from Anne to Lady Wingfield still exists but is undated and could have been in approximately 1532, as this is the period when Anne signed her name as Anne Rochford. Anne does say in the letter, after admitting that she had been neglected her old friend:

> '... and I trust you do know me for such a one that will write nothing to comfort you in your trouble, but I will abide by it as long as I live. And therefore I pray you leave your indiscreet trouble, both for displeasing of God, and displeasing of me, that does love you so entirely. And trusting in God that you thus do, I make an end. With the ill hand of your own assured friend during my life, Anne Rochford'.[12]

What Lady Wingfield did to displease Anner Boleyn so deeply cannot be proven. Her second husband, Imperial ambassador, Sir Nicholas Hervey, died in 1532,[13] and Lady Wingfield soon returned to court to marry courtier Sir Robert Tyrwhitt, of whom Anne Boleyn did not which may have been the issue.

Lady Wingfield had previously been at court since at least 1520, serving Queen Katharine. Her first husband had been Sir Richard Wingfield (father of her first ten children), a loyal courtier to Henry VII and Henry VIII, who had been married to Jasper Tudor's widow, Catherine Woodville, before marrying Lady Wingfield.[14] The couple were likewise loyal to Charles Brandon, Duke of Suffolk and his third wife, King Henry's sister, Mary Tudor, Queen of France. It is possible that any words about Anne Boleyn that Lady Wingfield whispered on her deathbed were relayed to the Duke of Suffolk, who had never approved of Anne Boleyn.[15]

Lady Wingfield's second husband, Sir Nicholas Hervey, was ambassador to Charles V, and Ambassador Chapuys knew the couple, furthering Lady Wingfield's conservative allies. Hervey was known to support Anne Boleyn over Queen Katharine regardless of his position among the loyal Catholics of court, and this is likely how Lady Wingfield and Anne Boleyn became friends. However, Lady Wingfield had a child each year of her six-year second marriage, meaning she could not be regularly at court. By 1532, Lady Wingfield had given birth sixteen times in nineteen years.

Lady Wingfield's third husband, Robert Tyrwhitt, came from a strong Yorkshire family, who was only months away from aiding the Pilgrimage of Grace uprising against the Reformation in 1536. Lady Wingfield's father-in-law, Sir Robert Tyrwhitt, was close to John, Lord Hussey, one of the leading nobles in the Pilgrimage of Grace and one of the nobles most against the Reformation and Anne Boleyn.[16] If Lady Wingfield knew something about Anne Boleyn's previous indiscretions, while dying after giving her final husband two children, her final words may have been shared with Tyrwhitt, who could speak against Anne to his friends.[17]

Lady-in-waiting Margery Horsman's brother was married to Elizabeth Hussey, providing an easy chain of conservative allies to supply Thomas Cromwell with information about inappropriate behaviour in the privy chamber, true or not. Whatever Lady Wingfield knew, or claimed to know, was obviously about Anne's distant past behaviour, but it had enough weight to it to join with the flimsy comments made by Margery Horsman, Nan Cobham, and Elizabeth Somerset. But Judge Spelman only wrote about this note from Anne Boleyn to Lady Wingfield, dated approximately 1532, and mentioned or reviewed no other evidence for the trial.

The Adultery

The instances in which Norris, Weston, Brereton, and Smeaton were supposedly meant to have slept with the queen were equally dubious. There is no basis for the dates these alleged trysts happened, and for many, the court was not even in the correct location for the indecencies to have occurred. The indictment read:

> 'Record of the Indictment found at Westminster on Wednesday next after three weeks of Easter (10 May): that whereas Queen Anne has been the wife of Henry VIII for three years and more, she, despising the solemn, not to mention most excellent and noble marriage between our lord the King and the same lady the Queen, but even as the same time having in her heart malice against our lord the King, seduced by evil and not having God before her eyes, and following daily her frail and carnal appetites, did falsely and traitorously procure by base conversations and kisses, touching, gifts and other unnamed crimes, divers of the King's daily and familiar servants to be her adulterers and concubines, so that several of the King's servants yielded to her vile provocations'.[18]

The papers spoke of sexual encounters between 1533 and 1536. First the jury concluded that Anne slept with Henry Norris twice, on 12 October and then on 19 November 1533, both times at Westminster. She had 'enticed' Norris with kisses and such a week before each tryst took place. But Princess Elizabeth had only been born on 7 September 1533, and Anne was still in confinement at Greenwich in October, making this first instance impossible.[19] The November encounter also had no basis behind it, as the king was at Westminster in mid-November, while Anne was at Greenwich.[20] Given that Anne was heavily pregnant in May 1534, the date was possibly chosen to make the parentage of Anne's second child suspicious.

William Brereton was then accused of sleeping with Anne on 27 November 1533 at Greenwich and 8 December 1533 at Hampton Court Palace, probably again to muddy the parentage of the second royal baby, and Brereton was 'enticed' (through kissing, touching, flirting) by Anne a week before each encounter. While these enticements a week before the sex took place are dated and catalogued, they are never explained. The issue is that on both 27 November and 8 December, Henry was at Westminster, where Brereton would have been in attendance while Anne stayed at Greenwich with her baby, making all these meetings impossible.[21]

The 1534 encounters made equally little sense. In January, Anne was already pregnant again and yet on 8 May, Anne supposedly enticed Sir Francis Weston into a sexual encounter, taking place on 20 May at Westminster. Anne was heavily pregnant at the time and staying at Richmond Palace.[22] The jury claimed Anne had slept with Mark Smeaton a day earlier, on 19 May at Greenwich, despite the fact Anne was also at Richmond that day.[23] Anne then apparently slept with Weston again on 20 June, two weeks after enticing him at Greenwich, despite the fact Anne was actually at Hampton Court at the time.[24] These dates are likely centred around the time Anne went into early labour and lost her child, which goes wholly unrecorded. The loss must have been devastating for Anne and Henry, and these trysts would have been an effective way to lay all the blame for the stillbirth on Anne.

Moving forward to 1535, Anne allegedly slept with Mark Smeaton on 26 April at Westminster, despite being in Greenwich at the time.[25] This date was completely random and there were no pregnancy rumours at the time (if Anne suspected she was pregnant around this time, it was not recorded, though Queen Katharine's pregnancies also suffered lacklustre records, so it is impossible to say). Soon after this imagined tryst with Smeaton, Henry and Anne went on their long and successful summer progress, where Anne fell pregnant in approximately October 1535.

Without evidence based in fact and without explanation, Anne and her lovers allegedly met, like some bizarre sort of lovers club, and discussed the king's death on 31 October 1535 at Westminster. But at the time, Anne was with King Henry at Windsor Castle.[26] After this, Anne was said to have slept with her brother, at Westminster on 5 November, a few days after 'enticing' him to do so. This fake affair was likely arranged so that it looked like the baby Anne sadly lost in January 1536 was her brother's child. Anne then allegedly had sex with her brother again on 29 December 1535 at Eltham Palace. This came hot on the heels of giving out lavish gifts to her lovers at Westminster throughout November 1535, suggested as bribes to her men.[27] Anne could not have been sleeping with her brother or giving out gifts at Westminster as she had remained with the king at Windsor Castle in November and December before spending Christmas at Eltham Palace.[28]

More gifts were given out to her lovers for New Year 1536 at Eltham Palace. The gift list for the New Year 1536 celebrations has conveniently disappeared (the only year missing), so it was only assumed gifts went to Anne's lovers. Anne may have given gifts to Norris, Weston, Brereton, and even Smeaton at this time, as she gave out gifts to everyone at court. The missing gift list for 1536 could have been destroyed at the same time as all other papers surrounding the trial.

The final affair date listed was 8 January 1536, the day on which pregnant Anne learned that her nemesis, Queen Katharine of Aragon, was finally dead. It was alleged Anne got her strange lovers club together again and conspired about the king's death now that Katharine was out of the way. Given Henry and Anne celebrated at court after Katharine's death, this notion of a meeting is based on no evidence. The prosecution discussed Anne's gift-giving as well as her apparent sexual favours:

> 'Moreover, the said lord Rochford, Norris, Brereton, Weston, and Smeaton, being thus inflamed with carnal love of the Queen, and having become very jealous of each other, gave her secret gifts and pledges while carrying on this illicit intercourse; and the Queen, on her part, could not endure any of them to converse with any other woman, without showing

great displeasure; and on the 27 Nov (1535) and other days before and after, at Westminster, she gave them great gifts to encourage them in their crimes. And further, the said Queen and these other traitors, 31 Oct (1535), at Westminster, conspired the death and destruction of the King, the Queen often saying she would marry one of them as soon as the King died, and affirming that she would never love the King in her heart. And the King having a brief time since become aware of the said abominable crimes and treasons against himself, took such inward displeasure and heaviness, especially from his said Queen's malice and adultery, that certain harms and perils have befallen his royal body'.[29]

But all the details in the case did not matter, the facts did not matter, and everyone in the court surely knew it. If the king had changed his mind at the last minute and did not want Anne convicted, the dates and details of these said affairs needed to be false, so the case could be invalidated at once. This would ensure that Cromwell, or anyone else, could not be punished by Henry if he changed his mind about Anne's downfall at the last minute. But Cromwell, hedging his bets either way according to Henry's future mood, could be of no help to the accused men. The record does not bother with details, saying:

> 'Mark Smeaton pleaded guilty of violation and carnal knowledge of the Queen and put himself in the King's mercy. Norris, Brereton, and Weston pleaded Not Guilty. The jury return a verdict of Guilty, and that they have no lands, goods, or chattels. Judgement against all four as in cases of treason; execution to be at Tyburn'.[30]

As these men had been found guilty, it meant that Anne had no way of beating her charges, after all, her alleged lovers could not have committed treason with anyone else.

It was time to arrange a French executioner for Anne Boleyn.

CHAPTER 18

Things Be So Abominable

There was much to do on the days between trials. Vicegerent Cromwell had an enormous list of tasks piling up while he dealt with the sham trials and the king's constant instability.[1] Another person to deal with was Henry Percy, Earl of Northumberland. Cromwell clearly never felt sure the false evidence and charges would work, as proven by the bonus option he arranged, and still needed to organise — his case proving that Anne Boleyn had been pre-contracted and possibly even slept with Henry Percy in the mid-1520s. The love match between Anne and Percy was well known, but the pair denied any kind of pre-contract when Wolsey informed them that they could not be together, and Percy was soon married to Lady Eleanor Talbot. When King Henry finally looked to marry Anne in 1532, Percy again swore there was no pre-contract between himself and Anne, clearing the way for the royal marriage.[2] No one had any issues, until now, when a pre-contract would come in very handy for Henry.

The Earl of Northumberland was known as a big spender, and in 1535 was forced to hand over a beautiful manor named Brooke House, located in Hackney, a five-mile walk northeast of Whitehall Palace.[3] Because of Percy's debts to the crown, he used the house as payment to the king, who happily took the manor and leased it to Thomas Cromwell, who was looking for property in the area at the time. Cromwell had not long purchased Sutton House for Ralph Sadler and his family and now had Brooke House for himself. Cromwell embarked on an extravagant building reconstruction for the manor, and by the time of the trial in 1536, it was all but complete and fit for a king. Cromwell and Ambassador Chapuys had dined there just once before the house was ready to be another home in Cromwell's magnificent personal collection. Cromwell's building costs for Hackney do not survive but given his costs for similar works on other buildings, he easily would have spent 2000*l*–3000*l* (over £1.1 million today) on Brooke House.[4] The only time the king had ever previously visited Cromwell at home was in

1535 when Henry visited Austin Friars to see Cromwell who was on his deathbed.[5] Now, Cromwell would have a home fit for a king to stay and visit on par with the homes of noblemen. By May 1536, Brooke House looked like an excellent bribe and a significant sacrifice for Cromwell. He gave the Hackney manor back to the king, so it could be gifted back to Henry Percy at no cost.[6] This was a serious move for Cromwell to make, and King Henry took this manor without any consideration. All Percy needed to do in return was say he was pre-contracted to Anne Boleyn.

Percy was staying at a manor at Newington Green, just two miles from Brooke House. Cromwell sent Percy a letter requesting his agreement to say there had been a pre-contract or consummation in place that Cardinal Wolsey would have ignored in the 1520s. This would have been great for Percy; it would have meant his loveless marriage to Eleanor Talbot would be invalid and the pair could be free of one another. It would also mean that Anne's marriage to Henry was invalid, and everything could be simply undone. But Percy would not budge and refused to say that he had a binding marriage agreement with Anne at any stage, even with the bribe of Brooke House. Percy told Cromwell on Saturday, 13 May:

> 'I perceive by Raynold Carnaby [messenger] that there is supposed a pre-contract between the Queen and me whereupon I was not only heretofore examined upon my oath before the archbishops of Canterbury and York [in 1532], but also received the blessed sacrament upon the same before the duke of Norfolk and other the King's highness' council learned in the spiritual law, assuring you, Mr. Secretary, by the said oath and blessed body, which afore I received and hereafter intend to receive, that the same may be to my damnation if ever there were any contract or promise of marriage between her and me'.[7]

Percy was not going to give Henry and Cromwell a straightforward way out of this whole mess and was going to have to sit in judgement of Anne Boleyn and her brother in court. Percy was a sick man with not a lot going for him, and yet he did not take this opportunity; he chose to tell the truth.

Meanwhile, Sir Edward Baynton was busy breaking up Anne Boleyn's household. She was not going to be the queen for much longer, and her staff needed to be discharged and her goods inventoried for the king. Baynton, alongside William Fitzwilliam and William Paulet, took charge of Anne's possessions, as they ultimately all belonged to the king and would be soon in the next queen's possession.[8] The staff would not have to travel far; they could help sort out all of Anne's things and merely wait for a new queen to arrive.

Over at the Tower, Sir Francis Weston was pragmatic about his conviction. He wrote up his list of debts owed, mostly to staff, merchants, friends, gambling debts, as well as the nobles he owed, such as the king, Thomas Boleyn, Henry Seymour, and unusually, Margery Horsman's uncle, John Horsman. The total was 925*l* 7*s* 2*d* (just over £400,000 today).[9] It was an enormous sum for a young man to owe, and Weston had been making foolish spending errors much like Henry Percy. Weston also wrote a letter to his family:

> 'Father and mother and wife, I shall humbly desire you, for the salvation of my soul, to discharge me of this bill, and for to forgive me of all the offences that I have done to you, and in especial to my wife, which I desire for the love of God to forgive me, and to pray for me: for I believe prayer will do me good. God's blessing has my children and mine… By me, a great offender to God'.[10]

King Henry was busy himself. Now that several of his powerful courtiers, Henry Norris and William Brereton were gone, many offices, lands and preferments now had no owners, and people were already circling Cromwell's offices looking for favours.[11] The king went through all these titles and tried to hand them out, hastily scribbled by Cromwell's secretary, Thomas Wriothesley. Most of the positions were given to deputies or already notable men in areas around the country. All were paid positions, so being awarded a role cannot have been unwelcomed. The king gave his son, Henry Fitzroy, all of Cheshire and North Wales, a sign of Henry's love and confidence in his son, who was about to turn 17.[12] But Fitzroy died of a lung infection on 9 July, a day after being becoming eligible to be the heir to the throne. Lord Lisle in Calais was desperate to gain a role and had his man, John Husee, harass Cromwell for favours, though many roles were simply handed out by the king so that the offices and lands could be run without any interruption. Cromwell himself had to take over multiple minor offices which he then gave to others, while many of his men, including Ralph Sadler and Thomas Wriothesley were given small roles as they gained the king's favour.[13] What the recipients of these grants thought of the whole trial and situation did not matter, as rejecting a role could be seen as disagreement with the king and no one was willing to take the risk.

A single piece of correspondence still survives of Vicegerent Cromwell mentioning Anne Boleyn. He wrote to Stephen Gardiner and John Wallop in Paris, but refused to divulge any details of the case:

> 'You have heard I doubt not the rumour, yet I shall express to you some pain of the coming out, and of the king preceding in the same. The queen's abomination both in incontinent living, and other offences towards the king's highness was so rank and common, that her ladies of her privy chamber and her chambers could not contain it within their breasts… certain persons of the privy chamber and others of her side were examined, in which examinations the matter appeared so evident, that beside that crime, with the accidents, there broke out a certain conspiracy of the king's death, which extended so far that all we that had the examination of it quaked at the danger his Grace was in, and on our knees gave Him laude and praise that He had preserved him so long from it, and now manifested the most wretched and detestable determination… certain men committed to the Tower for this cause, that is Mark and Norris, and her brother. Then was she apprehended, and conveyed to the same place, after her was sent thither for the crimes specified, Sir Francis Weston and William Brereton. And Norris, Weston, Brereton, and Mark be already condemned to death, upon arraignment in Westminster Hall on Friday last. She and her brother shall be arraigned tomorrow and will undoubtedly go the same way. I write no particularities, the things be so abominable, that I think the like was never heard…'[14]

Had Stephen Gardiner not kept his letters from Cromwell in 1536 there would almost no paperwork from Cromwell's offices that survived the careful destruction of all discussions, plans and rulings. Cromwell clearly knew how to ensure if there was any backlash to the whole debacle, there would be no written evidence for his part in the plan. We know both

Cromwell and King Henry wrote letters on the subject of Anne's crimes and trial, yet the frequent destruction of sensitive paperwork from Cromwell's offices will keep most of the secrets hidden forever.

Monday, 15 May

The King's Hall in the Tower had special seating built to accommodate 2000 people on the day of Anne and George Boleyn's trial. Thomas Howard, Duke of Norfolk sat under a cloth of estate as the Lord Steward with his white staff of office in his hand, with his son Henry Howard, Earl of Surrey sitting at his feet, holding the gold staff of the office of Earl Marshall for his father. Lord Chancellor Thomas Audley sat to Norfolk's right, and Charles Brandon, Duke of Suffolk sat to Norfolk's left.[15] Norfolk outwardly had no qualms about ruling that his niece and nephew had to die. The Duke of Suffolk had never supported Anne and always supported Henry. Audley was a puppet installed in his role by Thomas Cromwell and would do whatever he was told.

Around the trio sat the rest of the noble panel of judges.[16] Henry Courtenay, Marquis of Exeter, and Henry Pole, Lord Montagu were so strongly in favour of Mary that they had whispered of being prepared to spill blood in her name. Henry Percy, Earl of Northumberland, who had seemingly given up on life was prepared to do his duty. John de Vere, Earl of Oxford, Ralph Neville, Earl of Westmorland, Robert Radcliffe, Earl of Sussex, Thomas Manners, Earl of Rutland, and George Hastings, Earl of Huntingdon were long-time friends and supporters of the king and Queen Katharine. Charles Somerset, Earl of Worcester was going to hear his own wife's 'testimony' read out in court, that her 'indiscretions' were not as bad as the queen's. George Brooke, Lord Cobham was in the same position, ready to hear his wife, Nan Cobham's 'evidence.'

Henry Parker, Lord Morley was in an awkward position; he had to sit in judgement on his son-in-law, George Boleyn, while his daughter Jane Lady Rochford was left bewildered by the whole trial. William Lord Sandys was Lord Chamberlain and endlessly loyal to the king, while Thomas Fiennes, Lord Dacre was looking to gain favour from the king after almost being arrested for treason in 1534. Dacre went on to serve on many treason trials, as did John, Lord Mourdant, another courtier desperate to be in the king's good graces.[17] Thomas West, Lord De la Warr was a fervent Catholic there to support his king, while Andrew, Lord Windsor, a military man turned Keeper of the King's Wardrobe, was always anxious to impress the king.

Nepotism was high on the list on the jury too, with Edward, Lord Grey of Powys and Thomas, Lord Monteagle, two of the Duke of Suffolk's sons-in-law, while Jane Seymour's cousin Thomas, Lord Wentworth was also ready to sit in judgement.[18] Edward, Lord Clinton, husband of Bessie Blount (mother of the king's son Henry Fitzroy) was there to do his duty, as was William FitzAlan, Earl of Arundel, son of Margaret Woodville, and a deep Catholic. Alongside him was his son Henry FitzAlan, Lord Maltravers, a Conservative MP keen for royal favour. Edward Stanley, Earl of Derby was beloved by the king and supportive of Catholic rule, in addition to being the Duke of Norfolk's brother-in-law.[19] John Tuchet, Lord Audley was a cousin of the king through the Catholic Beaufort family and a nasty extra addition was Thomas, Lord Burgh.[20] He had worked as Anne Boleyn's Lord Chamberlain, and while being a reformer, also hated women, taking his rage out on his family, one member being Catherine Parr, who would later marry King Henry.[21]

All records of the trial were destroyed, likely weeks after Anne's death, and only snippets of information remain, along with eyewitness accounts of the day. Ambassador Chapuys did not attend, as he had been ill for several weeks, a shame considering how feverishly he recorded happenings in London. Thomas Cromwell was wise to ensure he was not on the panel of judges; conveniently, he was not a nobleman, so Attorney-General Sir Christopher Hales was placed in charge of the case in court. Whether Cromwell attended the trial at all goes unrecorded, and he is not mentioned at any stage.

Anne Boleyn was taken into the court by Sir William Kingston and Sir Edmund Walsingham, the same men in charge of her arrest and time in her rooms in the Tower. Lancelot de Carles, in his enormous missive on the case and trial wrote that:

> '[Anne] walked forth in fearful beauty … seemed unmoved as a stock, not as one who had to defend her cause, but with the bearing of one coming to great honour[22] … made an entry as though she were going to a great triumph… She presented herself with the true dignity of a queen, and curtseyed to her

> judges, looking round upon them all, without any sign of fear… She returned the salutations of the lords with her accustomed politeness… she stood undismayed, nor did ever exhibit any token of impatience, or grief, or cowardice.'[23]

Anne, seated on a platform in the middle of the hall before the judges, and accompanied only by Lady Mary Kingston and Lady Elizabeth Boleyn, had the charges against her read out by Christopher Hales and Anne listened while, 'her face said more than words, for she said little; but no one looking at her would have thought her guilty'.[24] Anne naturally pleaded not guilty to all the charges of incest, adultery, promising to marry Henry Norris, conspiring the king's death, and making jokes about the king and his attire. Anne, 'made so wise and discreet answers to all things laid against her, excusing herself with her words so clearly, as though she had never been guilty of the same'.[25] Anne was permitted to speak to the court and refute the charges, though surely, she knew it would do no good. The charges and evidence were the same as put to Norris, Weston, Brereton, and Smeaton three days earlier, and Smeaton had 'confessed.' Lancelot de Carles again wrote several records of Anne's speech in the court:

> 'My lords, I will not say your sentence is unjust, nor presume that my reasons can prevail against your convictions. I am willing to believe that you have sufficient reasons for what you have done; but then they must be other than those which have been produced in court, for I am clear of all the offences which you then laid to my charge. I have ever been a faithful wife to the King, though I do not say I have always shown him that humility which his goodness to me, and the honours to which he raised me, merited. I confess I have had jealous fancies and suspicions of him, which I had not discretion enough, and wisdom, to conceal at all times. But God knows, and is my witness, that I have not sinned against him in any other way. Think not I say this in the hope to prolong my life, for He who saveth from death hath taught me how to die, and He will strengthen my faith.
>
> Think not, however, that I am so bewildered in my mind as not to lay the honour of my chastity to heart now in mine

> extremity when I have maintained it all my life long, much as ever queen did. I know these, my last words, will avail me nothing but for the justification of my chastity and honour. As for my brother and those others who are unjustly condemned, I would willingly suffer many deaths to deliver them, but since I see it so pleases the King, I shall willingly accompany them in death, with this assurance, that I shall lead an endless life with them in peace and joy, where I will pray to God for the King and you, my lords'.[26]

These kinds of statements can only be taken as the truth, although all eyewitness accounts of events that day are undoubtedly embellished for effect. But there can be little doubt that Anne faced the occasion with great courage despite the overwhelming odds against her.[27] Crucially, the suggestion that Anne had given birth to a deformed child back in January 1536 was never mentioned. A deformity, at the time, could be seen as a sign of evil, or God's ill-will, or even as sign of wickedness in a mother, and yet this was not mentioned, serving to prove the suggestion was a story made up for effect many decades after Anne's death.

George Constantine also recorded Anne's trial, stating that her uncle, the Duke of Norfolk, had tears on his cheeks by the end of proceedings, which is deeply at odds with a man who had little love for his niece, or indeed anyone, but it does make for a dramatic story. Each of the peers of the jury pronounced Anne guilty of the charges and declared:

> 'Because thou hast offended against our sovereign the King's Grace in committing treason against his person, and here attainted of the same, the law of the realm is this, that thou hast deserved death, and thy judgement is this: that thou shalt be burned here within the Tower of London on the Green, else to have thy head smitten off, as the King's pleasure shall be further known of the same'.[28]

Tales of a woman, reportedly a childhood nurse of Anne, shrieking in panic seems to have appeared from nowhere, but it was reported that Henry Percy, Earl of Northumberland collapsed soon after the pronouncement, and had to be removed from the court, too ill to oversee

Lord Rochford's trial.[29] Lancelot de Carles wrote that Anne addressed the court again:

> 'I do not say that I have always borne towards the King the humility which I owed him, considering his kindness and the great honour he showed me and the great respect he always paid me; I admit too, that often I have taken it into my head to be jealous of him… But may God be my witness if I have done him any other wrong.'[30]

Ambassador Chapuys, receiving this information second-hand, also recorded that Anne maintained her composure throughout the trial and that she regretted that other innocents were to die for her after they had all been loyal to the king.[31] No sooner than Anne was taken away, it was time for George Boleyn, Lord Rochford to make his appearance. Again brought out by William Kingston and Edmund Walsingham, Rochford was indicted on counts of incest with his sister, and committing treason, to which he naturally pleaded not guilty. The case was laid out — how Rochford had slept with his sister on several occasions in late 1535 and had conspired to kill the king with Anne's merry band of lovers. The charges were a mixture of spiteful and vague, much like those laid before the other men already convicted:

> 'Also the Queen, 2 Nov. 27 Hen. VIII. and several times before and after, at Westminster, procured and incited her own natural brother, George Boleyn, lord Rocheford, gentleman of the privy chamber, to violate her, alluring him with her tongue in the said George's mouth, and the said George's tongue in hers, and also with kisses, presents, and jewels; whereby he, despising the commands of God, and all human laws, 5 Nov. 27 Hen. VIII., violated and carnally knew the said Queen, his own sister, at Westminster, which he also did on diverse other days before and after at the same place, sometimes by his own procurement and sometimes by the Queen's'.[32]

Chronicler Charles Wriothesley wrote that Rochford, 'made answer so prudently and widely to all articles laid against him, that marvel it was to hear, and never would confess anything, but made himself as clear as though he had never offended'.[33] The witness listening for Chapuys, likely one of his messenger servants, reported:

> 'Her brother was charged with having cohabited with her by presumption, because he had been once found a long time with her, and with certain other little follies. To all, he replied so well that several of those present wagered 10 to 1 that he would be acquitted, especially as no witnesses were produced against either him or her, as it is usual to do, particularly when the accused denies the charge'.[34]

There was one piece of evidence at Rochford's trial that was not mentioned during his sister's appearance. The case was made that Anne had said to Jane Boleyn, Lady Rochford, that King Henry, 'was not skilful in copulating and he had neither virtue nor potency'.[35] There was no proof that Lady Rochford said any such thing, nor Anne. Where this piece of alleged evidence came from goes completely unrecorded, like all of the witness statements. Given that none of Anne's ladies were ever interrogated means Lady Rochford, in particular, has long been slandered by those keen to find a source for such a statement.[36] This piece of evidence could not simply be relayed in court to 2000 people, so the statement was written down and handed to Rochford to read only to himself. Perhaps Rochford could see that he had no chance of freedom, that nothing he could say would be respected, and so he read the note aloud, to the shock of the enormous audience who became privy to the king's erectile dysfunction.

There was no evidence that the Boleyn siblings slept together, the only 'proof' being they spent time alone together. The suggestion that Lord Rochford did not think of Princess Elizabeth as the king's daughter was mentioned, to Rochford's indifference.[37] He was not going to say anything negative about his sister to help himself in any way. Rochford's sentence was pronounced as guilty by all in the jury, and Norfolk again was the one to read out the punishment:

> 'That he should go again to prison in the Tower from whence he came, and to be drawn from the said Tower of London through the City of London to the place of execution called

> Tyburn, and there to be hanged, being alive cut down, and then his members cut off and his bowels taken out of his body and burnt before him, and then his head cut off, and his body to be divided into quarter pieces, and his head and body to be set at such places as the King should assign.'[38]

Just like that, all was done. King Henry had what he wanted. Had Lord Rochford not gone to the king on the day of Anne's arrest, he may have been spared. His eagerness to speak up for his sister showed courage and determination against the crime playing out against Anne. No one spoke of the siblings having any kind of affair, nor was there any proof Lady Rochford had spoken a word on any matter about her husband or her sister-in-law. Thomas Boleyn, Earl of Wiltshire, had returned home to Hever after the oyer and terminer trials to grieve and was 'spared' any punishment over his daughter allegedly becoming the whore of the century. King Henry may have allowed Lord Rochford the same, had it not been for his panicked defiance. Without Anne, Rochford was simply another courtier with few supporters, much like everyone else. But now all was too late for both of the Boleyn siblings.

On the day of the trial, King Henry sent Sir Francis Bryan to Sir Thomas More's old manor in Chelsea, where Lady Jane Seymour waited for news, informing her that, 'Anne would be condemned by three in the afternoon'.[39] Never had a lack of truth mattered so little as in the case of Anne Boleyn.

CHAPTER 19

The Fall is Grievous from Aloft

Tuesday, 16 May

> 'Was with the King today, and declared the petition of lord Rochford, wherein I was answered. The said Lord desires to speak with you on a matter which touches his conscience. I wish to know your pleasure, because of my promise to him, and also to know the King's pleasure touching the Queen, as well for her confession as for the preparation of scaffolds. The King told me that my lord of Canterbury should be her confessor, and he was here today with her. The time is short, for the King supposes the gentlemen to die tomorrow.'[1]

Sir William Kingston was in charge of preparing the executions and seemed anxious to ensure everything went exactly to the king's wishes. He wrote to Cromwell about Lord Rochford, who had been busy trying to settle his debts,[2] and, 'wanted to ensure all was prepared before his death, despite only having two days' notice. Kingston had told Rochford he was likely to die on 17 May with the other condemned men, and he was ready to accept his fate, something Anne had not yet achieved. Lord Rochford wanted to discuss an issue with Cromwell; he wanted, 'the white monk from Tower Hill', to be appointed the abbot of Valle Crucis Abbey in Wales.[3] The previous abbot had been removed by Cromwell's inspectors for corruption, and the abbey was decaying, losing money, and did not meet the criteria for staying open under the Lesser Dissolutions Act in parliament. Cromwell later had John Heron alias Deram/Durham of Tower Hill appointed, who stayed in the position until the abbey was closed in 1537.[4] There are no clues as to why Lord Rochford was so keen to have this role finalised before his death, though he had promised the role to the monk months earlier, and perhaps simply wanted to help someone in need. Rochford was also concerned for

Gabriel Donne, the abbot of Buckfast Abbey in Devon, who needed to be paid 250*l* (£110,000 today).[5] Cromwell was Donne's patron and saw through these requests on Lord Rochford's behalf after his death.

Anne spent the day with Archbishop Thomas Cranmer who would be her confessor and comfort in the Tower. Cranmer also had the unpleasant task of ruling Henry and Anne's marriage annulled, despite her death sentence. Having Anne killed was not enough for Henry; he wanted his marriage to have never existed. What did Cranmer say to Anne in the Tower? Did he tell her about the annulment, and how her cooperation may find her some mercy from the king? Perhaps Cranmer thought that to be true. The notion of a pre-contract with Henry Percy remained, despite Percy's avid denials, though that seemingly never came to mind with Anne either. There was the issue that King Henry had slept with Anne's sister, possibly fathering one or two children. That was grounds for an annulment, as there had been no dispensation given for Henry and Anne's marriage to go ahead despite that level of affinity through Mary Boleyn. But whatever Archbishop Cranmer said to Anne in her rooms did give her some hope, as she told Kingston on 16 May that, 'she would go to a nunnery, and is in hope of life'.[6] No one could blame Anne for having moments of hope.

Not a single person appeared to believe Anne guilty of any crime. Even Ambassador Chapuys believed Anne, 'condemned on presumption and not evidence, without any witnesses or valid confession'.[7] Chapuys also reported that Cromwell, 'extolled beyond measure the sense, the wit, and the courage of the deceased royal mistress, as well as of her brother'.[8] Chapuys also told his master:

> 'Although everybody rejoices at the execution of the [whore], there are some who murmur at the mode of procedure against her and the others, and people speak variously of the King; and it will not pacify the world when it is known what has passed and is passing between him and Mrs. Jane Seymour. Already it sounds ill in the ears of the people, that the King, having received such ignominy, has shown himself more glad than ever since the arrest of the [whore]; for he has been going about banqueting with ladies, sometimes remaining after midnight, and returning by the river. Most part of the time he was accompanied by various musical instruments, and, on

> the other hand, by the singers of his chamber, which many interpret as showing his delight at getting rid of a 'skinny, old and evil thing', with hope of change, which is a thing specially agreeable to this King. He supped lately with several ladies in the house of the bishop of Carlisle [John Kite] and showed an extravagant joy.'[9]

Wednesday, 17 May

Time had truly run out. At Lambeth Palace, Archbishop Thomas Cranmer ruled, before Chancellor Audley, the Duke of Suffolk and John de Vere, Earl of Oxford, that Henry and Anne's marriage was invalid, though the grounds for this and the official records were not made public, simply seen through parliament on 10 June and the Convocation on 28 June, sealed, and then destroyed.[10] Ambassador Chapuys also noted that Cranmer ruled that Princess Elizabeth was the child of Henry Norris and not King Henry, but this was just a rumour, and nothing was put in writing or through parliament.[11] The Act of Succession needed to be updated as Princess Elizabeth was now illegitimate like Princess Mary and Henry Fitzroy, but her parentage did not need to be questioned for this process to occur. Chapuys was more likely listening to the myriad of rumours going around London at the time. Invalidating Henry and Anne's marriage was unnecessary given her execution, and yet the king had Cranmer go through the process anyway.

A scaffold had been hastily built for Anne's alleged lovers. The men were all notified that morning that the time had come and were, Kingston assumed, 'clean and ready to die'.[12] The men were taken to Tower Hill, to be despatched in order of rank: George Boleyn, Lord Rochford, Sir Henry Norris, Sir Francis Weston, Sir William Brereton, and then Mark Smeaton. The thought of having multiple high-ranking men close to the king killed all at once surely shocked even a people who had learned to live with the fact that the king could kill anyone at any time. The scaffold was a time to make peace with life and with God, and the impression left on those listening would hopefully cause them to treat the convict's family and friends with kindness in the future. Lord Rochford was to die first and gave a speech that left an impression on those present:

> 'Christian men, I am borne under the law, judged under the law, and die under the law, and the law has condemned me… Masters all, I am not come to preach, but to die, for I have deserved to die, for I have lived more shamefully than can be devised… I am a wretched sinner, and I have sinned shamefully. I have sinned so openly it would be no pleasure to you to hear them, nor for me to repeat them, for God knows all… Masters all, I pray you take heed by me, and especially my lords and gentlemen of the court, take heed by me and beware of such a fall… I pray to God, the Father, the Son, and the Holy Ghost that my death may be an example to you all. Beware, trust not in the vanity of the world… and especially in the flattery of the court. I cry for God's mercy, and ask the world's forgiveness, as willingly as I would have forgiveness from God… If I have offended any man that is not here now, either in thought, word, or deed, I pray you to heartily, on my behalf, pray them to forgive me for God's sake. I say you all, if I had followed God's word in deed as I did read it and set it forth to my power, I would not have come to this. I read the gospel of Christ, but I did not follow it; if I had, I would be among you now: so, I pray you… masters all, for God's sake, stick to the truth and follow it, for one good follower is worth three sinners, as God knows.'[13]

Three strokes of the axe took George Boleyn's life. Norris took to the block next, which already would be stained with the dark blood of the man before him. He too had a speech prepared, recorded second-hand by Gilbert Burnet from the second-hand information in the Spanish Chronicle (while George Constantine, Norris' servant, remarked that Norris said little[14]):

> 'I think no gentleman of the court owes more to the King than I do or has been more ungrateful than I have. But I loyally believe in my conscience, I think the Queen innocent of these things laid to her charge; but whether she was, I will not accuse her of anything. I will die a thousand times rather than ruin an innocent person… Most Sacred Heart of Jesus, I accept from Your hands whatever kind of death it may

> please You to send me this day with all its pains, penalties, and sorrows; in reparation for all my sins, for the souls in Purgatory, for all those who will die today and for Your greater glory. Amen.'[15]

Sir Francis Weston soon stood in the blood of Boleyn and Norris. His family had petitioned Cromwell, offering vast sums of money in return for freedom, money they could not afford.[16] French diplomats likewise petitioned on Weston's behalf, to no avail; while gossip in London suggested Weston might be saved, it was not to be.[17] Among the prayers said over the block, Weston uttered:

> 'I had thought to live in abomination for another twenty or thirty years, and then to have made amends… I thought little I would come to this. Everyone, you would do well to take the example of this, and to live clean lives under God.'[18]

Up next was the final man of the nobility, Sir William Brereton. He stood before the crowd on the scaffold, now with the sight of piled-up bodies to one side, heads tossed in a basket. Brereton was more defiant than the others, and rightly so, given that he had never had anything to do with Anne Boleyn. Brereton's wife, Lady Elizabeth believed in his innocence, though would have needed to ignore his additional corruption to think her husband a good man. Brereton saw to it that rather than admitting any culpability, he hoped others could see to his soul:

> 'I have offended God and the King; pray for me… I have deserved to die if it were a thousand deaths, but the cause whereof I die, judge me not. But if you judge, judge the best. But if you judge, judge the best. But if you judge, judge the best. But if you judge, judge the best'.[19]

Poor Mark Smeaton was last, a man of only around 23 years old; the youngest man on the block by several years. As a commoner, and possibly a foreigner, there was less sympathy for Smeaton, even if the population knew at large that nothing untoward had ever occurred. Smeaton's only crime was his supposed confession.

Once the bloodletting ceased, the bodies were moved to St Peter Ad Vincula, where George Boleyn, Lord Rochford would be placed in the Chapel Royal, and the others in the nearby churchyard. While Ambassador Chapuys, who was not present (Cromwell had informed Kingston no foreigners could be present at the executions[20]) mentioned that Anne had been moved to the Bell Tower to watch the killings, this was untrue, and Anne did not have to witness any of the torture. But Sir Thomas Wyatt did see everything from his Bell Tower cell, as mentioned in his poem, *Innocentia Veritas Viat Fides Circumdederunt me*:[21]

> The Bell Tower showed me such sight
> That in my head sticks day and night.
> There did I learn out of a grate,
> For all favour, glory, or might,
> That yet circa Regna tonat (it thunders around the throne).
>
> By proof, I say, there did I learn:
> Wit helpeth not defence too yerne,
> Of innocency to plead or prate.
> Bear low, therefore, give God the stern,
> For sure, circa Regna tonat.

Thursday, 18 May

Unsurprisingly, Anne Boleyn did not sleep the night before her execution. William Kingston had been in regular contact with Vicegerent Cromwell about making sure everything was right and proper for Anne, who had called for Thomas Cranmer several times so she could pray and be shriven before her death.[22] Kingston had also told Cromwell he was relieved a swordsman from Calais had been arranged, so all 'would be done well'. The French executioner must have been arranged after the guilty verdicts of Norris, Weston, Brereton, and Smeaton, to allow enough time for him to arrive.[23] Kingston's correspondence with Cromwell shows a man nervous to be the one seeing through these events, despite having the king's full permission. Henry had been the one to organise Anne's scaffold so that it would be a good vantage point for all viewers.[24] Henry had been the one who decided her death would be by beheading inside the tower walls and done with a French sword, the most chivalric way to execute a person.[25] The only person who thought Anne Boleyn guilty was the king, because he seemed to make himself believe it, to make himself a kind prince cruelly wronged by a woman. Henry wrote to Kingston on the same day the men were killed:

> 'We, moved by pity, do not wish the same Anne to be committed to be burned by fire. We, however, command that immediately after receipt of these presents, upon the Green within our Tower of London aforesaid, the head of the same Anne shall be caused to be cut off.'[26]

Sir William Kingston spent time throughout the night and early morning with Anne, and she spoke of her innocence so that Kingston could share her words. Anne's almoner, Bishop Nicholas Shaxton, also stayed at the Tower to pray with Anne.[27] One of the ladies in the Tower was spying for Ambassador Chapuys, likely Lady Anne Shelton given her previous relationship with him regarding Princess Mary, who reported that before and after receiving the Holy Sacrament, Anne continued to assert her innocence.[28] Had Anne lied at this time, it would have risked sending her soul to hell. Katharine of Aragon had made similar oaths that she was a virgin before her marriage to Henry and she loved him as his true wife. Both women had the chance to tell the truth at the moment of judgement and had sworn their innocence in the face of accusations thrown at them by Henry VIII.

On the morning of 18 May, Anne expected she would die, and called for Kingston, fearing the situation, as she wished to be dead before noon and past her pain. Kingston assured her there would be no pain, not that this could have soothed Anne's terror. Anne infamously replied, 'I heard the executioner was very good and I have a little neck', letting out a nervous laugh.[29] Anne seemed to have a dark humour about her in this time of great strife, telling her ladies her new nickname could be la Royne Anne Sana Tete, Queen Anne Lackhead. Anne had spent hours in prayer, but her death would not come on 18 May; Kingston had only just received his notice from Cromwell to clear the foreigners from the Tower for the event. Messages went between Kingston and Cromwell through his merchant friends Sir Richard Gresham, Robert Whethill and William Lok (who was also Anne Boleyn's garment maker).[30] There was no plan for Anne to die on 18 May, as the call would have come early that morning and Henry had not given the command, but no one had bothered to tell Anne.

Outside the Tower, Ambassador Chapuys was informing his masters about Jane Seymour. Given that the king was now free to remarry, the option of giving Henry an Imperial bride would have made the elusive Chapuys-Cromwell alliance complete, but Jane Seymour was more than ready to supplant Anne Boleyn. King Henry had convinced himself that rushing into another marriage was a clever idea. Chapuys told Antoine Perrenot de Granvelle, Emperor Charles' man in the Netherlands:

> '[Jane] is sister of one Edward Semel, (of the privy chamber) of middle stature and no great beauty, so fair that one would call her rather pale than otherwise. She is over 25 years old. I leave you to judge whether, being English and having long frequented the Court, if she would be conscious of having not provided [marital relations] and be warned what it is to have a wedding [night]. Perhaps this King will only be too glad to be so far relieved from trouble. Also, according to the account given of him by the Concubine, he has neither vigour nor virtue; and besides, he may make a condition in the marriage that she be a virgin, and when he has a mind to divorce her, he will find enough of witnesses. The said Semel is not a woman of great wit, but she may have good understanding. It is said she inclines to be proud and haughty. She bears great love and reverence to the Princess. I know not if honours will make her change hereafter.'[31]

Princess Mary was the subject of much scrutiny from her supporters. She had maintained total silence during the case against Anne Boleyn, and now Chapuys and her domestic supporters expected that she would become the heir to the kingdom. King Henry had made no such assertions, but Cromwell was preparing to ensure Mary's safety after the proceedings with Anne. Ultimately, it had been for Princess Mary that so many had turned against Anne, rather than because of Henry's infatuation with Jane Seymour. Cromwell still wanted his Imperial alliance and Mary's name as heir-presumptive was a condition. Failing that, Cromwell's only other option was to change the Act of Succession in parliament, which was scheduled for 8 June. But first, no one would be safe until Anne Boleyn was dead and Henry had no more time to change his mind.

Friday, 19 May

The call came early on a spring Friday morning that death had arrived for Anne. Led out of the queen's rooms with Sir William Kingston, and flanked by ladies she did not like, Anne passed the Great Hall and through the Cold Harbour Gate to the west side of the White Tower in the centre of the great fortress.[32] Approximately just over one metre high (around three to four feet), the platform was draped in black fabric, which would do a good job of soaking up a queen's blood. A crowd of around 1000 people stood firm, among them Vicegerent Cromwell, Chancellor Audley, the Duke of Suffolk, and Henry Fitzroy. The Mayor and most of the aldermen and merchants of the city came along, most friends with Cromwell. Anne and Cromwell had hated each other since they first met, and one of them had to step aside for control of the kingdom. The king may have thought he was the powerful one on the throne, but Anne and Cromwell had spent years jostling for the control of the king.

Wearing a grey damask gown lined with fur and an ermine mantle, an English gable hood over her hair, Anne took the steps of the scaffold on her own, and was able to address the enormous crowd:

> 'Good Christian people, I have not come to preach a sermon; I have come hither to die. For according to the law and by the law, I am judged to die, and so I will speak nothing against it. I am come hither to accuse no man, nor to speak of that whereof I am accused and condemned to die, but I pray to God to save the King and send him long to reign over you, for a gentler nor more merciful prince was there never, and to me he was ever a good, a gentle, and sovereign lord. And if any person will meddle of my cause, I need them to judge the best. And thus, I take my leave of the world and of you all, and I heartily desire you all to pray for me'.[33]

Anne did not speak of repentance for her sins, for there was no need. Instead, she paid her executioner and gave him forgiveness. Removing her ermine and hood, the ladies on the scaffold gave Anne a simple linen cap for her hair, though conflicting reports differ on whether she was blindfolded. She knelt, no need for a block, and many joined her in kneeling for the dramatic moment. Anne prayed, 'O Lord have mercy on me, to God I commend my soul. To Jesus Christ I commend my soul; Lord Jesus, receive my soul.'[34]

Later attempts to identify the executioner and his sword have turned up no evidence, despite claims to the contrary. Queen Mary of Hungary, Governor of the Netherlands, wrote to her uncle, King Ferdinand of Romans, 'I hope the English will not do much against us now, as we are free from his lady, who was a good Frenchwoman. That the vengeance might be executed by the Emperor's subjects, he sent for the executioner of St Omer, as there were none in England good enough'.[35] The executioner of St Omer, a town forty miles southeast of Calais, was recorded as being Jean Rimbaud, swordsman of Calais. However, there is no record of who Cromwell arranged to undertake the execution, so none of this can be confirmed. Getting a French executioner meant that the person who cut off Anne's head, and the sword used for the task, could remain anonymous. Some things remain better off unknown.

Whether Anne Boleyn received a coffin is a tale distorted by time. One witness account from the period stated a plain coffin was provided,[36] while another, of dubious origins, stated she was put in a box made for bow staves,[37] and this tale has taken flight for centuries, continually made into a horrifying tale of distressed women trying to hide a queen's body. Despite reports that Anne's head would be placed on a spike for the public, which seems not to have borne out, she was quickly buried close to her brother at St Peter ad Vincula, a burial site largely undisturbed for almost 500 years.

CHAPTER 20

All is Washed Away

It was the king's desire, and the country's duty, to move on from the tale of Anne Boleyn. But Anne dying 'boldly' spread like wildfire.[1] King Henry and Jane Seymour were betrothed on 20 May, and Thomas Cranmer prepared a dispensation due to the couple being fifth cousins through King Edward III, like most of the royal court.[2] Jane Seymour had moved closer to the king on 17 May, before the previous queen had died, to reside just a mile from the court, in preparation for becoming England's new queen. Anyone who thought that Jane Seymour was a weakling only fooled themselves; she had stayed quiet and steady as she watched the man who presented his affection to her also slaughter six people so they could marry. It took the bravest, or perhaps, most ruthless, woman to sit through such an audacious plan. Not everyone was so thrilled that the king had spiralled in anger, killed an innocent woman, and had another ready to be queen. Disgruntled whispers started to appear in London as early as 20 May, when Chapuys reported that Jane Seymour had already been moved to London to meet the king at 9 a.m. for their official betrothal. Henry wanted to keep his engagement to Jane a secret until Whitsuntide on 4 June, for propriety, but, 'everybody begins already to murmur by suspicion, and several affirm that long before the death of the other, there was some arrangement which sounds ill in the ears of the people,' Chapuys claimed.[3]

On 25 May, Mary of Hungary, Governor of the Netherlands, who had grown up in Margaret of Austria's household, where Anne had briefly lived, wrote to her uncle, King Ferdinand:

> '…people think [Henry] invented this device to get rid of [Anne]. Anyhow, not much wrong can be done to her, even in being suspected as méchante [evil], for that has long been her character. It is to be hoped, if hope be a right thing to entertain about such acts, that when he is tired of this one [Jane], he

will find some occasion of getting rid of her. I think wives will hardly be well contented if such customs become general. Although I have no desire to put myself in this danger, yet being of the feminine gender I will pray with the others that God may keep us from it.'[4]

But despite all the horrific acts of the previous week, one issue remained. So many backed Jane Seymour because she was the key to wooing Henry away from Anne and making Princess Mary the heir-apparent to the country. The moves to solidify Mary's power had still not come into effect. Princess Mary had been moved away from her usual place with Princess Elizabeth three days after Anne's arrest, and had her own household again, causing optimism for both Mary and her supporters. But Chapuys had fears, which were based on solid foundations, that Mary could not simply head back to court and into her father's affections; first, she would need to acknowledge her father as Head of the Church and accept her own illegitimacy, signing the Oath of Supremacy. Chapuys wrote to the Emperor:

> 'What I most fear as regards [to Mary] is, that when the King is asked by Parliament to restore her to her rights, he will refuse his consent unless the Princess first swears to the statutes invalidating the first marriage and the Pope's authority. To this, I think, she will not easily yield, although I should advise her to acquiesce in everything as far as she can without prejudice to her conscience and her own rights.'[5]

King Henry was still refusing to discuss the subject of Princess Mary, making those who supported Jane and Mary as nervous as ever.[6] Ambassador Chapuys and Vicegerent Cromwell at once had to continue with internal diplomatic relations. Jane Seymour had not spent her time batting her eyelashes at the king, she had been discussing the restoration of Princess Mary, despite the risk she surely knew that would carry. Even before Anne Boleyn's arrest:

> 'The King, speaking with Mistress Jane Seymour of their future marriage, the latter suggested that the Princess should be replaced in her former position; and the King told her

> she was a fool, and ought to solicit the advancement of the children they would have between them, and not any others. She replied that in asking for the restoration of the Princess she conceived she was seeking the rest and tranquillity of the King, herself, her future children, and the whole realm.'[7]

Jane Seymour seemed happy to poke the angry bear that was King Henry. Both Cromwell and Chapuys were keen to support Mary's safety, and Chapuys' unnamed sources told him that parliament was ready to push Henry to support Mary once again. Henry tried to keep his betrothal to Jane quiet, but word soon crept around London and then abroad,[8] while Cromwell was left to tidy up all the loose ends of the plan. Anne's debts had to be settled, and her household and her belongings were catalogued to be given to Jane once she came back to court.[9] Jane Boleyn, Lady Rochford wrote to Cromwell, complaining that the money she was left to live on now her husband was dead was just 100 marks a year (around 60*l* or £25,000 today), and, 'is very hard for me to shift the world withal'.[10]

The only part left in the plan to murder Anne Boleyn was ensuring Princess Mary's position, which Cromwell moved quickly to achieve. Henry's mood had not soothed despite being able to get his new bride. Mary wrote to Cromwell on 26 May, looking for his help in establishing a relationship with her father,[11] finally feeling safe enough to do so. Henry permitted Mary to write to him on 4 June, perhaps feeling generous on account of his five-day-old marriage being proclaimed to the court.[12] Cromwell sent Mary a letter to copy out, talking of how she would accept her father's will in all things, but it was not enough.[13] Princess Mary was locked in her room at Hunsdon by the Duke of Norfolk until she signed the Oath of Supremacy, which she did, along with writing humble repentance to her father.[14] Chapuys immediately sent for Mary's absolution from the Pope for saying her father was the Head of the Church.

Princess Mary did get her eventual reconciliation with her father, meeting Henry and Jane on 7 July, at the Hackney property Cromwell had just relinquished to the king, out of sight of the court, where the slow process of recovering the royal relationship could begin.[15] Ambassador Chapuys was always there for Princess Mary, serving at the English court until 1545 when he grew ill, but he lived for another eleven years in retirement in Europe, long enough to see Queen Mary I on the throne. Without Chapuys' letters, what happened in April and May 1536 would be near impossible to decipher.

Vicegerent Cromwell pushed the revised Act of Succession through the new parliament session, which stated that the king could choose his heir, rather than needing it chosen by legitimacy, birth, or gender.[16] This was almost a win for Princess Mary's supporters, who would never relent in their push for her rightful place as heir, supporting her for decades to come. Displacing Anne never got Princess Mary or her supporters that longed for heir-apparent title, though with the sudden death of her half-brother Henry Fitzroy in July 1536,[17] Mary's supporters knew they only had to bide their time (although support for Mary somewhat did falter after the birth of her brother, Prince Edward).

King Henry and Jane Seymour married on 30 May 1536, in the queen's closet at Whitehall Palace.[18] A coronation plan started to form immediately for Michaelmas in late September,[19] and Sir Edward Seymour became Lord Beauchamp, the new favoured brother-in-law in the privy chamber. The ceremony was presided over by Bishop Stephen Gardiner, the same man who had 'overheard' the rumours of Anne's adultery in France back in December 1535. Queen Jane was publicly proclaimed on 4 June 1536, after being accepted at a banquet on the edge of the Thames, where 400 canons fired from the Tower. The king had moved quickly to ensure his bed was still warm, but those who wanted to see Mary restored and the Reformation stalled still worried. The whole saga of naming Anne Boleyn an adulterer and Jane Seymour some kind of Catholic saviour had caused the most atrocious act a king could commit, and yet what that meant for Mary had not changed. On 6 June, Chapuys reported that:

> '[Cromwell] himself had been authorised and commissioned by the King to prosecute and bring to an end the mistress's trial, to do which he had taken considerable trouble. [Cromwell] said it was he who had discovered and followed up the affair of the Concubine, and that, owing to the displeasure and anger he had incurred upon the reply given to me by the King on the third day of Easter [the infamous argument between Henry and Cromwell over an Imperial alliance], he had set himself to fantasise and conspire the affair, and one of the things which had roused [Cromwell's] suspicion and made him enquire into

> the matter was a prognostic made in Flanders threatening the king with a conspiracy of those who were nearest his person'.[20]

Why Cromwell chose to share the Flanders prophecy to Chapuys goes unmentioned. It could have simply been an extra way to justify his behaviour while destroying a queen. Cromwell had eyes and ears all over the court, and perhaps did ask people to listen out for rumours of conspiracy, only for them to hear innocent remarks that boiled over into the idea that Anne could be an adulterer. The easiest way to destroy a woman has always been to accuse her of promiscuity and it worked this time with remarkable efficiency.

After Cromwell admitted to Chapuys that he had organised the plan to make Anne an adulterer, he also praised Anne and her brother for their wit and courage.[21] The king had asked for a new wife, and Cromwell had delivered, and yet peace around the throne never returned. Within months, the north of England was in uprising due to the Pilgrimage of Grace, a demand to return England to the Catholic faith and for Princess Mary to be reinstated as heir to the throne. Still Henry would not budge. International relations and marriage alliance talks resumed at once, and yet Princess Mary never received the longed-for restoration as a legitimate child of a king, nor restoration to the succession under any of Cromwell's parliaments. Despite years of diplomatic relations, Cromwell and Chapuys never got as close to an Anglo-Imperial alliance as they did on that fateful night of 18 April 1536. Princess Mary also never got a serious marriage alliance.

Seventeen months after Anne's murder, Queen Jane died of childbed fever, though King Henry had his Prince Edward, a healthy son at last.[22] The queen that the Catholics and Mary supporters wanted was gone so soon after their victory over Anne Boleyn. But the heir to the throne did grow up to be in favour of the Reformation, thanks to Sir Edward Seymour's careful placement of Protestant teachers in Prince Edward's household.[23] Thomas Cromwell also placed strong reformist tutors and governesses in Princess Elizabeth's household, ensuring the girl grew up with her mother's ideals.[24]

Thomas Boleyn, Earl of Wiltshire and Ormond, relinquished his role at court as Lord Privy Seal and retired to Hever Castle (and asked Cromwell to give a farewell speech on his behalf[25]) to be with his wife, Elizabeth, who had been sick for some time by May 1536. Boleyn did not stay away from court permanently, helping with the Pilgrimage of Grace uprising, and staying connected with Thomas Cromwell,[26] lending him luxurious items, and offering his assistance wherever he could. In 1537, Boleyn attended Prince Edward's christening as one of the earls of the realm and enjoyed a reasonable amount of respect and comfort from his peers.[27] Lady Elizabeth Boleyn died in April 1538, and Boleyn passed away a year later, both at Hever Castle. Their surviving daughter, Mary Boleyn, her husband William Stafford, and Mary's daughter Catherine Carey were all invited back to court by Cromwell in late 1539,[28] and while Mary Boleyn died in 1543, her descendants are still on the throne today.

Master Secretary and Vicegerent Thomas Cromwell needed to get straight back to work after the Anne Boleyn saga. The Pilgrimage of Grace, a Yorkshire-based uprising that started as a protest against tax collections and monastery closures, had ballooned into an army of men marching to cut off Cromwell's head, did not cause the king to lose any love for Cromwell. Made Lord Privy Seal on 2 July 1536, and given that he already ran the kingdom for the king, he was named Thomas Lord Cromwell, Baron of Wimbledon, and given lands around the Wimbledon, Mortlake, and Wandsworth areas where he grew up.[29] Cromwell was granted Mortlake Manor, a luxurious home on the Thames (where his relatives once worked as servants), usually given to the Archbishop of Canterbury. Mortlake was taken from Thomas Cranmer as retribution for standing up for Anne during her imprisonment.[30] Cromwell continued to gain official offices, eventually becoming the Earl of Essex and the Great Lord Chamberlain, in addition to being Lord Privy Seal, Master Secretary, Chancellor of the Exchequer, a member of the Noble Order of the Garter, having full control over parliament, and more than forty other major titles. The first two years after Anne's death went well for Cromwell; he married his son Gregory to Queen Jane's sister, Elizabeth, and managed to push through many changes to religion, changes Anne Boleyn would have liked to have seen, such as creating the English Bible in England and legislating unity in religion. But Lord Cromwell was also burdened with much of the king's international diplomatic relations, which included finding a European bride for the king after the death of Jane Seymour, a role nobody wanted. When Cromwell almost died in 1539 from another bout of malaria, he spent four months bedridden, missing a parliament session that saw the Duke of Norfolk roll back Catholic doctrine into law.[31] It was too late for the monasteries, as the dissolution legislation had extended to cover all monasteries of all sizes, and the last Catholic religious house closed in March 1540.[32]

Eventually, Lord Cromwell managed to secure Anna von der Marck, Duchess of Cleves as a bride for the king; a Catholic woman with a powerful Lutheran brother, Duke Wilhelm of Julich-Cleves-Burg. The Duke of Cleves was one of the Lutheran nobles in the Schmalkaldic League, and Duchess Anna's sister was Sybille, Duchess of Saxony, wife to the most influential reformist leader in Europe, Fredrick, Duke of Saxony. This marriage gave England evangelical allies while receiving a religiously moderate 'middle-way' bride for Henry.[33] In return, England had to back the duchy of Julich-Cleves-Burg against Emperor Charles in matters of war and religion. King Henry instantly panicked and wanted to back out when war came over the horizon in November 1539, leaving Lord Cromwell and poor Anna of Cleves in a crisis. King Henry then beheaded Cromwell as a way of showing Emperor Charles he did not plan to back the German duchy in a war against the Empire. Queen Anna managed to survive and divorce, but was forever exiled from her family and homeland. The Reformation and England's finances quickly fell into collapse without Lord Cromwell, the country virtually bankrupted by 1544 and all the money made from the dissolution of the monasteries lost during petty battles with France.

Archbishop Thomas Cranmer struggled with the arrival of Queen Jane after Anne Boleyn's death but pushed on with his alliance with Thomas Cromwell to create the English Bible and oversee the reform of monasteries across the country. But losing Cromwell in 1540 meant Cranmer no longer had the dedicated support he needed, especially after throwing his weight behind Cromwell in defiance of the king.[34] Cranmer was almost destroyed and potentially executed several times throughout the rest of Henry's reign. He managed to push through some reformist doctrine under King Edward, only to be burned at the stake by Queen Mary in 1556.[35] Two of Cranmer's enemies stayed close to Mary; Bishop Stephen Gardiner and Thomas Howard, Duke of Norfolk were both in the Tower for the whole of King Edward's reign (Norfolk for treason before King Henry's death and Gardiner for his views after Edward's accession). Gardiner, who had started the rumour of Anne Boleyn's adultery, became Queen Mary's Lord Chancellor, but became disillusioned by Mary's Spanish marriage and died in 1555. The Duke of Norfolk died only a year into Queen Mary's reign, dying of old age, after a long life which included seeing two of his nieces as queens of England who were beheaded.

None of Anne Boleyn's ladies were harmed after the trial. Jane Boleyn, Lady Rochford, was given a prime position in Queen Jane's court, and her father, Lord Morley, was granted lands after his work on the adultery trials.[36] Nan Cobham continued to have children with her husband George Brooke, Lord Cobham, and the pair enjoyed Cromwell's patronage and friendship.[37] Margery Horsman married Sir Michael Lyster, son of one of the judges of the Chief Justice of the King's Bench, six months after the trial of Anne Boleyn, and became close with Queen Jane and was the Keeper of the Queen's Jewels.[38] Lady Elizabeth Somerset, Countess of Worcester, had her baby after Anne Boleyn was killed, naming her daughter after the fallen queen, and did not return to court. Lady Worcester's baby, Anne Somerset, grew up to be a devout Catholic and tried to lead an uprising against Queen Elizabeth in favour of Mary, Queen of Scots.[39]

Anne's cousins, the Shelton sisters, Mary and Margaret, left court and married in the 1540s; Mary, after her contribution to the Devonshire manuscripts, married Sir Anthony Heveningham and Margaret married MP and soldier, Thomas Woodhouse.[40] Their parents, Sir John and Lady Anne Shelton, continued to run Princess Elizabeth's household, without the cruelty previously shown to Princess Mary.[41] Margaret Coffin, who attended Anne in the Tower and readily volunteered herself to relay news, joined Queen Jane's household as a reward for her service, while her husband was rewarded with lands.[42] It was not such a good time to be a lady-in-waiting connected to the Howard family, as Jane Seymour had no desire to have the family around her.

It was Chancellor Thomas Audley, not Lord Cromwell, who benefitted most from the deaths of George Boleyn, Henry Norris, and William Brereton. He scooped up lands, titles, and offices all over the country, enriching himself with the king's blessing. While Cromwell did get the power he needed in Wales to start instituting a proper legal system, it was Audley's bank accounts that flourished as a result of the deaths. Audley remained a puppet installed in the role of Lord Chancellor before dying without being missed, in 1544.[43]

Sir Thomas Wyatt struggled after the death of Anne Boleyn, as seen in a poem about the murders possibly written by him, in May 1536.[44] Wyatt was still in the Tower when the cannons boomed across London to celebrate Henry's marriage to Jane. His father, Sir Henry Wyatt, wrote to Cromwell after the executions, thanking him for protecting his son. Released one month later, Wyatt was given a job by Cromwell, who sent him abroad as ambassador to Spain. Wyatt did poorly in the position and was heard to complain bitterly about his time in the Tower and what Henry had done to him and Anne.[45] Wyatt was recalled to England by an exasperated Cromwell in 1540, before dying of illness in 1542.

Sir Richard Page was released from the Tower at the same time as Wyatt, without ever being interrogated for his part in the Anne Boleyn scandal.[46] Page took the arrest personally, and no longer wished to be friendly with Cromwell, a rarity among courtiers who worked for a living. A comparable situation happened with Sir William Fitzwilliam, who was involved in bringing down Anne Boleyn as much as Cromwell. Fitzwilliam was made the Earl of Southampton in thanks for his cooperation, but both he and his brother, Sir Anthony Browne, leaned away from the Reformation and their associations with Cromwell. Though Fitzwilliam died of illness in 1542, Browne slowly faded into a quiet life as a trusted but unremarkable courtier. Fading much quicker was Henry Percy, Earl of Northumberland, who died of illness in June 1537,[47] after defying his family and supporting King Henry during the Pilgrimage of Grace, rather than his northern family and allies, despite what the king did to Anne Boleyn.

Given how much Sir Nicholas Carew and his wife had pushed to support Princess Mary and remove Anne Boleyn, all the work, and risk, was largely in vain. While Mary was returned to being a beloved daughter of the king, life for the remaining White Roses of York was short and brutal. King Henry had his cousins Henry Courtenay, Marquis of Exeter, Henry Pole, Lord Montagu, along with Sir Edward Neville executed for treason in 1538.[48] Sir Nicholas Carew had not been supportive of King Henry's decision to kill or imprison the remaining White Roses (despite serving on the jury), and was himself then convicted of treason, and was executed in March 1539.[49] Cromwell supported Lady Elizabeth Carew and their young son, a privilege not given to the Courtenay and Pole families.[50] Lady Elizabeth Carew's brother, Sir Francis Bryan, nicknamed the Vicar of Hell by both Cromwell and Wolsey before him,[51] remained in the king's favour, and was named chief gentleman of the privy chamber in 1536,[52] and was high in King Edward VI's esteem as Lord Justice of Ireland.

Chief among the sufferers of the events of 1536 were the Norris, Weston, and Brereton families. Sir Henry Norris' children, Henry and Mary, were raised partly by their uncle, Sir John Norris, and then by John Williams (a relative of Thomas Cromwell). Henry Norris married Margery Williams, before living a life beloved by Queen Elizabeth.[53] Young Mary Norris married Sir George Carew, and then Arthur Champernowne, kinsman to Queen Elizabeth's beloved childhood governess, Kat Ashley, and the couple remained high in Elizabeth's esteem.

Sir Richard Weston, father of Sir Francis Weston, maintained his friendship with Thomas Cromwell after his son's death.[54] The pair regularly spent time together and sent gifts to each other on special occasions.[55] Richard Weston cared for his grandchildren Henry and Anne Weston as their mother soon remarried, had another son named Henry and then ten more siblings.[56] Henry Weston grew up to be a member of parliament, and all his siblings were either married into noble houses, knighted and ennobled or joined parliament. Henry Weston had better prospects than contemporaries Henry and Thomas Brereton; their mother Elizabeth died in 1545, still believing in her husband William Brereton's innocence.[57] But their uncle, Sir Urian Brereton, maintained power in the Welsh Marshes, providing the boys with family and security, and neither of the boys grew up to spend time at the royal court.

Anne Boleyn's attempts to place reformist men in positions of power in religion did slowly start to pay off after her death. Her almoner, John Skipp, who had preached against King Henry and Vicegerent Cromwell served as Bishop of Hereford for thirteen years.[58] Her chaplain Matthew Parker served as Queen Elizabeth's Archbishop of Canterbury for almost two decades. Bishop Hugh Latimer, despite having to quit his bishopric in 1539, never gave up on the Reformation and was burned at the stake by Queen Mary in 1555.[59] Anne's chaplain, Bishop Nicholas Shaxton, was likewise forced to give up in bishopric in 1539, but eventually recanted and participated in the trials that saw fellow reformers of his time burned at the stake, a total departure from all he had believed in under Anne. Bishop Edward Foxe never gave up on the Reformation, but died of illness in 1538,[60] while Bishop Nicholas Heath, another supporter of Anne and her religious beliefs, flip-flopped his way between the two religions dependent on the beliefs of the monarch, eventually settling on supporting Queen Elizabeth after giving up his roles as Archbishop of York and Lord Chancellor.[61] Some of Anne's younger reformist supporters were not as faithful. Thomas Goodricke was a passionate reformer and became Bishop of Ely but bowed down to Queen Mary and became Catholic at the first opportunity.[62] After his death, his replacement Thomas Thirlby become Bishop of Ely as a Catholic and oversaw many burnings, including Thomas Cranmer's.[63] Not all those who supported the Reformation had the courage to stand up for it in the way Anne Boleyn could.

Only two months passed between Anne Boleyn asking John Skipp to preach against King Henry, and Henry presenting his new wife Queen Jane to the court. A poem sprang up about how unseemly it was that Henry and Jane had married so fast, despite the fact Anne Boleyn had never been liked by the public.[64] No one ever seemed to believe that she was a guilty woman. England spent the second half of 1536, the year of three queens, at war with itself as upwards of 40,000 marched towards London in the defence of the Catholic faith and Princess Mary, but the shock at what happened to Anne was not soon forgotten. King Henry VIII had planned the murder of Anne Boleyn, and in turn, made her immortal.

Bibliography

Archive Sources

British Library, London

Additional MSS Charters

Arundel MSS

Cotton MSS

Cotton MSS Appendix

Cotton MSS Cleopatra

Cotton MSS Galba

Cotton MSS Nero

Cotton MSS Othello

Cotton MSS Titus

Cotton MSS Vespasian

Cotton MSS Vitellius

Egerton MS

Harley MSS and Harley Charters

Landsdowne MSS

Longleat House MSS

Royal MSS

Haus-, Hof- und Staatsarchiv, *Wien, Austrian State Archives,* Department of House, Court and State Archives

State Papers published under the authority of His Majesty's Commission, King Henry VIII 11 vols. (London 1830–52) and State Archives State Papers Online, 1509–1714: https://www.gale.com/uk/primary-sources/state-paper online

The National Archives, Kew

SP 1; SP 2; SP 6; SP 10; SP 11; SP 12; SP 15; SP 46: State Papers, Domestic, Henry VIII– Elizabeth

SP 3: Lisle correspondence
SP 5: Exchequer: King's Remembrancer papers
SP 7: Wriothesley correspondence

Primary Sources

Amyot, T., *Transcript of an original manuscript, containing a memorial from George Constantyne to Thomas, Lord Cromwell, Archaeologia, or, Miscellaneous Tracts Relating to Antiquity Vol. 23.* (The Society of Antiquaries of London, 1831.)

Anstis, J., *The register of the most noble Order of the Garter... usually called the Black Book.* 2 vols. (Barber, London, 1724.)

Ascoli, G., *La Grande-Bretagne devant l'opinion française, depuis la guerre de Cent ans, jusqu'à la fin du XVIe siècle.* (Librairie universitaire J. Gamber, Paris, 1927.)

Ashmole, E., *The history of the most noble Order of the Garter: Wherein is set forth an account of the town, castle, chappel, and college of Windsor; ... To which is prefix'd, a discourse of knighthood in general, ... Collected by Elias Ashmole, ... The whole illustrated with proper sculptures.* (A. Bell, E. Curll, J. Pemberton, and A. Collins; W. Taylor and J. Baker, London, 1715.)

Beveill, R. S., *Old English Manuscripts in the Early Age of Print: Matthew Parker and his Scribes.* (PhD dissertation, University of Tennessee, 2016.)

Brewer, J. S. (ed.), *Letters and Papers, Foreign and Domestic, Henry VIII, Volume 1, 1509–1514.* (Her Majesty's Stationery Office, London, 1920.)

Brewer, J. S. (ed.), *Letters and Papers, Foreign and Domestic, Henry VIII, Volume 2, 1515– 1518.* (Her Majesty's Stationery Office, London, 1864.)

Brewer, J. S. (ed.), *Letters and Papers, Foreign and Domestic, Henry VIII, Volume 3, 1519– 1523.* (Her Majesty's Stationery Office, London, 1867.)

Brewer, J. S. (ed.), *Letters and Papers, Foreign and Domestic, Henry VIII, Volume 4, 1524– 1530.* (Her Majesty's Stationery Office, London, 1875.)

Brock, R. E., *The Courtier in Early Tudor Society.* (London Univ. Ph.D. thesis, London, 1964.)

Bruce, J., Perowne, T. T. (eds.), *The Correspondence of Matthew Parker, D.D., Archbishop of Canterbury: Comprising Letters Written by and to Him, from A.D. 1535 to His Death, A.D. 1575.* (University Press, Cambridge, 1853.)

Burnet, G., *The History of the Reformation.* (T.H. for Richard Chiswell, London, 1679.)

Camusat, N., *Meslanges Historiques (Lettres de Roy Francois Premier... pour de dir Roy de'Angleterre).* (1619.)

Castelnau, M., *Memoirs of The Reigns of Francis II, And Charles IX, Of France, Containing A Particular Account of The Three First Civil Wars Raised and Carried On By The Huguenots In That Kingdom. Wherein The Most Remarkable Passages in The Reigns of King Henry VIII, Of England, Queen Elizabeth, And The Unfortunate Mary Queen Of Scots, Are Set In A True Light.* (London, 1724.)

Chirbury, E. Lord Herbert, *The Life and Raigne of King Henry the Eighth.* (London, 1649.)

Crapelet, G. A., Simon, E. T., *Lettres de Henri VIII à Anne Boleyn, pub. D'après les originaux de la Bibliothèque du Vatican.* (Imprimé de Crapelet, Paris, 1835.)

Cox, J. E. (ed.), *Miscellaneous Writings and Letters of Thomas Cranmer.* (Cambridge University Press, Cambridge, 1846.)

De Carles, *Épistre Contenant le Procès Criminel Faict à l'Encontre de la Royne Anne Boullant d'Angleterre.* (Lyon, 1545.)

De Gayangos, P. (ed.), *Calendar of State Papers of Spain Volume 5 Part 2.* (1888.)

Du Bellay, J., Scheurer, R. (eds.), *Correspondance du cardinal Jean Du Bellay (in French).* Vol. I: 1529–1535. (C. Klincksieck, Paris, 1969.)

Ellis, H., *Original Letters illustrative of English History... from autographs in the British Museum and... other collections.* 11 vols. (Bentley, London, 1824, 1827, 1846.)

Flower, W., Norcliffe, C. B. (eds.), *The Visitation of Yorkshire in the Years 1563 and 1564, Made by William Flower, Esquire, Norroy king of Arms. Publications of the Harleian Society.* Vol. XVI. (Mitchell and Hughes, Printers, London, 1881.)

Foxe, J., *The Unabridged Acts and Monuments Online* or TAMO. (HRI Online Publications, Sheffield, 2011). Available from: http//www.johnfoxe.org.

Foxe, J., *The first volume of the ecclesiasticall history contaynyng the actes and monuments of thynges passed in every kynges tume in this realme... The second volume of the ecclesiastical history, contenynyng the actes and monumentes of martyrs.* (Daye, London, 1570.)

Foxe, J., *Actes and monuments of matters most speciall and memorable, happenyng in the Church.* (London, 1583, RSTC 11225.)

Fuller, T., *A Pisgah-sight of Palestine and the confines thereof with the history of the Old and New Testament acted thereon.* (J. F. for John Williams, London, 1650.)

Gairdner, J. (ed.), *Letters and Papers, Foreign and Domestic, Henry VIII, Volume 5, 1531– 1532.* (Her Majesty's Stationery Office, London, 1880.)

Gairdner, J. (ed.), *Letters and Papers, Foreign and Domestic, Henry VIII, Volume 6, 1533.* (Her Majesty's Stationery Office, London, 1882.)

Gairdner, J. (ed.), *Letters and Papers, Foreign and Domestic, Henry VIII, Volume 7, 1534.* (Her Majesty's Stationery Office, London, 1883.)

Gairdner, J. (ed.), *Letters and Papers, Foreign and Domestic, Henry VIII, Volume 8, January – July 1535.* (Her Majesty's Stationery Office, London, 1885.)

Gairdner, J. (ed.), *Letters and Papers, Foreign and Domestic, Henry VIII, Volume 9, August – December 1535.* (Her Majesty's Stationery Office, London, 1886.)

Gairdner, J. (ed.), *Letters and Papers, Foreign and Domestic, Henry VIII, Volume 10, January – July 1536.* (Her Majesty's Stationery Office, London, 1887.)

Gairdner, J. (ed.), *Letters and Papers, Foreign and Domestic, Henry VIII, Volume 11, August – December 1536.* (Her Majesty's Stationery Office, London, 1888.)

Gairdner, J. (ed.), *Letters and Papers, Foreign and Domestic, Henry VIII, Volume 12 Part 1, January – May 1537.* (Her Majesty's Stationery Office, London, 1890.)

Gairdner, J. (ed.), *Letters and Papers, Foreign and Domestic, Henry VIII, Volume 12 Part 2, June – December 1537.* (Her Majesty's Stationery Office, London, 1891.)

Gairdner, J. (ed.), *Letters and Papers, Foreign and Domestic, Henry VIII, Volume 13 Part 1, January – July 1538.* (Her Majesty's Stationery Office, London, 1892.)

Gairdner, J. (ed.), *Letters and Papers, Foreign and Domestic, Henry VIII, Volume 13 Part 2, August – December 1538.* (Her Majesty's Stationery Office, London, 1893.)

Gairdner, J., and Brodie, R. H. (eds.), *Letters and Papers, Foreign and Domestic, Henry VIII, Volume 14 Part 1, January – July 1539.* (Her Majesty's Stationery Office, London, 1894.)

Gairdner, J., and Brodie, R. H. (eds.), *Letters and Papers, Foreign and Domestic, Henry VIII, Volume 14 Part 2, August – December 1539.* (Her Majesty's Stationery Office, London, 1895.)

Gairdner, J., and Brodie, R. H. (eds.), *Letters and Papers, Foreign and Domestic, Henry VIII, Volume 15 1540.* (Her Majesty's Stationery Office, London, 1896.)

Giles, J. A. (ed.), *The Chronicles of the White Rose of York: A Series of Historical Fragments, Proclamations, Letters, and Other Contemporary Documents Relating to the Reign of King Edward the Fourth.* (J. Bohn, London 1845.)

Greenaway, D. E., *Fasti Ecclesiae Anglicanae 1066–1300: Volume 2, Monastic Cathedrals (Northern and Southern Provinces).* (Institute of Historical Research, London, 1971.)

Hall, E., Ellis, H. (eds.), *Hall's Chronicle containing the history of England, during the reign of Henry the Fourth, and the succeeding monarchs, to the end of the reign of Henry the Eighth, in which are particularly described the manners and customs of those periods. Carefully collated with the editions of 1548 and 1550.* (J. Johnston, London, 1809.)

Hardy, W. J., *Documents Illustrative of English Church History.* (Macmillan, London, 1910.)

Henry, G., Hardy, W. J., *Documents illustrative of English Church History.* (MacMillan and co., London, 1910.)

Holyrode, A., *Prophecy and the Fall of Anne Boleyn.* (MA dissertation, University of Huddersfield, 2017.)

Hume, M. A. S., *Chronicle of King Henry VIII of England.* (Bell and Sons, London, 1889.)

Kaulek, J. (ed.), *Correspondance politique de mm. de Castillon et de Marillac, ambassadeurs de France en Angleterre (1537–1542); pub. sous les auspices de la Commission des archives diplomatiques.* (F. Alcan, Paris, 1885.)

Langbaine, G., *The true subiect to the rebell, or, The hurt of sedition, how greivous it is to a common-wealth written by Sir John Cheeke ... ; whereunto is newly added by way of preface a briefe discourse of those times, as they may relate to the present, with the authors life.* (Leonard Lichfield, Oxford, 1641.)

Loke, W., Heath, J. B (eds.), *An account of materials furnished for the use of Queen Anne Boleyn, and the Princess Elizabeth by ... 'the king's mercer,' between the 20th Jany. 1535 ... and 27th April 1536.* (Philobiblon Society, London, 1862–3.)

LP – *Letters and Papers, Foreign and Domestic, Henry VIII – see Brewer et al. and Gairdner et al.*

Madden, F., *Privy Purse Expenses of the Princess Mary, Daughter of the King Henry VIII afterward Queen Mary.* (William Pickering, London, 1831.)

Madden, F., Bandinel, B., Gough Nichols, J., *Collectanea Topographica Et Genealogica: Volume 5.* (J. B. Nichols and son, London, 1838.)

Mattingly, G., *Calendar of State Papers, Spain: Further Supplement to Volumes 1 and 2, Documents from Archives in Vienna.* (London, 1947.)

Melanchthon, P., *The Augsburg Confession The confession of faith, which was submitted to His Imperial Majesty Charles V at the diet of Augsburg in the year 1530.* (Philip Melanchthon, 1530)

MS Jesus College 74: *Thomas Master collection for Lord Herbert's Life of Henry VIII.* (Western manuscripts at the Bodleian Libraries.)

Nicolas, N. H., *Privy Purse Expenses of Elizabeth of York : Wardrobe Accounts of Edward the Fourth. With a memoir of Elizabeth of York, and notes.* (William Pickering, London, 1830.)

Nichols, J. G., *The Reminiscences of John Louth, Archdeacon of Nottingham in the Narratives of the Days of the Reformation.* (Camden Society, London, 1859.)

Singer, S. W. (ed.), *The Life of Cardinal Wolsey by George Cavendish.* (Harding, Triphook & Lepard, London, 1825.)

St. C. Byrne, M., *The Lisle Letters 6 vols.* (University of Chicago Press, London and Chicago, 1981.)

Stevenson, J., (ed.) *Calendar of State Papers Foreign: Elizabeth, Volume 1, 1558–1559.* (London, 1863.)

Strype, J., *The Life and Acts of Matthew Parker, vol 1.* (Clarendon Press, London, 1821.)

Tait, M. B., *The Bridgettine monastery of Syon (Middlesex) with special references to its monastic usages.* (PhD Thesis, University of Oxford, 1975.)

Thompson, E. M. (ed.), *Letters of Dean Prideaux.* (Camden Society, London, 1875.)

Trokelowe, J., Hearne, T., Blanforde, H. (ed.), *Johannis de Trokelowe annales Edvardi II. Henrici de Blaneforde Chronica, et Edvardi II Vita.* (E Teatro Sheldoniano, Oxford, 1729.)

Wilkins, D. (ed.), *Concilia Magnae Britanniae et Hiberniae Vol. III.* (R. Gosling, London, 1737.)

Wood, M. A. E., *Letters of Royal and Illustrious Ladies of Great Britain.* Vol. II. (Henry Colburn, London, 1846.)

Wriothesley, C. (ed.), Hamilton, E. D., *A Chronicle of England, 1485-1559.* (Camden Society, London, 1877.)

Secondary Sources

Angus, C., *Henry VIII's Children.* (Pen & Sword, Yorkshire, 2023.)

Angus, C., *The Private Life of Thomas Cromwell.* (Pen & Sword, Yorkshire, 2022.)

Aubrey, J., Edward, J., *Wiltshire: The Topographical Collections of John Aubrey, F. R. S., A. D. 1659–70, With Illustrations.* (Wiltshire Archaeological and Natural History Society, London, 1862.)

Bandello, M., Payne, P. (eds.), *The Novels of Matteo Bandello Bishop of Agen now first done into English prose and verse.* (London, 1890.)

Bannerman, B. (ed.), *The Visitations of the County of Sussex, Vol. 53.* (The Harleian Society, London, 1805.)

Bernard, G. W., *Anne Boleyn.* (Yale University Press, London, 2010.)

Bindoff, S. T., *The House of Commons, 1509–1558, Volume 1.* (Secker & Warburg, London, 1982.)

Brook, V. J. K., *A life of Archbishop Parker.* (Clarendon Press, Oxford, 1962.)

Burke, J., *Burke's genealogical and heraldic history of peerage, baronetage and knightage.* (G.P. Putnam's Sons, New York, 1914.)

Burnett, C., Mann, N., *Britannia Latina: Latin in the culture of Great Britain from the Middle Ages to the twentieth century.* (Warberg Institute, London 2005.)

Caley, J., Hunter, J., (eds.), *Valor ecclesiasticus temp. Henr. VIII: auctoritate regia institutus, Volume iv.* (Record Commission, London, 1821.)

Cattley, S. R. (ed.), *The Acts and Monuments of John Foxe. Vol. IV.* (R. B. Seeley and W. Burnside, London, 1857.)

Chambers, R. (ed.), *The Book of Days: A Miscellany of Popular Antiquities in Connection with the Calendar, Including Anecdote, Biography, & History, Curiosities of Literature and Oddities of Human Life and Character, Volume 1.* (W. & R. Chambers Limited, London, 1832.)

Chisholm, H., (ed.). *Encyclopædia Britannica. Vol. 25.* (Cambridge University Press, Cambridge, 1911.)

Clarke, E., Lee, S. (ed.), *Weston, Francis, Dictionary of National Biography. Vol. 60.* (Smith, Elder & Co, London, 1889.)

Clifford H., *The life of Jane Dormer, Duchess of Feria.* (E.E. Estcourt and J. Stevenson, London, 1887.)

Cokayne, G., E., Gibbs, V. (eds.), *The Complete Peerage, Vol. I* (St Catherine Press, London, 1910.)

Copinger, W. A., *The Manors of Suffolk: Notes on their History and Devolution; The Hundreds of Blything and Bosmere and Claydon; With Some Illustrations of Old Manor Houses. Vol. 2.* (Taylor, Garnett, Evans & Co, Manchester, 1908.)

Dalder, J., *Collected Poems of Sir Thomas Wyatt.* (Oxford University Press, Oxford, 1975.)

Dashwood, G., *Visitation of Norfolk in the Year 1563, Vol. 1.* (Norwich, 1878, p. 104.)

Demaus, R., *Hugh Latimer: A Biography.* (The Religious Tract Society, London, 1904.)

Dowling, M., *Humanism in the age of Henry VIII.* (Croom Helm, London, 1986.)

Dugdale, W., *Derbyshire Visitation Pedigrees 1569 and 1611.* (London, 1895.)

Edwards, A.S.G. (ed.), *George Cavendish, Metrical Visions.* (Columbia University of South Carolina Press, South Carolina, 1980.)

Elton, G. R., *Policy and Police: The Enforcement of the Reformation in the Age of Thomas Cromwell.* (Cambridge University Press, Cambridge, 1985.)

Erickson, C., *Anne Boleyn.* (Papermac, London, 1984.)

Foster, J. (ed.), *Alumni Oxonienses: The Members of the University of Oxford.* (Parker and Co., Oxford, 1891.)

Fraser, A., *Mary, Queen of Scots.* (Weidenfeld & Nicolson, London, 1969.)

Gachard, L.P., *Analectes historiques.* (Hayez, Brussels, 1856.)

Gristwood, S., *Tudors in Love.* (OneWorld, London, 2021.)

Grueninger, N., *The Final Year of Anne Boleyn.* (Pen & Sword, Yorkshire, 2022.)

Gunn, S. J., *Charles Brandon, Duke of Suffolk, c. 1484–1545.* (The American Historical Review, Volume 95, Issue 4, New York: Basil Blackwell. New York, 1988.)

Haigh, C., *English Reformations: Religion, Politics, and Society Under the Tudors.* (Clarendon, London, 1993.)

Halsted, C. A, *Richard III, as Duke of Gloucester and King of England.* (Carey and Hart, Philadelphia, 1844.)

Harrison, F., *Annals of an Old Manor House.* (Macmillan and Co., London, 1899.)

Hayward, M., *Dress at the Court of Henry VIII.* (Taylor & Francis Publishing, London, 2007.)

Heale, M., *The Abbots and Priors of Late Medieval and Reformation England.* (Oxford University Press, Oxford, 2016.)

Hillebrand, H. N., *The Early History of the Chapel Royal.* (Modern Philology, Vol. 18, No. 5, September 1920.)

Horn, J. M. (ed.), *Fasti Ecclesiae Anglicanae 1300–1541: Volume 2, Hereford Diocese.* (Institute of Historical Research, London, 1962.)

Hoyle, R.W., *The Pilgrimage of Grace and the Politics of the 1530s* (Oxford University Press, Oxford, 2001.)

Hutchinson, J., *Catalogue of Notable Middle Templars: With Brief Biographical Notices.* (The Honourable Society of the Middle Temple, London, 1902.)

Huth, H., Startridge, F. Hazlitt, W. C., *The Huth library : A catalogue of the printed books, manuscripts, autograph letters, and engravings, collected by Henry Huth, with collations and bibliographical descriptions, Volume 1.* (Ellis and White, London, 1880.)

Ives, E. (ed.), *Letters and Accounts of William Brereton of Malpas. The Record Society of Lancashire and Cheshire. Vol. 116.* (Record Society of Lancashire and Cheshire, Old Woking, 1976.)

Ives, E., *The Life and Death of Anne Boleyn.* (Blackwell, Oxford, 2004.)

Ives, E., *William Brereton and the Pork Barrel: Travails of Political Ascendancy.* (Lecture Delivered to the Worldwide Brereton Family Reunion, Holly Lodge, Holmes Chapel, Cheshire, 30 July 2001.)

James, S. E., *Kateryn Parr: The Making of a Queen.* (Ashgate Publishing, Aldershot, 1999)

Lee, S. (ed.), *Norris, Henry (d.1536) Dictionary of National Biography. Vol. 41.* (Smith, Elder & Co, London, 1895.)

Lee, S., *Seymour, Edward , Dictionary of National Biography. Vol. 51.* (Smith, Elder & Co, London, 1897.)

Leedham-Green, E., *A Concise History of the University of Cambridge.* (Cambridge University Press Cambridge, 1996.)

Levin, C., Bertolet, A. R., Carney, J. E. (ed.), *A Biographical Encyclopedia of Early Modern Englishwomen: Exemplary Lives and Memorable Acts, 1500–1650.* (Routledge, New York, 2016.)

Loades, D. (ed.), *The Papers of George Wyatt Esquire.* (Offices of The Royal Historical Society, London, 1968.)

Loades, D., *Jane Seymour: Henry VIII's Favourite Wife.* (Amberley, Gloucestershire, 2013.)

Lysons, D., *Beddington, in The Environs of London: Volume 1, County of Surrey.* (T. Cadell and W. Davies, London, 1792.)

Lyttleton, H., *Lyster D., Memorials of an ancient house: a history of the family of Lister or Lyster.* (Ballantyne Hanson, Edinburgh, 1913.)

MacCulloch, D., *The Reformation: A History.* (Penguin, London, 2005.)

MacCulloch, D., *Thomas Cranmer: A Life.* (Yale University, London, 1996.)

MacCulloch, D., *Thomas Cromwell: A Life.* (Viking, London, 2018.)

MacLean, J., *Manor of Tockington and the Roman Villa, Transactions of the Bristol & Gloucestershire Archaeological Society, For 1887–88. Vol. XII.* (Bristol & Gloucestershire Archaeological Soc., 1888.)

Magalhães, A., Romera Pintor, I., Sirera, J. L (eds.), *Le Comédies bibliques di Margherita di Navarra, tra evangelismo e mistero medievale, in La mujer: de los bastidores al proscenio en el teatro del siglo XVI.* (Publicacions de la Universitat de València, Valencia, 2011.)

McEntegart, R., *Henry VIII, the League of Schmalkalden, and the English Reformation.* (Boydell Press, Suffolk, 2002.)

Merriman, R. B., *Life and Letters of Thomas Cromwell Vol. I.* (Clarendon Press, Oxford, 1902.)

More, C., Hunter, J. (eds.), *The Life of Sir Thomas More.* (William Pickering, London, 1828.)

Mosley, C., (ed.) *Burke's Peerage, Baronetage & Knightage, 107th edition, 3 vols.* (Genealogical Books, Delaware, Burke's.)

Murphy, B., *Bastard Prince: Henry VIII's Lost Son.* (History Press, Gloucestershire, 2010.)

Norton, E., *Jane Seymour: King Henry's True Love.* (Amberley, Gloucestershire, 2009.)

Penn, T., *Winter King: Henry VII and the Dawn of Tudor England.* (Penguin, London, 2011.)

Pocock, N. (ed.), *Records of the Reformation, The Divorce 1527–1533.* (Clarendon, Oxford, 1870.)

Richardson, D., Everingham, K. G., (ed.) *Magna Carta Ancestry: A Study in Colonial and Medieval Families.* (CreateSpace, 2011.)

Richardson, D., Everingham, K. G., (eds.) *Plantagenet Ancestry: A Study in Colonial and Medieval Families, Vol. II (2nd ed.).* (CreateSpace, 2011.)

Ridgway, C., *The Fall of Anne Boleyn: A Countdown.* (MadeGlobal Publishing, 2012.)

Rodger, N.A.M., *The Safeguard of the Sea: A Naval History of Britain. Vol. 1 660–1649.* (HarperCollins, London, 1997.)

Russell, G., *Young and Damned and Fair: the Life of Catherine Howard.* (William Collins, London, 2017.)

Sanders, N., *Rise and Growth of the Anglican Schism.* (Burns & Oates, London, 1877.)

Seymour, W., *Ordeal by Ambition: An English Family in the Shadow of the Tudors.* (Sidgwick & Jackson, London, 1972.)

Shaw, W. A., *The Knights of England, Vol I.* (Sherrat and Hughes, London, 1906.).

Shulman, N., *Graven With Diamonds: The Many Lives of Thomas Wyatt: Courtier, Poet, Assassin, Spy in the Court of Henry VIII.* (Faber Short Books, London, 2012.)

Smith, D. M. (ed.), *The Heads of Religious Houses in England and Wales, III, 1377–1540.* (Cambridge, University Press, Cambridge, 2008.)

Smith, L. B., *The Elizabethan World.* (Houghton Mifflin, Boston, 1967.)

Soberton, S. B, *Ladies in Waiting: Women Who Served Anne Boleyn.* (Golden Age, 2022.)

Southall, R., *The Devonshire Manuscript of Early Tudor Poetry, 1532–41.* (The Review of English Studies, 1964.)

Thomas, M., *The King's Pearl.* (Amberley Publishing, Gloucestershire, 2017.)

Thornton, T., *Cheshire and the Tudor State 1480–1560. Royal Historical Society Studies in History New Series Vol. 18.* (Boydell & Brewer, Suffolk, 2000.)

Thornton, T., *The Channel Islands, 1370–1640: Between England and Normandy.* (The Boydell Press, Woodbridge, 2012.)

Vasoli, S., *Anne Boleyn's Letter from the Tower: New Updated Edition.* (GreyLondon Press, London, 2022.)

Waters, R. E. C., *Genealogical memoirs of the kindred families of Thomas Cranmer, Archbishop of Canterbury, and Thomas Wood, Bishop of Lichfield, London.* (Robson and Sons, London, 1877.)

Webb, S., Webb, B., *English Local Government: English Poor Law History, Part 1.* (Longmans, Green & Co, London, 1927.)

Wegemer, G., *Thomas More: Portrait of Courage.* (Scepter, Ohio, 1998.)

Weir, A., *Henry VIII: King and Court.* (Pimlico, London, 2002.)

Weir, A., *The Lady in the Tower: The Fall of Anne Boleyn.* (Vintage, London, 2009.)

Wilkinson, J., *Anne Boleyn.* (Amberley, Gloucestershire, 2011.)

Wyatt, M., *Italian Encounter with England.* (Cambridge University Press, 2012.)

Wyatt, T., Rebholz, R. A. (ed.), *The Complete Poems.* (Penguin, Harmondsworth, 1978.)

Wyatt, T., Yeowell, J. (ed.), *The Poetical Works of Sir Thomas Wyatt.* (George Bell and Sons, London, 1898.)

Zevin, E. M., *The Life of Edward Stanley, Third Earl of Derby: Noble Power and the Tudor Monarchy.* (Edwin Mellen Press, New York, 2010.)

Notes

Chapter 1: Defying the Heroes of History

1. SP I/452.
2. Arch. xvi. 23.
3. LP x no. 37.
4. Otho. C. x. 216 and f. 216b.
5. Arch. xvi. 23.
6. Ibid.
7. LP x no. 76.
8. Ibid.
9. Ibid.
10. Wien, Rep. P. C., Fasc. 236, no.3.
11. LP x no. 141.
12. Add. MSS. 25,114 f. 126.
13. Sanders, p.131–132.
14. Wien, Rep. P. C., Fasc. 229, no. 6.
15. S. E., L. 865, f. 86.
16. LP x no. 141.
17. Ibid.
18. LP vii no. 690.
19. Cleop. E. iv. 203.
20. Wien, Rep. P. C., Fasc. 230, 1–4.
21. Wien. Rep. P. C., Fasc. 228, no. 43.
22. Wien, Rep. P. C., Fasc. 236, no.3.
23. LP x no. 256.
24. Otho C. x. 220.
25. Thomas, p.148.
26. LP x no. 141.

27. Ibid.
28. Wien, Rep. P. C., Fasc. 236, no. 3.
29. Ibid.
30. Ibid.
31. LP x no. 307.
32. LP x no. 151.
33. Wien, Rep. P. C., Fasc. 229, no. 6.
34. Add MS 28,588, f. 145.

Chapter 2: Power Vacuum

1. Add. MS. 28,588, f. 161.
2. MacCulloch, 2018, p.269.
3. Add. MSS. 25,114, f. 175 is a great example of Cromwell being passive-aggressive with Gardiner.
4. Angus, 2022, p.75–78.
5. Greenway, p.85.
6. SP 1/44 f. 3.
7. LP Spanish Calendar, 5 no. 267.
8. Angus, 2022, p.61.
9. Cavendish, p.274.
10. LP iv no. 6294.
11. LP iv no. 6757.
12. Submission of the Clergy, see Pocock, II. 257; Restraint of Appeals, see Cleo. E. VI. 185.
13. MacCulloch, 2018, p.133.
14. An early example is LP iv. no. 3741.
15. Angus, 2022, p.87–89.
16. MacCulloch, 1996, p.45–51.
17. MacCulloch, 2018, p.192.
18. Ibid.
19. TNA, SP 70/7 ff. 3–13, at ff. 6r–7r.
20. Thomas, p.165.
21. Castelnau's Memoirs vol I. no. 405.
22. CSP Foreign: Elizabeth, Volume 1 no. 1303.

23. Ibid.
24. Ibid.

Chapter 3: Pride Before the Fall

1. LP xii no. 242.
2. Hayward, p.108.
3. Hall, p.697.
4. LP x no. 427.
5. LP x no. 200.
6. Wriothesley, p.33.
7. Add. MSS. 25,114, f. 137.
8. Grueninger, p.132–133.
9. Wriothesley, p.33.
10. Wien, Rep. P. C., Fasc. 229, no. 6.
11. Ibid.
12. Sanders, p.25.
13. LP x no. 282.
14. Wien, Rep. P. C., Fasc. 229, no. 6.
15. Wriothesley, p.33.
16. Wien, Rep. P. C., Fasc. 229, no. 6.
17. LP x no. 352.
18. LP x no. 199.
19. LP x no. 282.
20. Chisholm, p.386–387.
21. Norton, p.41.
22. Norton, p.13.
23. Norton, p.39–40.
24. Ibid, p.33.
25. Seymour, p.26.
26. MacCulloch 2018, p. 422.
27. Aubrey, p.377.
28. Loades, p.28.
29. Norton, p.9.
30. Titus, B. I. 429.

31. Clifford, p.41.
32. Norton, p.41.
33. LP vii no. 9.
34. Thornton, p.71.
35. Grueninger, p.101 for the Seymour visit. This excellent book also details the entire royal progress of 1535.
36. Lee, p.245.
37. LP x no. 908.
38. Madden, 1838, p.21–24.
39. Flower, p.166.
40. LP Spanish Calendar 5 ii no. 43a.

Chapter 4: The Empire Strikes Back

1. LP x no. 284.
2. Ibid.
3. Ibid.
4. Huth Library Catalogue, v.1692.
5. LP x no. 284.
6. Ibid.
7. LP x no. 199.
8. Add. MS. 28,588, f. 171.
9. Corpus Reform., iii. 49.
10. Wien, Rep. P. C., Fasc. 229, ii. 10—2.
11. Ibid.
12. R. MS. 7 F. xiv. f. 83.
13. Foxe, 1570, 1385.
14. Angus, 2022, p.108.
15. SP 1/83 f. 88.
16. Wien. Rep. P. C., Fasc. 229½, ii. f.29.
17. LP x no. 351.
18. LP viii no. 1105.
19. LP x no. 351.
20. Ibid.
21. Ibid.
22. Ibid.

23. Ibid.
24. Ibid.
25. LP Spanish Calendar 5 ii no. 29.
26. Ibid.

Chapter 5: Cold Shoulders of the Great Families of England

1. SP 1/142 f. 202rv.
2. Ibid.
3. LP xiv i no. 190.
4. SP 1/142 f. 202v.
5. Ibid.
6. Ibid.
7. Madden, 1831, p.52.
8. Lysons, p.49–67.
9. Ibid.
10. Weir, 2002, p.241,
11. Wien. Rep. P. Fasc. 225, no. 50.
12. Weir, 2002, p.320.
13. Wien. Rep. P. Fasc. 227, no. 39.
14. Anstis' Garter ii. p.398.
15. Angus, 2023, p.103.
16. LP i no. 82.
17. Weir, 2022, p.217.
18. LP xiv.i no. 498.
19. Harl. MS. 6,989 f. 56.
20. Vit. B. xiv. 278.
21. SP 1/65 f. 238.
22. Cleo. E. v.172.
23. LP x no. 663.
24. Otho, C. x.176.
25. Vesp. F. XIII. 203.
26. LP v no. 429.
27. Lysons, p.60.
28. Grueninger, 2022, p.160.
29. CSP Foreign: Elizabeth, Volume 1 no. 1303.

30. Wien, Rep. P. C., Fasc. 229, ii. 10-2.
31. Wood, p.112.
32. LP x no. 601.
33. Ives, p.231.
34. Ibid.
35. Ives, p.125.
36. Soberton, p.170. The author has multiple excellent books on this topic.
37. Richardson, *Magna Carta*, p.371.
38. Ibid.

Chapter 6: Factions in a Queen's Household

1. Richardson, p.460.
2. Halsted, p.37.
3. Angus, 2023, p.191.
4. LP vii no. 1257.
5. LP xiv. no. 285.
6. Bindoff, p.312.
7. Ives, p.211.
8. Grueninger, pp. 95–96.
9. LP xiv. ii no. 782, f. 117.
10. Richardson, *Magna Carta* p.51.
11. Penn, p.141.
12. Ibid.
13. Angus, 2023, p.88.
14. Southall, p.146.
15. Soberton, p.173.
16. LP vi no. 728.
17. Soberton, p.177.
18. Soberton, p.171.
19. MacCulloch, 2018, p.422.
20. LP xiv ii no. 782.
21. Southall, p.146.
22. McCulloch, 2018, p.34.
23. McCulloch, 2018, p.132.
24. Dugdale, p.87.

25. Richardson, *Magna Carta*, pp.216–17.
26. Titus B.I. 383a.
27. Soberton, p.149.
28. Ives, p.265.
29. Ibid.
30. LP xiv. ii no. 782, f. 117, f. 59.
31. Ellis, p.32.
32. Richardson, *Magna Carta*, pp.380–81.
33. Shulman, p.88.
34. McCulloch, 2018, p.385.
35. Ibid.
36. Ibid.
37. Madden, 1838, p.283.
38. Lyttleton, p.260–261.
39. Madden, 1831, p.182.
40. SP 3/10 f. 70.
41. Mosley, p.587.
42. Ibid.
43. Ives, p.265.

Chapter 7: Dissolution of True Reform

1. LP x no. 243 Parl. Roll 27 Hen. VIII.
2. McCulloch, 2018, p.328.
3. Murphy, p.170.
4. Murphy, p.30.
5. LP x no. 243.
6. Ibid.
7. Parl. Roll 27 Hen. VIII.
8. 28 Hen. 8. c. 24.
9. Cleo. E. VI. 185.
10. Cleo. E. VI. 262.
11. 27 Hen. 8 c.8.
12. 27 Hen. 8 c.10.
13. Caley, *Valor Ecclesiasticus* 1821 copy.
14. SP 1/101 f. 28.

15. Cleo. E. iv, f. 8.
16. Cleo. E. iv, f. 7.
17. Hardy, p.257.
18. Caley, *Valor Ecclesiasticus* 1821 copy.
19. Ibid.
20. Angus, 2022, p.41–46.
21. Angus, 2022, p.102.
22. Ibid.
23. Ibid.
24. McCulloch, 2018, p.261.
25. Loades, 1968, p.155–160.
26. SP 3/6 f. 144.
27. SP 3/6 f. 144.
28. McCulloch, 2018, p.274.
29. 27 Hen. 8. c. 28.
30. LP x no. 445.
31. SP1/102 f. 177.
32. Ibid.
33. Cleo. E. iv. 144.
34. SP 1/140 f. 73.
35. Merriman, p.17.
36. Titus B. I. 360.
37. SP 3/14 f. 47.
38. Loades, 1968, p.159–60.
39. SP 3/14 f. 47.
40. More, p.263.
41. Pendrill, p.144.
42. SP 1/134 f. 248 is just one example of Rich's bad attitude.
43. TNA E 315/232 ff. 1v-7v.
44. LP Spanish Calendar 5 ii 83-84.
45. BL MS Royal 18 CVI.
46. Ibid.
47. Webb, p.45.
48. BL MS Royal 18 CVI.
49. Ibid.
50. Ibid.
51. LP vii no. 1035.

52. LP ix 523.
53. LP ix no. 358.
54. LP xii.ii no. 660.
55. BL MS Royal 18 CVI.
56. Webb, p.46.
57. Dowling, p.239.

Chapter 8: Rise of the Seymours

1. Add. 28,588, f. 223.
2. Add. 28,588, f. 228.
3. Ibid.
4. SP 1/104 f. 211.
5. Wien, Rep. P. C., Fasc. 230, 1–4.
6. Ibid.
7. Ives, p.127.
8. Wien, Rep. P. C., Fasc. 230, 1–4.
9. Norton, p.7.
10. Norton, p.8.
11. Ibid.
12. Wien, Rep. P. C., Fasc. 230, 1–4.
13. Ibid.

Chapter 9: Two Sides of the Same Reformed Coin

1. Cleop. E. iv. 230.
2. Cleop. E. iv. 230.
3. LP xi no. 233.
4. McCulloch, 2018, p.133.
5. Wien, Rep. P. C., Fasc. 229½.
6. Ibid.
7. Bandello, vol 4. p.117.
8. Foxe, 1570, p.138.
9. Chambers, p.77.
10. SP I/65 f. 122.

11. Friedmann, p.44.
12. Bernard, p.188.
13. SP 1/68 f. 58.
14. Ives, p.18–33.
15. LP i no. 2655.
16. Ives, p.18–33.
17. LP i no. 2941.
18. Herbert, p.161.
19. LP ix no. 378.
20. Magalhães, p.171–201.
21. Wilkinson, p.57–58.
22. LP iii. no. 1011.
23. Nichols, p.55-56
24. Wegemer, p.131.
25. LP v no. 291 (201).
26. Nichols, pp.51–53.
27. Ibid.
28. Galba B. x 338.
29. Ibid.
30. Harl. 419. f. 103.
31. Erickson, p.130–131.
32. TNA SP1/72 f.18v.
33. Cavendish, Metrical Visions, p.49.
34. LP viii 985.
35. One example is LP ix no. 723.
36. TNA SP1/92 f. 37.
37. Tait, p.217–219.
38. Elton, p.117.
39. E Leedham-Green, p.44.
40. Ibid.
41. MacCulloch, 2018, p.86.
42. LP xiv.i no. 245.
43. Harl. MS. 6,989, f. 56.
44. Ives, p.261–262.
45. Pollard, p.946.
46. Horn, p.1–3.

47. *The Primer in English, most necessary for the Educacyon of Children, abstracted out of the Manuall of Prayers, or Primer in Englishe and Latin, set forth by John, laet bysh. of Rochester*, 1539, is just one book dedicated to Cromwell from Hilsey.
48. Ives, p.261.
49. House of Commons, I 626.
50. Strype, J, *The Life and Act of Matthew Parker*, I p.16.
51. Hillebrand, p.245.

Chapter 10: Battle for the Pulpit

1. MacCulloch, 1996, p.21.
2. SP 1/49 f. 196.
3. SP 1/44 ff. 144–5.
4. Thompson, p.21, p.48.
5. LP v no. 1326.
6. LP v no. 1326.
7. Waters, p.16.
8. Harl. 7032, f. 141 b.
9. Ibid.
10. MacCulloch, 2018, p.298–299.
11. Wien, Rep. P. C., Fasc. 230, 1–4.
12. Ibid.
13. Ibid.
14. Wien, Rep. P. C., Fasc. 230, 1–4.
15. Ibid.
16. Ibid.
17. Ibid.
18. Ibid.
19. Ibid.
20. LP x no. 615 1-12.
21. Ibid.
22. Ibid.
23. Ibid.
24. 27 Hen 8 c 28.

25. LP vi no. 1468.
26. Titus B.I. 489 is one example.
27. Chambers, p.399.
28. Holyrode, *Prophecy and the Fall of Anne Boleyn.*
29. LP x no. 1069 is Cromwell's first recorded mention of the prophecy.
30. LP x no. 663 Vaughan is in Antwerp in April, before being called home in June.
31. At the time of publication, The 480,000 items in the ETSC were unavailable from the British Library after its cyber-attack so the papers cannot be cited. Yes, I should have copied down the file number the first time!
32. Thomas, p.21.
33. Holyrode, *Prophecy and the Fall of Anne Boleyn.*
34. MacCulloch, 2018, p.487–489.
35. LP x no. 1069.

Chapter 11: The Dinner

1. 27 Hen. 8. c. 42.
2. 27 Hen. 8. c. 10 and 16.
3. 27 Hen. 8. c. 26.
4. Vit. B. xiv. 177.
5. Harl. MS. 6,989, f. 56.
6. LP x 663.
7. Vit. B. xiv. 177.
8. Ibid.
9. LP x no. 699.
10. Ibid.
11. Ibid.
12. LP Spanish Calendar 5 ii no.43a.
13. Ibid.
14. Ibid.
15. Ibid.
16. Wien. Rep. P. C., Fasc. 229½, 1–4.
17. Ibid.
18. Galba, B. VII. 102.

19. LP x no. 699.
20. Ibid.
21. LP Spanish Calendar 5 ii no.43a.
22. Ibid.

Chapter 12: An Affair to Invent

1. LP x no. 748.
2. LP x no. 753.
3. Ibid.
4. LP x no. 700.
5. Cokayne, p.33.
6. Anstis' Order of the Garter. ii. p.398.
7. Anstis' Order of the Garter. ii. p.100.
8. LP x no. 752.
9. LP x no. 753.
10. Add. MS. 25, 114, f. 14 b.
11. Harl. MS. 539, f. 147.
12. Cleop. E. vi. 257.
13. TNA E 315/232 ff. 1v-8r.
14. LP x no. 720.
15. Add. MS. 25,114, f. 139.
16. LP x no. 848 iii.
17. CSP Foreign: Elizabeth, Volume 1 no. 1303.
18. Richardson, *Magna Carta*, p.225.
19. Giles, p.168.
20. Penn, p.141.
21. Cokayne, p.260.
22. BL MS 71009 f. 17.
23. Rodger, p.174.
24. LP iv no. 461.
25. R. Brock, p.17.
26. SP 1/78 f. 104.
27. LP v no. 748.
28. TNA SP1/129 f.174.
29. Ibid.

30. LP x no. 383.
31. Pocock, p.574.
32. Ibid.
33. Ibid.

Chapter 13: Indecision of a King

1. Harl. MS. 282, f. 7.
2. LP x no. 713.
3. Harl. MS. 282, f. 7.
4. Add. MS. 25,114, f. 293.
5. Calig, B. ii. 233.
6. Ibid.
7. LP x no. 738.
8. LP x no. 752.
9. MacCulloch, 1996, p.316.
10. CSP Foreign: Elizabeth, Volume 1 no. 1303.
11. MSS Julius C. V. 186.
12. Longleat House, Add. MS. 4622, f. 133.
13. Ibid.
14. Ibid.
15. LP ix no. 216 xv.
16. Titus, B. I. 424 and 424b.
17. See *The Augsburg Confession*.
18. Ibid.
19. MacCulloch, 2018, p.447.
20. McEntegart, p.85 — it was well-noted that Henry VIII could not be trusted with reform.
21. CSP Foreign: Elizabeth, Volume 1 no. 1303.
22. MacCulloch, 2018, p.274–281 shows Cranmer's constant battles against his own clergymen throughout 1535.
23. Bruce, p.59.
24. Brook, p.16.
25. Brook, pp.20–26.
26. Bruce p.59.
27. Smith, p.57.

28. See Beveill, *Old English Manuscripts in the Early Age of Print*.
29. Close Roll, 28 Hen. VIII. m. 43 d.
30. Ibid.
31. Ibid.
32. LP x nos.734–774.
33. Close Roll, 28 Hen. VIII. m. 43 d.
34. 28 Hen. 8. c. 24.
35. 28 Hen. 8. c. 10.
36. 28 Hen. 8. c. 11.
37. LP Spanish Calendar 5 ii no.47.
38. Foster, p.1422.
39. Pollard, p.403–405.
40. Ibid.
41. MacCulloch 1996, p.200–201, 204.
42. Vitellius, B. XII, f.12.
43. Camusat, 14.
44. Harl. MS. 6,989, f. 56.
45. Harl. MS. 6,989, f. 58.
46. LP x no. 752.
47. Ibid.

Chapter 14: Creating One's Own Proof

1. SP 3/8 f. 65.
2. Ibid.
3. LP x no. 793.
4. Ibid.
5. Grueninger, 2022, p.156.
6. See Loke, W, *Account of materials.*
7. MacCulloch, 2018, p.45.
8. Lee, Sidney, p.121–122.
9. Richardson, *Magna Carta*, p.350.
10. Ibid.
11. Ibid.
12. Copinger, p.6.
13. Ridgway, p.71.

14. Russell, p.90.
15. LP x no. 878.
16. Singer, p.451.
17. LP x no. 793.
18. Otho, C. x. 225.
19. 26 Hen. 8. c. 13.
20. Otho, C. x. 260b.
21. Ives, p.193.
22. CSP Foreign: Elizabeth, Volume 1 no. 1303.
23. Angus, 2023, p.116.
24. LP x no. 779.
25. Amyot, p.50–78.
26. Ibid.
27. Ibid.
28. CSP Foreign: Elizabeth, Volume 1 no. 1303.
29. LP x no. 819.

Chapter 15: Planning the Murder of Anne Boleyn

1. Grueninger, 2022, p.160.
2. Constantine, p.64.
3. Ibid.
4. Ibid.
5. LP x no. 782.
6. Ibid.
7. Ibid.
8. Wriothesley, p.36.
9. Ibid.
10. Singer, p.451.
11. SP 1/736 f. 76.
12. Otho. C. x. 224b.
13. Ibid.
14. Otho, C. x. 225.
15. Ibid.
16. Ibid.
17. LP x no. 782.

18. LP xi no. 108.
19. LP x no. 792.
20. LP x no. 838.
21. LP x no. 785.
22. Ibid.
23. LP x no. 788.
24. Rot. Reg. 11 B. xlvii.
25. Otho, C. x. 222b.
26. LP x no. 798.
27. Otho, C. x. 222.
28. LP ii Revels no. 7, 25 Dec 1514.
29. LP iv no. 426 ii.
30. LP iv no. 1939 xiv.
31. Du Bellay, p.105.
32. Cattley, p.657.
33. Singer II 1825, p.22.
34. Wyatt, p.12.
35. TNA C 1/224/62.
36. Otho, C. x. 209 b.
37. Otho, C. x. 226.
38. Ibid.
39. Otho, C. x. 226.
40. LP x no. 809.
41. Harl 1124, f. 17.
42. Ibid.
43. Ibid.
44. Ibid.
45. Burke, p.207.
46. Ives, *Brereton accounts*, p.11, 33.
47. LP iv no. 4755.
48. 27 Hen. 8. c. 26.
49. Ives, Brereton speech, 2001.
50. Ibid.
51. Ibid.
52. Ibid.
53. Amyot, pp.50–78.
54. Thornton, p.214.

55. LP x no. 825.
56. Privy Purse Expenses of Elizabeth of York, p.23,p. 84, p.99.
57. Richardson, p.487.
58. Clarke, p.360–361.
59. Bannerman, p.26.
60. Bindoff, p.199.
61. Clarke, p.363–364.
62. Otho, C. x. 225
63. Hall's Chronicle p.598–9.

Chapter 16: Some Force Other Than Reason

1. Otho, C. x. 222.
2. Vasoli, pp.83–85 does an excellent job of breaking the truth around the letter.
3. Ibid.
4. LP xv no. 1027.
5. Hatfield House, Cecil Papers, 124–7.
6. Otho, C. x. 228.
7. Ibid.
8. Ascoli, pp.349–84.
9. Otho, C. x. 222.
10. LP x no. 819.
11. LP x no. 865.
12. Ibid.
13. LP x no. 835.
14. LP x no. 827.
15. Cleo E iv ff.109v-110.
16. Add. MSS. 25,114, f. 137.
17. Cleop. E. iv. 89.
18. Even the 1538 trial of Henry Courtenay, Henry Pole, and John Neville, who were arrested and convicted on dubious evidence, had more convincing evidence, witness accounts, interrogations and a full trial. Cromwell had personally overseen this case, and even with flimsy evidence, the investigation was thorough, and is a rare surviving example of Cromwell's organisation of a trial.

19. LP x no. 834 i, ii.
20. LP x no. 840.
21. Ibid.
22. LP x no. 843.

Chapter 17: Dead Men Walking

1. LP x no. 848 i.
2. LP x no. 818 iii.
3. LP x no. 848 vii.
4. LP x no. 848.
5. Ives, p.339.
6. Ibid.
7. Ives, p.338.
8. Wien Rep. P. C., Fasc. 230, No. 28.
9. Otho, C. x. 209b.
10. SP 6/4 ff. 266 is a record of 1538, busy with gifts and money, although every year has many examples.
11. Spelman, I p.71.
12. LP v no. 12.
13. Ives, 2004, p.378.
14. Ibid.
15. Gunn, p.118.
16. Hoyle, p.407.
17. LP xi no. 533, 534, 539.
18. Baga de Secretis, National Archives, but quoted by Weir, 2009, p.229–231.
19. LP vi no. 1221 and 1293.
20. LP vi no. 1440.
21. LP vi no. 1481 xxvii and 1508.
22. Har. MS. 6,148, f. 79b.
23. Ibid.
24. LP vi no. 820, 823, 824.
25. LP viii no. 592 and 594.
26. LP ix no. 710.
27. LP ix no. 779.

28. LP ix no. 820, 823, 905.
29. Wriothesley, Vol. I appendix II, p.242.
30. LP x no. 848 ix.

Chapter 18: Things Be So Abominable

1. Titus, B. i. 444.
2. Singer, p.459.
3. MacCulloch, 2018, p.517.
4. Angus, 2022, pp.132, 133.
5. Wien, Rep. P. C., Fasc. 230, no.23.
6. MacCulloch, 2018 p.517.
7. Otho, C. x. 221.
8. LP x no. 912, 913, 914.
9. Ibid.
10. LP x no. 969.
11. LP x no. 870.
12. LP x no. 865.
13. LP x no. 870.
14. Add. MSS. 25,114, f. 160.
15. Wriothesley, p.37.
16. LP x no. 876.
17. Hutchinson, p.169.
18. LP x no. 876.
19. Zevin, chapter V gives a good rundown of the loyalty between the families.
20. James, pp.60–63.
21. Richardson, *Magna Carta* p.838.
22. Ascoli p.821–1046.
23. Ibid.
24. Wriothesley, p.37–39.
25. Ibid.
26. Ascoli, pp.1002–1012.
27. Wriothesley, p.37–39.
28. Ibid.
29. LP x no. 876.

30. Ascoli, p.1002–1012.
31. LP x no. 876.
32. Ibid.
33. Wriothesley, p.37–39.
34. LP x no. 908.
35. Ibid.
36. Herbert, p.384.
37. Ibid.
38. Wriothesley, p.37–39.
39. LP x no. 895.

Chapter 19: The Fall Is Grievous From Aloft

1. Harl. MS. 283, f. 134.
2. Ibid.
3. Ibid.
4. Smith, pp.344–5.
5. LP x no. 902.
6. Harl. MS. 283, f. 134.
7. LP x no. 908.
8. Wien, Rep. P. C., Fasc. 230, No. 32.
9. Ibid.
10. Wilkins, iii p.803.
11. LP x no. 909.
12. LP x no. 902.
13. Wriothesley p.39–40.
14. Amyot, pp.50–78.
15. Weir, 2009, p.311, quoting Gilbert Burnet, Bishop of Salisbury.
16. LP x no. 865.
17. Ibid.
18. Weir, 2009 p.311.
19. Ibid.
20. Otho, C. x. 223.
21. Dalder, poem 143.
22. LP x no. 902.
23. Otho, C. x. 223.

24. TNA C. 193/3 f.80. Thank you to Natalie Grueninger for allowing me to quote her transcription from the original, provided by Sean Cunningham after his discovery of the original document.
25. Grueninger p.179; Gristwood, p.188.
26. TNA C. 193/3 f.80. Thank you to Natalie Grueninger for allowing me to quote her transcription from the original, provided by Sean Cunningham after his discovery of the original document.
27. Otho, C. x. 223.
28. LP x no. 908.
29. Otho, C. x. 223.
30. Otho, C. x. 223.
31. LP x no. 901.
32. LP x no. 919.
33. *Hall's Chronicle*, p.819.
34. Crapelet, *Lettres de Henry VIII*. p.167.
35. Gachard, 1 S.17.
36. Ives, p.359.
37. Ibid.

Chapter 20: All Is Washed Away

1. LP x no. 919.
2. LP x no. 915.
3. LP x no. 926.
4. LP x no. 965.
5. LP x no. 908.
6. Otho. C. x. 280.
7. Wien, Rep. P. C., Fasc. 230, No. 29.
8. LP x no. 926.
9. LP x no. 912 913 914.
10. Vesp. F. XIII. f. 109.
11. Otho, C. x. 276.
12. Otho. C. x. 280.
13. Otho, C. x. 262 b and Otho, C. x. 261. B.
14. LP xi no. 40.
15. Ibid.

16. 28 Hen. 8. c. 7.
17. LP xi no. 148.
18. LP x no. 1000.
19. Add. MS. 9835, f. 22.
20. LP x no. 1069.
21. Ibid.
22. Nero C. x. l.
23. Langbaine, pp.15–17.
24. LP xi no. 639.
25. LP xi no. 17.
26. LP xii.ii no. 629.
27. Trokelowe, p.271.
28. Kaulek, no. 23.
29. LP xi no. 202 iii, xiv.
30. MacCulloch, 2018, p.361.
31. MSS Cleo. E. VI., 285.
32. Heale, p.323.
33. Kaulek, no. 137.
34. Cox, p.401.
35. MacCulloch 1996, pp.600–605.
36. LP x no. 1256 ii.
37. LP xiv. ii no. 782, f.117.
38. Levin, p.478.
39. Antonia Fraser, *Mary, Queen of Scots*, p.485.
40. Dashwood, p.104.
41. Angus, 2023, p.140.
42. LP x no. 1256 ii.
43. Ashmole, p.525.
44. Dalder, poem no. 149.
45. LP xiii no. 270.
46. LP xi no. 920.
47. LP xii.ii no. 201.
48. LP xiii.ii no. 771-803.
49. LP xiv.i no. 189.
50. LP xiv.i no. 489.
51. Add. MSS. 25,114, f. 160.
52. Weir, 2002, p.382.

53. Lee, Vol. 41. P.122–124.
54. Russell, p.90.
55. LP xi no. 242 shows Cromwell staying with the Westons on progress. Richard Weston and Thomas Cromwell remained on good terms post-1536.
56. Harrison, pp.87–96.
57. Ridgway, p.201.
58. Newcombe, p.1885–1900.
59. Demaus, p.508.
60. LP xiii no. 953.
61. Chisholm, Vol. 13 pp.157–158.
62. Chisholm, Vol. 12, p.238.
63. Burnet, i. no. 531.
64. LP x no. 909.

Index